# Grammar Sense 2A

## SECOND EDITION

**SERIES DIRECTOR**
Susan Kesner Bland

**AUTHOR**
Cheryl Pavlik

OXFORD
UNIVERSITY PRESS

## OXFORD
### UNIVERSITY PRESS

198 Madison Avenue
New York, NY 10016 USA

Great Clarendon Street, Oxford, OX2 6DP, United Kingdom

Oxford University Press is a department of the University of Oxford.
It furthers the University's objective of excellence in research, scholarship,
and education by publishing worldwide. Oxford is a registered trade
mark of Oxford University Press in the UK and in certain other countries

General Manager, American ELT: Laura Pearson
Publisher: Stephanie Karras
Associate Publishing Manager: Sharon Sargent
Managing Editor: Alex Ragan
Director, ADP: Susan Sanguily
Executive Design Manager: Maj-Britt Hagsted
Electronic Production Manager: Julie Armstrong
Senior Designer: Yin Ling Wong
Image Manager: Trisha Masterson

Publishing and Editorial Management: hyphen S.A.

ISBN: 978 0 19 448914 0 Student Book 2A with Online Practice pack
ISBN: 978 0 19 448904 1 Student Book 2A as pack component
ISBN: 978 0 19 448928 7 Online Practice as pack component

Printed in China

This book is printed on paper from certified and well-managed sources

ACKNOWLEDGEMENTS

*Although every effort has been made to trace and contact copyright holders before
publication, this has not been possible in some cases. We apologize for any apparent
infringement of copyright and if notified, the publisher will be pleased to rectify any
errors or omissions at the earliest opportunity.*

*The authors and publisher are grateful to those who have given permission to
reproduce the following extracts and adaptations of copyright material:*

pp. 4–5. "Mysterious Island." This article first appeared in The Christian
Science Monitor on June 16, 1998, and is reproduced with permission. ©
1998 The Christian Science Publishing Society. All rights reserved.

*Illustrations by*: Thanos Tsilis (hyphen): 4, 39, 41, 121, 149, 192, 217, 303,
318,360, 371, 391,413; Alexandros Tzimeros / SmartMagna (hyphen): 56,
74, 95, 103, 118, 129, 138, 195, 207, 213, 230, 252, 269, 338, 420.

*We would also like to thank the following for permission to reproduce the following
photographs*: Devation - Edwin Verbruggen / www.shutterstock.com,
Andreas Gradin / shutterstock.com, homydesign / www.shutterstock.com,
marekuliasz / www.shutterstock.com, Travel Ink / Getty Images, Cover l
to r and interior; Marcin Krygier / iStockphoto, Front matter and back
cover (laptop); Pingebat / istockphoto, pg 4 (map); Akos Major / Getty
Images, pg 4; G Fletcher / Getty Images, pg. 5; Joe McDonald / Corbis,
pg. 8; Wally McNamee / Corbis, pg. 14; Juniors Bildarchiv / Alamy, pg. 18;
Layne Kennedy / Corbis, pg. 19; Photodisc / OUPpicturebank, pg. 31; Henry
Diltz / Corbis, pg. 48; M&N / Alamy, pg. 49; Bettmann / Corbis, pg. 52; Jim
Sugar / Corbis, pg. 54; Digital Vision / OUPpicturebank, pg. 59 (tl); Reda /
Shutterstock, pg. 59 (cl); Blend Images / OUPpicturebank, pg. 59 (bl); Jim
Craigmyle / Corbis, pg. 59 (tr); Somos Images / Alamy, pg. 59 (cr); Cultura /
Corbis, pg. 59 (br); Courtesy of the Rosenberg Library Galveston, Texas,
pg. 70; Corbis / Corbis, pg. 71; Jim Reed / Jim Reed Photography - Severe
& / Corbis, pg. 82; Parque / Corbis, pg. 90; Pingebat / istockphoto, pg. 90
(map); Michele Burgess / Corbis, pg. 107; Moodboard / OUPpicturebank,
pg. 112 (l); C.Devan / Corbis, pg. 112 (r); Comstock / OUPpicturebank,
pg. 113 (l); Tanya Constantine / Blend Images / Corbis, pg. 113 (r); Photodisc
/ OUPpicturebank, pg. 135; Klaus Tiedge / Corbis, pg. 145; CHIP EAST /
Reuters / Corbis, pg. 156; Photodisc / OUPpicturebank, pg. 157; Denkou
Images / Alamy, pg. 166; Tim Kiusalaas / Corbis, pg. 171; Stephen Frink /
Monsoon / Photolibrary / Corbis, pg. 175; Digital Vision / OUPpicturebank,
pg. 178; Blue Jean Images / OUPpicturebank, pg. 201; Corbis / Corbis,
pg. 225 (l); Corbis / Corbis, pg. 225 (r); James Green / Robert Harding World
Imagery / Corbis, pg. 240; David Loftus Limited / the food passionates /
Corbis, pg. 268; Corbis / Digital Stock / OUPpicturebank, pg. 282 (pitcher
plant); David Frazier / Corbis, pg. 282 (cobralily); Patrick Endres / Visuals
Unlimited / Corbis, pg. 282 (sundew); Visuals Unlimited / Corbis, pg. 283;
Photodisc / OUPpicturebank, pg. 295 (cactus); Wave / OUPpicturebank,
pg. 295 (butterfly); Christopher Talbot Frank / Photex / Corbis, pg. 295
(maple tree); Clive Nichols / Corbis, pg. 295 (rose); Jones, Huw / the food
passionates / Corbis, pg. 295 (green pepper); Tobias Bernhard / Corbis,
pg. 295 (shark); Corbis / Digital Stock / OUPpicturebank, pg. 296; Photodisc
/ OUPpicturebank, pg. 313 (sweater); Comstock / OUPpicturebank, pg. 313
(sofa); OUP / OUPpicturebank, pg. 313 (box); OUP / OUPpicturebank, pg. 313
(purse); OUP / OUPpicturebank, pg. 313 (toy airplane); olaf.kowalzik /
OUPpicturebank, pg. 313 (hat); Ian Shaw / OUPpicturebank, pg. 346; Image
Source / OUPpicturebank, pg. 363; Sarah Rice / Star Ledger / Corbis,
pg. 366; Nation Wong / Corbis, pg. 382; Bettmann / Corbis, pg. 396; Martin
Sundberg / Corbis, pg. 408; Andrzej Tokarski / Alamy, pg. 413

# Reviewers

*We would like to acknowledge the following individuals for their input during the development of the series:*

**Marcia Adato**, Delaware Technical and Community College, DE
**Donette Artenie**, Georgetown University, DC
**Alexander Astor**, Hostos Community College/CUNY, Bronx, NY
**Nathalie Bailey**, Lehman College, CUNY, NY
**Jamie Beaton**, Boston University, MA
**Michael Berman**, Montgomery College, MD
**Linda Best**, Kean University, NJ
**Marcel Bolintiam**, Kings Colleges, Los Angeles, CA
**Houda Bouslama**, Virtual University Tunis, Tunis, Tunisia
**Nancy Boyer**, Golden West College, Huntington Beach, CA
**Glenda Bro**, Mount San Antonio Community College, CA
**Shannonine Caruana**, Kean University, NJ
**Sharon Cavusgil**, Georgia State University, GA
**Robin Rosen Chang**, Kean University, NJ
**Jorge Cordon**, Colegio Internacional Montessori, Guatemala
**Magali Duignan**, Augusta State University, GA
**Anne Ediger**, Hunter College, CUNY, NY
**Begoña Escourdio**, Colegio Miraflores, Naucalpan, Mexico
**Marcella Farina**, University of Central Florida, FL
**Carol Fox**, Oakton Community College, Niles, IL
**Glenn S. Gardner**, Glendale Community College, Glendale, CA
**Ruth Griffith**, Kean University, NJ
**Evalyn Hansen**, Rogue Community College, Medford, OR
**Liz Hardy**, Rogue Community College, Medford, OR
**Habiba Hassina**, Virtual University Tunis, Tunis, Tunisia
**Virginia Heringer**, Pasadena City College, CA
**Rocia Hernandez**, Mexico City, Mexico
**Kieran Hilu**, Virginia Tech, VA
**Rosemary Hiruma**, California State University, Long Beach, CA
**Linda Holden**, College of Lake County, Grayslake, IL
**Elke Holtz**, Escuela Sierra Nevada Interlomas, Mexico City, Mexico
**Kate de Jong**, University of California, San Diego, CA
**Gail Kellersberger**, University of Houston-Downtown, ELI, Houston, TX

**Pamela Kennedy**, Holyoke Community College, MA
**Elis Lee**, Glendale Community College, Glendale, CA
**Patricia Lowy**, State University of New York-New Paltz, NY
**Jean McConochie**, Pace University, NY
**Karen McRobie**, Golden Gate University, CA
**Hafid Mekaoui**, Al Akhawayn University, Ifrane, Morocco
**Elizabeth Neblett**, Union County College, NJ
**Patricia Palermo**, Kean University, NJ
**Maria E. Palma**, Colegio Lationamericano Bilingue, Chihuahua, Mexico
**Mary Peacock**, Richland College, Dallas, TX
**Dian Perkins**, Wheeling High School, IL
**Nancy Herzfeld-Pipkin**, Grossmont College, El Cajon, CA
**Kent Richmond**, California State University, Long Beach, CA
**Ellen Rosen**, Fullerton College, CA
**Jessica Saigh**, University of Missouri-St. Louis, St. Louis, MO
**Boutheina Lassadi-Sayadi**, The Faculty of Humanities and Social Sciences of Tunis, Tunis, Tunisia
**Anne-Marie Schlender**, Austin Community College-Rio Grande, Austin, TX
**Shira Seaman**, Global English Academy, NY
**Katharine Sherak**, San Francisco State University, CA
**Maxine Steinhaus**, New York University, NY
**Andrea Stewart**, Houston Community College-Gulfton, Houston, TX
**Nancy Storer**, University of Denver, CO
**Veronica Struck**, Sussex Community College, Newton, NJ
**Frank Tang**, New York University, NY
**Claude Taylor**, Baruch College, NY
**Marshall Thomas**, California State University, Long Beach, CA
**Christine Tierney**, Houston Community College, Houston, TX
**Anthea Tillyer**, Hunter College, CUNY, NY
**Julie Un**, Massasoit Community College, MA
**Marvaette Washington**, Houston Community College, Houston, TX
**Cheryl Wecksler**, California State University, San Marcos, CA
**Teresa Wise**, Associated Colleges of the South, GA

# Contents

# Welcome to Grammar Sense

## A Sensible Solution to Learning Grammar

**Grammar Sense Second Edition** gives learners a true understanding of how grammar is used in authentic contexts.

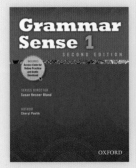 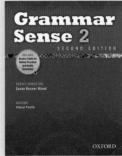 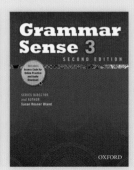 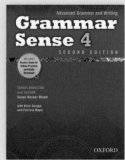

## With Grammar Sense Online Practice

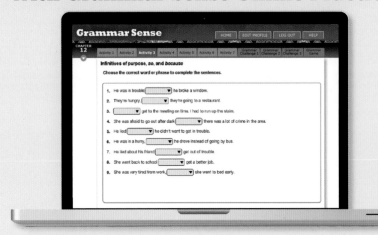

- **Student Solutions:** a **focus on Critical Thinking** for improved application of grammatical knowledge.

- **Writing Solutions:** a **Writing section in every chapter** encourages students to see the relevance of grammar in their writing.

- **Technology Solutions:** *Grammar Sense Online Practice* provides additional practice in an easy-to-use **online workbook**.

- **Assessment Solutions:** the Part Tests at the end of every section and the Grammar Sense Test Generators allow **ongoing assessment**.

Each chapter in *Grammar Sense Second Edition* **follows** this format.

## The Grammar in Discourse section introduces the target grammar in its natural context via high-interest readings.

**Pre- and post-reading tasks** help students understand the text.

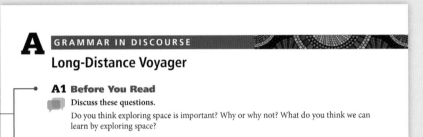

# A GRAMMAR IN DISCOURSE

## Long-Distance Voyager

### A1 Before You Read

Discuss these questions.

Do you think exploring space is important? Why or why not? What do you think we can learn by exploring space?

### A2 Read

CD1 T9 Read the magazine article on the following page to find out about a famous spacecraft.

### A3 After You Read

Write *T* for true or *F* for false for each statement.

___T___ 1. *Voyager* is a spacecraft.

_____ 2. *Voyager* is traveling through space.

_____ 3. *Voyager* is coming back to Earth soon.

_____ 4. *Voyage*

_____ 5. We are

_____ 6. *Voyage*

Exposure to **authentic readings** encourages awareness of the grammar in daily life: in textbooks, magazines, newspapers, websites, and so on.

LONG-DISTANCE
# Voyager

*Voyager 1* is a spacecraft that left Earth in 1977. Its purpose was to explore our solar system. Scientists expected to receive information about Jupiter and Saturn from *Voyager* for ten to fifteen years. They were wrong. They are still receiving messages from *Voyager* today. *Voyager* is currently moving away from
5 Earth at a speed of over 38,000 miles per hour (over 61,000 kilometers per hour). Now it is so far away that its messages take over fifteen hours to travel to Earth.
   How far away is *Voyager 1* now and what is it exploring? *Voyager* is many billions of miles from us. It is farther from Earth than any other human-made object. It is traveling in a part of our solar system beyond all the planets. In fact,
10 it is approaching the outer boundaries of our solar system. These days, *Voyager's* messages are giving us information about this most distant part of our solar system. Large antennas on Earth are receiving its signals.
   Soon *Voyager* will leave our solar system. Then it will send us information about interstellar space—the space between our Sun and other stars. *Voyager* will
15 continue into interstellar space, and we will continue to learn from *Voyager*. Finally, sometime between about 2020 and 2025, *Voyager* will stop sending information and will travel silently through space.

# The Form section(s) provides clear presentation of the target grammar, detailed notes, and thorough practice exercises.

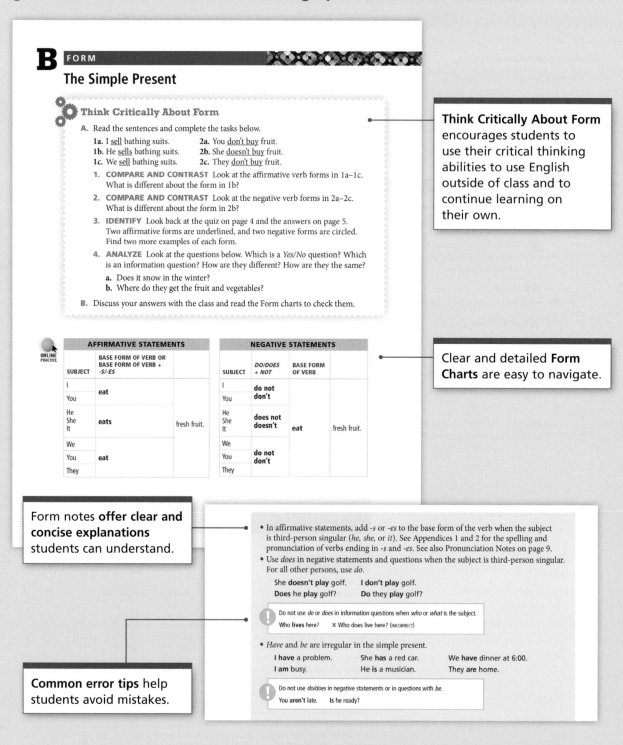

## B FORM

### The Simple Present

#### Think Critically About Form

A. Read the sentences and complete the tasks below.

1a. I <u>sell</u> bathing suits.    2a. You <u>don't buy</u> fruit.
1b. He <u>sells</u> bathing suits.   2b. She <u>doesn't buy</u> fruit.
1c. We <u>sell</u> bathing suits.   2c. They <u>don't buy</u> fruit.

1. **COMPARE AND CONTRAST** Look at the affirmative verb forms in 1a–1c. What is different about the form in 1b?

2. **COMPARE AND CONTRAST** Look at the negative verb forms in 2a–2c. What is different about the form in 2b?

3. **IDENTIFY** Look back at the quiz on page 4 and the answers on page 5. Two affirmative forms are underlined, and two negative forms are circled. Find two more examples of each form.

4. **ANALYZE** Look at the questions below. Which is a *Yes/No* question? Which is an information question? How are they different? How are they the same?

   a. Does it snow in the winter?
   b. Where do they get the fruit and vegetables?

B. Discuss your answers with the class and read the Form charts to check them.

**Think Critically About Form** encourages students to use their critical thinking abilities to use English outside of class and to continue learning on their own.

**ONLINE PRACTICE**

### AFFIRMATIVE STATEMENTS

| SUBJECT | BASE FORM OF VERB OR BASE FORM OF VERB + -S/-ES | |
|---|---|---|
| I | | |
| You | eat | |
| He She It | eats | fresh fruit. |
| We | | |
| You | eat | |
| They | | |

### NEGATIVE STATEMENTS

| SUBJECT | DO/DOES + NOT | BASE FORM OF VERB | |
|---|---|---|---|
| I | do not | | |
| You | don't | | |
| He She It | does not doesn't | eat | fresh fruit. |
| We | do not | | |
| You | don't | | |
| They | | | |

Clear and detailed **Form Charts** are easy to navigate.

Form notes **offer clear and concise explanations** students can understand.

- In affirmative statements, add *-s* or *-es* to the base form of the verb when the subject is third-person singular (*he, she,* or *it*). See Appendices 1 and 2 for the spelling and pronunciation of verbs ending in *-s* and *-es*. See also Pronunciation Notes on page 9.
- Use *does* in negative statements and questions when the subject is third-person singular. For all other persons, use *do*.

  She **doesn't play** golf.   I **don't play** golf.
  **Does** he **play** golf?   **Do** they **play** golf?

  > Do not use *do* or *does* in information questions when *who* or *what* is the subject.
  > Who **lives** here?   ✗ Who does live here? (INCORRECT)

- *Have* and *be* are irregular in the simple present.

  I **have** a problem.   She **has** a red car.   We **have** dinner at 6:00.
  I **am** busy.   He **is** a musician.   They **are** home.

  > Do not use *do/does* in negative statements or in questions with *be*.
  > You **aren't** late.   Is he ready?

**Common error tips** help students avoid mistakes.

**The Meaning and Use** section(s) offers clear and comprehensive explanations of how the target structure is used, and exercises to practice using it appropriately.

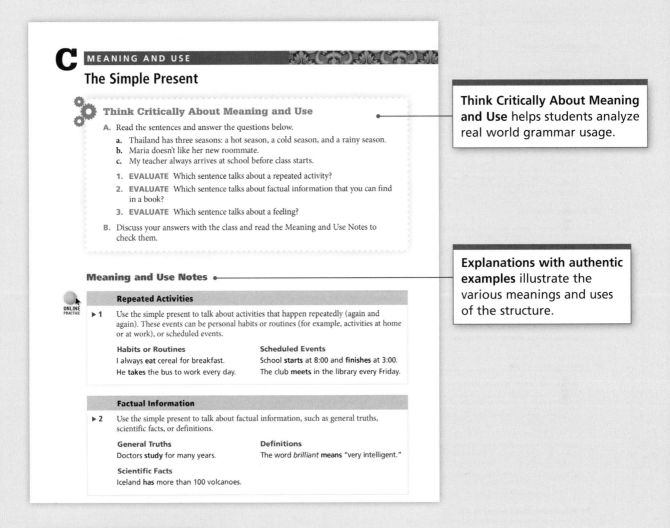

**C  MEANING AND USE**

## The Simple Present

### Think Critically About Meaning and Use

A. Read the sentences and answer the questions below.

   **a.** Thailand has three seasons: a hot season, a cold season, and a rainy season.
   **b.** Maria doesn't like her new roommate.
   **c.** My teacher always arrives at school before class starts.

   **1.** EVALUATE  Which sentence talks about a repeated activity?
   **2.** EVALUATE  Which sentence talks about factual information that you can find in a book?
   **3.** EVALUATE  Which sentence talks about a feeling?

B. Discuss your answers with the class and read the Meaning and Use Notes to check them.

**Think Critically About Meaning and Use** helps students analyze real world grammar usage.

### Meaning and Use Notes

ONLINE PRACTICE

**Repeated Activities**

▶ 1  Use the simple present to talk about activities that happen repeatedly (again and again). These events can be personal habits or routines (for example, activities at home or at work), or scheduled events.

| **Habits or Routines** | **Scheduled Events** |
| I always **eat** cereal for breakfast. | School **starts** at 8:00 and **finishes** at 3:00. |
| He **takes** the bus to work every day. | The club **meets** in the library every Friday. |

**Factual Information**

▶ 2  Use the simple present to talk about factual information, such as general truths, scientific facts, or definitions.

| **General Truths** | **Definitions** |
| Doctors **study** for many years. | The word *brilliant* **means** "very intelligent." |
| **Scientific Facts** | |
| Iceland **has** more than 100 volcanoes. | |

**Explanations with authentic examples** illustrate the various meanings and uses of the structure.

**Practice exercises** enable students to **use the grammar structure appropriately and fluently**.

**C1  Listening for Meaning and Use**    ▶ Notes 1, 2

CD1 T5  Listen to each statement. Is the speaker describing a personal routine or a general truth? Check ( ✓ ) the correct column.

|  | PERSONAL ROUTINE | GENERAL TRUTH |
|---|---|---|
| 1. | | ✓ |
| 2. | | |
| 3. | | |
| 4. | | |
| 5. | | |
| 6. | | |

# Special sections appear throughout the chapters with clear explanations, authentic examples, and follow-up exercises.

**Beyond the Sentence** demonstrates how structures function differently in extended discourses.

**Informally Speaking** clarifies the differences between written and spoken language.

---

## Beyond the Sentence

### Combining Ideas

When you compare people or things, it is important to combine your ideas by using additions with *and . . . too, and . . . either, and so, and neither,* and *but.* If you do not combine ideas, your writing will be very repetitive. Compare these two paragraphs. Notice how combining ideas makes the second paragraph sound less repetitive.

*Repetitive*

My best friend and I have many similarities. I have a sister. Carol has a sister. I like vanilla ice cream. Carol likes vanilla ice cream. I'm not good at math. Carol isn't good at math. There is one big difference. Carol lives in the United States. I don't live in the United States. I live in Costa Rica.

*Not Repetitive*

My best friend and I have many similarities. I have a sister, **and so does** Carol. I like vanilla ice cream, **and** Carol does, **too.** I'm not good at math, **and neither** is Carol. There is one big difference. Carol lives in the United States, but I don't. I live in Costa Rica.

### D6 Avoiding Repetition

Read this paragraph. Underline the parts that are repetitive. Then rewrite the paragraph combining sentences where possible.

The United States and the United Kingdom have many similarities and differences. One of the similarities is language. People in the United States speak English. People in the United Kingdom speak English. Some people say that Americans don't speak very clearly. Some people say that the British speak very clearly. American and British food is also similar in some ways. Americans like to eat meat and potatoes. The British like to eat meat and potatoes. The two countries also both have strong traditions of volunteer work. Many Americans give some of their time to help others. Many Britons also give some time to help others. One big difference is the political system. The United Kingdom has a queen. The United States doesn't have a king or a queen. In the United States, voters elect a president. In the United Kingdom, voters don't elect a

---

## Pronunciation Notes

### Pronunciation of Verbs Ending in *-s* or *-es*

The letters *-s* or *-es* at the end of third-person singular verbs are pronounced in three different ways, depending on the final sound of the base form of the verb.

1. The *-s* or *-es* is pronounced /s/ if the base form of the verb ends with the sound /p/, /t/, /k/, or /f/.

    stop — stops /staps/    like — likes /laɪks/    laugh — laughs /læfs/

2. The *-s* or *-es* is pronounced /z/ if the base form of the verb ends with the sound /b/, /d/, /g/, /v/, /ð/, /m/, /n/, /ŋ/, /l/, /r/, or a vowel sound.

    leave — leaves /livz/    run — runs /rʌnz/    go — goes /gouz/

3. The *-es* is pronounced /ɪz/ if the base form of the verb ends with the sound /s/, /z/, /ʃ/, /ʒ/, /tʃ/, /dʒ/, or /ks/. This adds an extra syllable to the word.

    notice — notices /'noʊtəsɪz/  buzz — buzzes /'bʌzɪz/  watch — watches /'wɑtʃɪz/

### B3 Pronouncing Verbs Ending in *-s* or *-es*

🎧 CD1 T4  A. Listen to the pronunciation of each verb. What ending do you hear? Check (✓) the correct column.

|   |           | /s/ | /z/ | /ɪz/ |
|---|-----------|-----|-----|------|
| 1.| lives     |     | ✓   |      |
| 2.| practices |     |     |      |
| 3.| works     |     |     |      |
| 4.| closes    |     |     |      |
| 5.| arranges  |     |     |      |
| 6.| tells     |     |     |      |

B. Work with a partner. Take turns reading these sentences aloud. Be sure to pronounce the verb endings correctly.

1. Pablo lives in San Diego.
2. The team practices every day.
3. The computer works just fine.
4. My mother closes the window at night.
5. Tony arranges all the meetings.
6. Sheryl tells everyone's secrets.

CHAPTER 1 | 9

**Pronunciation Notes** show students how to pronounce forms of the target language.

---

## Informally Speaking

### Reduced Form of *Going To*

🎧 CD1 T34  Look at the cartoon and listen to the conversation. How are the underlined forms in the cartoon different from what you hear?

> Are you going to see Mary tonight?

> No, I'm going to study. I have a lot of homework.

In informal speech, *going to* is often pronounced /gənə/.

| Standard Form | What You Might Hear |
|---|---|
| They are going to call. | "They're /gənə/ call." |
| He is going to buy a new phone. | "He's /gənə/ buy a new phone." |
| I am going to stay home. | "I'm /gənə/ stay home." |

### B5 Understanding Informal Speech

🎧 CD1 T35  Listen and write the standard form of the words you hear.

1. We ___are going to make___ dinner soon.
2. I _____ to the beach.
3. We _____ him in Seattle.
4. Our class _____ next Wednesday.
5. The store _____ in five minutes.
6. Mark _____ at Lincoln University.
7. The children _____ happy about this.
8. They _____ the test tomorrow.

---

## Vocabulary Notes

### Adverbs and Time Expressions with the Present Continuous

**Still and the Present Continuous** *Still* is an adverb that is often used with the present continuous. *Still* emphasizes that the activity or state is in progress. It often suggests surprise that the activity or state has not ended. Place *still* after *be* in affirmative statements, before *be* in negative statements, and after the subject in questions.

| **Affirmative Statement** | **Negative Statement** |
|---|---|
| He is **still** living with his parents. | He **still** isn't living on his own. |
| **Yes/No Question** | **Information Question** |
| Is he **still** living with his parents? | Why is he **still** living with his parents? |

**Time Expressions with the Present Continuous** Time expressions are also commonly used with the present continuous. Some time expressions refer to an exact moment in the present. These include *now, right now,* and *at the moment.*

Others refer to a longer time period that includes the present moment. These include *this morning, this afternoon, this evening, this week, this month, this semester, this year, these days,* and *nowadays.*

Time expressions can occur at the beginning or end of a sentence.

| **Exact Moment** | **Longer Time Period** |
|---|---|
| **Now** I'm making dinner. | She's working hard **this morning.** |
| He's sleeping **right now.** | **This week** I'm doing research at the library. |
| He's taking a shower **at the moment.** | She's feeling much better **these days.** |

### C4 Using Adverbs and Time Expressions with the Present Continuous

In your notebook, write sentences about yourself and people you know. Use the present continuous and these subjects and time expressions.

1. I/right now
    *I am studying English right now.*
2. My best friend/these days
3. Some of my friends/still
5. My family/nowadays
6. I/still
7. I/this year

40

**Vocabulary Notes** highlight the connection between the key vocabulary and grammatical structures.

# The Writing section guides students through the process of applying grammatical knowledge to compositions.

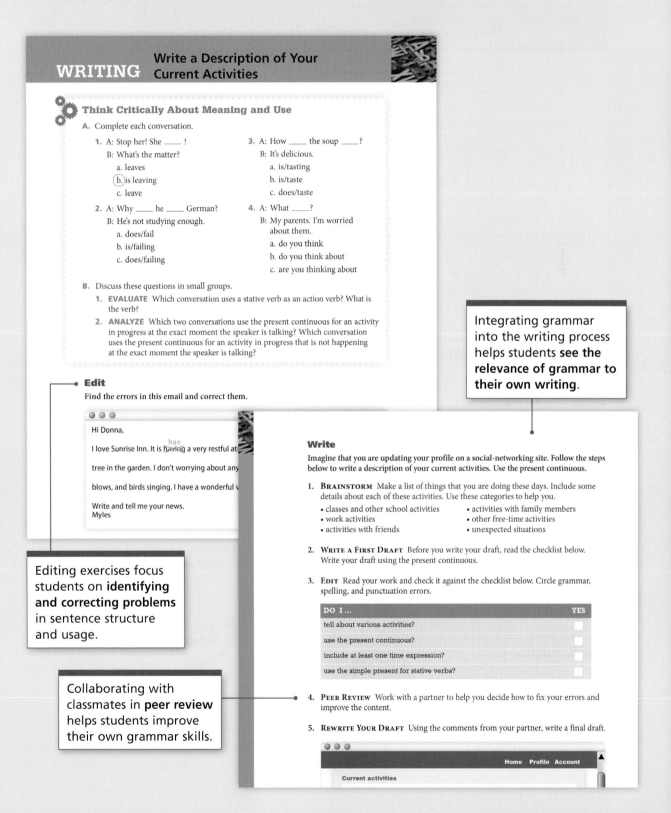

**WRITING** Write a Description of Your Current Activities

### Think Critically About Meaning and Use

**A.** Complete each conversation.

1. A: Stop her! She ____ !
   B: What's the matter?
   a. leaves
   b. is leaving
   c. leave

2. A: Why ____ he ____ German?
   B: He's not studying enough.
   a. does/fail
   b. is/failing
   c. does/failing

3. A: How ____ the soup ____?
   B: It's delicious.
   a. is/tasting
   b. is/taste
   c. does/taste

4. A: What ____?
   B: My parents. I'm worried about them.
   a. do you think
   b. do you think about
   c. are you thinking about

**B.** Discuss these questions in small groups.

1. **EVALUATE** Which conversation uses a stative verb as an action verb? What is the verb?

2. **ANALYZE** Which two conversations use the present continuous for an activity in progress at the exact moment the speaker is talking? Which conversation uses the present continuous for an activity in progress that is not happening at the exact moment the speaker is talking?

### Edit

Find the errors in this email and correct them.

Hi Donna,
                                        has
I love Sunrise Inn. It is having a very restful at
tree in the garden. I don't worrying about any
blows, and birds singing. I have a wonderful v
Write and tell me your news.
Myles

Integrating grammar into the writing process helps students **see the relevance of grammar to their own writing**.

Editing exercises focus students on **identifying and correcting problems** in sentence structure and usage.

Collaborating with classmates in **peer review** helps students improve their own grammar skills.

### Write

Imagine that you are updating your profile on a social-networking site. Follow the steps below to write a description of your current activities. Use the present continuous.

1. **BRAINSTORM** Make a list of things that you are doing these days. Include some details about each of these activities. Use these categories to help you.
   - classes and other school activities
   - work activities
   - activities with friends
   - activities with family members
   - other free-time activities
   - unexpected situations

2. **WRITE A FIRST DRAFT** Before you write your draft, read the checklist below. Write your draft using the present continuous.

3. **EDIT** Read your work and check it against the checklist below. Circle grammar, spelling, and punctuation errors.

| DO I ... | YES |
|---|---|
| tell about various activities? | |
| use the present continuous? | |
| include at least one time expression? | |
| use the simple present for stative verbs? | |

4. **PEER REVIEW** Work with a partner to help you decide how to fix your errors and improve the content.

5. **REWRITE YOUR DRAFT** Using the comments from your partner, write a final draft.

Home   Profile   Account

Current activities

# Assessment

## PART 1
## TEST | The Present

Choose the correct word or words to complete each sentence.

1. _____ write in the margins of your test booklet, class.

   a. Doesn't     c. Not

   b. Don't     d. No

2. Please _____ the bottom of this form, sir.

   a. sign     c. signing

   b. signs     d. to sign

3. Many economists believe the world economy _____ right now.

   a. am shrinking     c. are shrinking

   b. is shrinking     d. shrinking

4. Naomi and Emily _____ two brothers.

   a. are having     c. has

   b. having     d. have

> **Part Tests** allow ongoing assessment and evaluate the students' mastery of the grammar.

# Teacher's Resources

## Teacher's Book

- Creative techniques for presenting the grammar, along with troubleshooting tips, and suggestions for additional activities

- Answer key and audio scripts

- Includes a *Grammar Sense Online Practice* Teacher Access Code

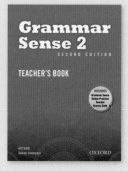

## Test Generator CD-ROM

- Over 3,000 items available!

- Test-generating software allows you to customize tests for all levels of Grammar Sense

- Includes a bank of ready-made tests

Grammar Sense Teachers' Club site contains additional teaching resources at www.oup.com/elt/teacher/grammarsense

## Class Audio

- Audio CDs feature exercises for discriminating form, understanding meaning and use, and interpreting non-standard forms

**ONLINE PRACTICE**

# Grammar Sense Online Practice is an online program with all new content. It correlates with the *Grammar Sense* student books and provides additional practice.

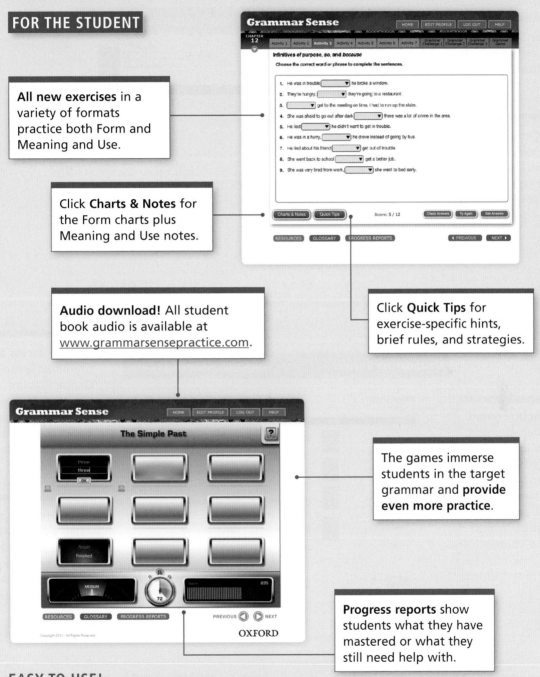

**All new exercises** in a variety of formats practice both Form and Meaning and Use.

Click **Charts & Notes** for the Form charts plus Meaning and Use notes.

**Audio download!** All student book audio is available at www.grammarsensepractice.com.

Click **Quick Tips** for exercise-specific hints, brief rules, and strategies.

The games immerse students in the target grammar and **provide even more practice**.

**Progress reports** show students what they have mastered or what they still need help with.

**EASY TO USE!**

Use the access code printed on the inside back cover of this book to register at www.grammarsensepractice.com. See the last page of the book for registration instructions.

# FOR THE TEACHER AND THE ADMINISTRATOR

**Flexible** enough for use in the classroom or easily assigned as homework.

*Grammar Sense Online Practice* automatically **grades** student exercises and tracks progress.

The easy-to-use online management system allows you to **review, print, or export** the reports you need.

You can **access all** *Grammar Sense Online Practice* **activities**, download the student book audio, and utilize the additional student resources.

The **straightforward online management system** allows you to add or delete classes, manage your classes, plus view, print, or export all class and individual student reports.

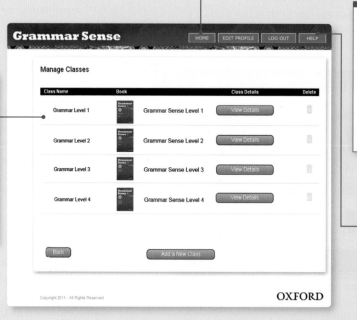

Click Help for simple, step-by-step support that is **available in six languages**: English, Spanish, Korean, Arabic, Chinese, and Japanese.

## FOR ADDITIONAL SUPPORT
Email our customer support team at grammarsensesupport@oup.com and you will receive a response within 24 hours.

## FOR ADMINISTRATOR CODES
Please contact your sales representative for an Administrator Access Code. A Teacher Access Code comes with every Teacher's Book.

# PART

# 1

## The Present

# CHAPTER

# 1

# The Simple Present

# Mysterious Island

## A1 Before You Read

 Discuss these questions.

What do you think about when you imagine an island? Do you imagine warm weather or cold weather? Can you name any islands that are countries?

## A2 Read

 CD1 T2  Read this geography quiz to find out more about Iceland.

QUIZ

Iceland

EUROPE

Mysterious Island

ICELAND IS A TRULY UNIQUE ISLAND—in fact, it's like nowhere else on Earth. The interior of this island nation contains incredible contrasts. It has tundras, huge glaciers, volcanoes, and waterfalls.

Read these amazing facts about Iceland. Then guess the answers to the questions.
5 Check your guesses on page 5.

1 Swimsuit maker Speedo® sells a very large number of bathing suits in Iceland. Is it warm here all year?

2 The island's climate is cool, but most 10 people don't pay much money for heat. Energy is very cheap and it doesn't cause pollution. What kind of energy do Icelanders use?

3 Icelanders eat fresh fruit and 15 vegetables all year, but they rarely buy them from other countries. Where do they get them?

4 Icelanders like to play golf all night during the summer. How do they see 20 the ball?

## ANSWERS

**1** No. Winters are cold in Iceland, but the people of Iceland swim all year in heated swimming pools.

**2** They use geothermal heat from under the ground. Icelanders use water from volcanoes, hot springs,
25 and geysers. Pipes carry the heated water throughout the country. The water heats buildings.

**3** They get them from greenhouses. Icelanders use geothermal energy to grow fruit and vegetables in greenhouses, even in the winter. This means they
30 don't need to import produce.

**4** Iceland is very close to the Arctic Circle. In the summer the sun doesn't go down, so people can play sports all night.

A geyser in Iceland

Adapted from *The Christian Science Monitor*

**climate:** the typical weather conditions of a place
**geyser:** a hot spring that shoots water into the air
**glacier:** a large body of ice that moves slowly over land
**greenhouse:** a glass building used for growing plants

**produce:** foods such as fruit and vegetables
**tundra:** a large, flat area of frozen land without trees
**volcano:** a mountain from which hot melted rock, gas, smoke, and ash can escape from a hole in its top

## A3 After You Read

**Write *T* for true or *F* for false for each statement.**

__F__ **1.** Iceland is warm in the winter.

_____ **2.** Icelanders use geothermal energy.

_____ **3.** Geothermal energy comes from the sun.

_____ **4.** Icelanders heat their houses with oil.

_____ **5.** Icelanders don't grow fresh fruit.

_____ **6.** The sun shines all night in Iceland in the summer.

# B | FORM

# The Simple Present

## Think Critically About Form

**A.** Read the sentences and complete the tasks below.

**1a.** I <u>sell</u> bathing suits.　　**2a.** You <u>don't buy</u> fruit.
**1b.** He <u>sells</u> bathing suits.　　**2b.** She <u>doesn't buy</u> fruit.
**1c.** We <u>sell</u> bathing suits.　　**2c.** They <u>don't buy</u> fruit.

1. **COMPARE AND CONTRAST** Look at the affirmative verb forms in 1a–1c. What is different about the form in 1b?

2. **COMPARE AND CONTRAST** Look at the negative verb forms in 2a–2c. What is different about the form in 2b?

3. **IDENTIFY** Look back at the quiz on page 4 and the answers on page 5. Two affirmative forms are underlined, and two negative forms are circled. Find two more examples of each form.

4. **ANALYZE** Look at the questions below. Which is a *Yes/No* question? Which is an information question? How are they different? How are they the same?

   **a.** Does it snow in the winter?
   **b.** Where do they get the fruit and vegetables?

**B.** Discuss your answers with the class and read the Form charts to check them.

ONLINE PRACTICE

| AFFIRMATIVE STATEMENTS | | |
|---|---|---|
| **SUBJECT** | **BASE FORM OF VERB OR BASE FORM OF VERB + -S/-ES** | |
| I You | **eat** | fresh fruit. |
| He She It | **eats** | |
| We You They | **eat** | |

| NEGATIVE STATEMENTS | | | |
|---|---|---|---|
| **SUBJECT** | **DO/DOES + NOT** | **BASE FORM OF VERB** | |
| I You | **do not don't** | **eat** | fresh fruit. |
| He She It | **does not doesn't** | | |
| We You They | **do not don't** | | |

| YES/NO QUESTIONS | | | |
|---|---|---|---|
| *DO/DOES* | SUBJECT | BASE FORM OF VERB | |
| Do | you | | |
| Does | she | **eat** | fresh fruit? |
| Do | they | | |

| SHORT ANSWERS | | | | | | |
|---|---|---|---|---|---|---|
| *YES* | SUBJECT | *DO/DOES* | | *NO* | SUBJECT | *DO/DOES+ NOT* |
| | I | **do.** | | | I | **don't.** |
| Yes, | she | **does.** | | No, | she | **doesn't.** |
| | they | **do.** | | | they | **don't.** |

| INFORMATION QUESTIONS | | | | |
|---|---|---|---|---|
| *WH-* WORD | *DO/DOES* | SUBJECT | BASE FORM | |
| Who | **do** | you | **teach** | on Tuesdays? |
| What | **does** | he | **eat**? | |
| When | | | | |
| Where | **do** | they | **travel** | in the winter? |
| Why | | | | |
| How | | | | |

| *WH-* WORD (SUBJECT) | | BASE FORM OF VERB + *-S/-ES* | |
|---|---|---|---|
| Who | | **works** | on Tuesdays? |
| What | | **happens** | there? |

- In affirmative statements, add *-s* or *-es* to the base form of the verb when the subject is third-person singular (*he, she,* or *it*). See Appendices 1 and 2 for the spelling and pronunciation of verbs ending in *-s* and *-es*. See also Pronunciation Notes on page 9.

- Use *does* in negative statements and questions when the subject is third-person singular. For all other persons, use *do*.

  | | |
  |---|---|
  | She **doesn't play** golf. | I **don't play** golf. |
  | **Does** he **play** golf? | **Do** they **play** golf? |

Do not use *do* or *does* in information questions when *who* or *what* is the subject.

Who **lives** here?    X Who does live here? (INCORRECT)

- *Have* and *be* are irregular in the simple present.

  | | | |
  |---|---|---|
  | I **have** a problem. | She **has** a red car. | We **have** dinner at 6:00. |
  | I **am** busy. | He **is** a musician. | They **are** home. |

Do not use *do/does* in negative statements or in questions with *be*.

You **aren't** late.    **Is** he ready?

Form **CHAPTER 1** | 7

## B1 Listening for Form

🔊 CD1 T3    **Listen to this paragraph. Write the verb forms you hear.**

Many people in Hawaii _____live_____ in two different worlds—the world of traditional
                              1

Hawaiian culture and the world of modern American culture. Keenan Kanaeholo

_____ a typical Hawaiian. He _____ on the island of Oahu. Like many
     2                                    3

Hawaiians, Keenan _____ two languages. At home, he and his family
                          4

_____ English. They _____ to each other in Hawaiian. Keenan
     5                            6

_____ in a large hotel. At work, he _____ English. Keenan's wife, Emeha,
     7                                          8

_____ in the hotel. She _____ at an elementary school. Both Keenan
     9                              10

and Emeha _____ to dance. They _____ dancing on the weekends. Emeha
              11                             12

also _____ the hula, but Keenan _____ .
          13                                 14

## B2 Working on Affirmative and Negative Statements

**Complete this paragraph with the correct form of the verbs in parentheses.
Use contractions where possible.**

An okapi _____looks_____ (look) like the child of
                1

a zebra and a giraffe, but it _____ (not/be).
                                     2

It _____ (have) stripes like a zebra, and it
      3

_____ (have) a body like a giraffe. The
     4

okapi's stripes _____ (hide) it from its
                       5

enemies. The okapi _____ (be) a relative
                           6

of the giraffe, but it _____ (not/have)
                              7

a long neck. It _____ (not/need) one
                       8

to find food because it _____ (eat) fruit
                                9

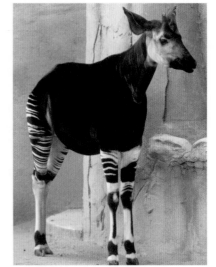

An okapi

and leaves near the ground. Okapis _____ (play) in a strange way. They
                                           10

_____ (put) their heads down, _____ (move) their tails, and _____
     11                                    12                                      13

(run) in circles. Okapis _____ (live) only in Central Africa and _____ (be)
                               14                                             15

very rare.

## Pronunciation Notes

### Pronunciation of Verbs Ending in *-s* or *-es*

The letters *-s* or *-es* at the end of third-person singular verbs are pronounced in three different ways, depending on the final sound of the base form of the verb.

1. The *-s* or *-es* is pronounced /s/ if the base form of the verb ends with the sound /p/, /t/, /k/, or /f/.

   stop — stops /stɑps/          like — likes /laɪks/          laugh — laughs /læfs/

2. The *-s* or *-es* is pronounced /z/ if the base form of the verb ends with the sound /b/, /d/, /ʊ/, /v/, /ð/, /m/, /n/, /ŋ/, /l/, /r/, or a vowel sound.

   leave — leaves /livz/          run — runs /rʌnz/          go — goes /goʊz/

3. The *-es* is pronounced /ɪz/ if the base form of the verb ends with the sound /s/, /z/, /ʃ/, /ʒ/, /tʃ/, /dʒ/, or /ks/. This adds an extra syllable to the word.

   notice — notices /ˈnoʊtəsɪz/  buzz — buzzes /ˈbʌzɪz/  watch — watches /ˈwatʃɪz/

## B3 Pronouncing Verbs Ending in *-s* or *-es*

 CD1 T4 **A.** Listen to the pronunciation of each verb. What ending do you hear? Check ( ✓ ) the correct column.

|     |           | /s/ | /z/ | /ɪz/ |
|-----|-----------|-----|-----|------|
| 1.  | lives     |     | ✓   |      |
| 2.  | practices |     |     |      |
| 3.  | works     |     |     |      |
| 4.  | closes    |     |     |      |
| 5.  | arranges  |     |     |      |
| 6.  | tells     |     |     |      |

**B.** Work with a partner. Take turns reading these sentences aloud. Be sure to pronounce the verb endings correctly.

1. Pablo lives in San Diego.
2. The team practices every day.
3. The computer works just fine.
4. My mother closes the window at night.
5. Tony arranges all the meetings.
6. Sheryl tells everyone's secrets.

## B4 Forming *Yes/No* Questions

**A.** Use these words and phrases to form *Yes/No* questions. Punctuate your sentences correctly.

1. study/do/a lot/you _Do you study a lot?_____

2. teacher/does/your/speak/language/your _____

3. have/do/homework/you/a lot of _____

4. a/do/use/you/dictionary _____

5. speak/you/do/English/of/class/outside _____

6. your/computers/school/does/have/many _____

**B.** Work with a partner. Take turns asking and answering the questions in part A.

*A: Do you study a lot?*
*B: Yes, I do.* OR *No, I don't.*

## B5 Changing Statements into Questions

**A.** Write an information question about each underlined word or phrase.

1. <u>Water</u> freezes at 32° Fahrenheit. _What freezes at 32° Fahrenheit?_____

2. <u>Kim</u> has a test today. _____

3. A power plant makes <u>electricity</u>. _____

4. Niagara Falls is <u>in North America</u>. _____

5. <u>Dan</u> drives Lee to school every day. _____

6. Dan drives <u>Lee</u> to school every day. _____

7. It is hot in Chicago <u>in the summer</u>. _____

8. The eucalyptus tree is from <u>Australia</u>. _____

**B.** In your notebook, write a *Yes/No* question about each sentence in part A.

*Does water freeze at 32° Fahrenheit?*

# The Simple Present

## Think Critically About Meaning and Use

**A.** Read the sentences and answer the questions below.

   **a.** Thailand has three seasons: a hot season, a cold season, and a rainy season.

   **b.** Maria doesn't like her new roommate.

   **c.** My teacher always arrives at school before class starts.

   **1. EVALUATE** Which sentence talks about a repeated activity?

   **2. EVALUATE** Which sentence talks about factual information that you can find in a book?

   **3. EVALUATE** Which sentence talks about a feeling?

**B.** Discuss your answers with the class and read the Meaning and Use Notes to check them.

## Meaning and Use Notes

ONLINE
PRACTICE

### Repeated Activities

▶ **1**    Use the simple present to talk about activities that happen repeatedly (again and again). These events can be personal habits or routines (for example, activities at home or at work), or scheduled events.

| **Habits or Routines** | **Scheduled Events** |
|---|---|
| I always **eat** cereal for breakfast. | School **starts** at 8:00 and **finishes** at 3:00. |
| He **takes** the bus to work every day. | The club **meets** in the library every Friday. |

### Factual Information

▶ **2**    Use the simple present to talk about factual information, such as general truths, scientific facts, or definitions.

| **General Truths** | **Definitions** |
|---|---|
| Doctors **study** for many years. | The word *brilliant* **means** "very intelligent." |

**Scientific Facts**
Iceland **has** more than 100 volcanoes.

*(Continued on page 12)*

## States or Conditions

▶ **3** Use the simple present with stative verbs (verbs that do not express action) to talk about states or conditions, such as physical descriptions, feelings, relationships, knowledge, beliefs, or possession. Some common stative verbs are *be, have, seem, like, want, know, understand, mean, believe, own,* and *belong*. See Appendix 7 for a list of common stative verbs.

| | |
|---|---|
| He **is** tall and **has** dark hair. | She **knows** the answer. |
| She **seems** angry. | I don't **understand**. |
| You **like** sports. | I **believe** you. |
| They **want** a new car. | We **belong** to the soccer club. |

## Adverbs of Frequency with the Simple Present

▶ **4** Use adverbs of frequency with the simple present to express how often something happens. Adverbs of frequency usually come before the main verb, but after the verb *be*.

She **always** has ballet from 3:00 to 6:00 P.M.

The cafeteria food is **usually** bad.

My mother **often** cooks for us.

It **sometimes** rains here in the summer.

My brother and I **seldom** fight.

He **never** cleans his room.

## C1 Listening for Meaning and Use

▶ Notes 1, 2

CD1 T5 Listen to each statement. Is the speaker describing a personal routine or a general truth? Check ( ✓ ) the correct column.

| | PERSONAL ROUTINE | GENERAL TRUTH |
|---|---|---|
| 1. | | ✓ |
| 2. | | |
| 3. | | |
| 4. | | |
| 5. | | |
| 6. | | |

## C2 Talking About Routines

▶ Notes 1, 4

**A.** Read these statements. Check ( ✓ ) the ones that are true for you.

_____ **1.** I always wash the dishes after dinner.

_____ **2.** I often ride the bus in the morning.

_____ **3.** My friends sometimes visit me on Saturdays.

_____ **4.** I often get up at 7:00 A.M.

_____ **5.** I usually recycle paper.

_____ **6.** I never go to bed before midnight.

_____ **7.** My friends and I sometimes study together in the evenings.

_____ **8.** I never stay home on Saturday nights.

**B.** Work with a partner. Look at the statements in part A that you did not check. Take turns talking about them.

A: *I don't always wash the dishes after dinner. I sometimes leave them for the next day.*

B: *I seldom ride the bus in the morning. I have a car.*

## C3 Asking for Definitions

▶ Note 2

**A.** Work with a partner. How much do you remember from the quiz about Iceland on page 4? Take turns asking and answering questions about the meaning of these words. If you don't remember the meaning of a word, look at the definitions on page 5.

**1.** tundra

A: *What does the word* tundra *mean?*

B: *The word* tundra *means "a large, flat area of frozen land."*

**2.** glacier

**3.** greenhouse

**4.** climate

**5.** geyser

**6.** volcano

**B.** Look back at the quiz on page 4. Find a word that is new to you and ask your partner what it means. If your partner doesn't know, look in a dictionary.

**A. Complete this paragraph with the correct form of the verbs in parentheses.**

Bobsledding ____is____ (be) a dangerous sport. A bobsled
1

_____ (weigh) about 600 pounds and _____ (carry) four people. Each
2                                                           3

person on a bobsled team _____ (have) an important job. First, all four
4

people _____ (move) the sled back and forth. When it _____ (start) to
5                                                              6

move, they _____ (push) it very hard, and the pilot _____ (jump) into the
7                                                              8

bobsled to steer. Then, the person on each side _____ (jump) in.
9

The brakeman _____ (stay) at the back and _____ (push) for a few more
10                                            11

seconds. Then he or she _____ (get) in, too. The bobsled _____ (be) very
12                                                    13

fast. It _____ (go) up to 90 miles per hour.
14

**B. Describe another sport. In your notebook, write five or six facts about the sport, using the simple present.**

> Ice hockey is a popular sport in cold places like Canada and the northeastern United States. This game has two teams of players. The players wear ice skates and play on an ice-skating rink...

## Think Critically About Meaning and Use

**A.** Look at these topics. Check ( ✓ ) the ones you can discuss or write about using the simple present.

✓ **1.** Traditions in your country

—— **2.** Your childhood

—— **3.** A concert you went to last night

—— **4.** The geography of a country

—— **5.** The life of a 19th-century politician

—— **6.** A vacation you took

—— **7.** How a machine works

—— **8.** Your best friend's personality

**B.** Discuss these questions in small groups.

**1. GENERATE** Create two simple present sentences about one of the topics.

**2. SYNTHESIZE** What are some other topics to discuss in the simple present?

## Edit

Find the errors in this paragraph and correct them.

Which large American city ~~are~~ *is* on three islands? New York City! New York is on Manhattan Island, Long Island, and Staten Island. Most people thinks of Manhattan when they think of New York City. This is because Manhattan have the tall buildings that New York is famous for. Sometimes people travel from Staten Island to Manhattan by boat. However, most people in New York not use boats to go from one part of the city to another. Large bridges connects the islands. Trains and cars also uses long tunnels under the water to move between the islands. In fact, New Yorkers usually forget that they lives on an island.

## Write

Write a factual paragraph about an unusual animal. Follow the steps below to write the paragraph. Use the simple present.

1. **BRAINSTORM** Think about an unusual animal and research it on the Internet. Look for information about the animal and its habits. Take notes about what you want to say. Use these questions to help you.

   - What does this animal look like?
   - Where does it live?
   - What does it eat?
   - When and where does it sleep?
   - What are its habits?
   - How is this animal unusual and interesting?

2. **WRITE A FIRST DRAFT** Before you write your draft, read the checklist below. Write your draft using the simple present.

3. **EDIT** Read your work and check it against the checklist below. Circle grammar, spelling, and punctuation errors.

| DO I ... | YES |
|---|---|
| give basic facts and show how the animal is unusual? | ☐ |
| use the simple present? | ☐ |
| include at least one positive statement? | ☐ |
| include at least one negative statement? | ☐ |
| use correct forms for irregular *have* and *be*? | ☐ |

4. **PEER REVIEW** Work with a partner to decide how to fix your errors and improve the content.

5. **REWRITE YOUR DRAFT** Using the comments from your partner, write a final draft.

> Moles are small mammals. They live in North America, Europe, and Asia. They are usually underground. A mole has tiny eyes and doesn't see much...

# 2

# Imperatives

# Dos and Don'ts with Bears

### A1 Before You Read

Discuss these questions.

Do you like to walk in the woods? Are there wild animals in the woods in your area? Are they dangerous?

### A2 Read

 CD1 T6 Read the webpage on the following page to find out about what to do if you see a bear.

### A3 After You Read

Write *T* for true or *F* for false for each statement.

___F___ **1.** Bears often attack cars.

_____ **2.** If a bear attacks you, you should run.

_____ **3.** Bears attack when they feel threatened.

_____ **4.** Bears are great tree climbers.

_____ **5.** Garbage attracts bears because they think it is food.

_____ **6.** Bears are slow and weak.

## BLACK BEAR MOUNTAIN PARK

# Dos and Don'ts with Bears

About 250 black bears live in Black Bear Mountain Park. If you run into a bear in the park, it is important to know what to do.

5  Talk loudly, sing, or clap as you walk through the woods. Bears don't like surprises. Singing or clapping will probably frighten the bears off before you even see them.

  Don't hike through the woods at night.
10 Bears are most active at nighttime.

  If you are in a car and see a bear, stay inside. Close the windows. Most bears will not attack a car, so you are safest inside. Don't get out to take a photograph.

15  If you are outside and see a bear, stay calm. Stand still and don't run. Slowly move backward. Bears are nervous animals. They are more likely to attack you if they feel threatened.

20  If a bear attacks you, don't fight. Lie still and be quiet. Maybe the bear will lose interest and wander off.

  Do not climb a tree to get away from a bear. Bears are great tree climbers!

25  Do not keep food or cosmetics in your tent. Put them in a bag and hang them in a tree that is at least 100 yards from your tent. Bears like anything that resembles food. Remove food, cosmetics, and toothpaste
30 from your tent so you won't attract their attention.

  Burn food waste. Bears cannot tell the difference between food and garbage. They will go after both.

35 Remember bears are dangerous animals. They are very fast and very strong. Be safe. Don't be sorry!

---

**attract:** to cause someone or something to feel interest

**dos and don'ts:** rules about what you should and should not do in a situation

**resemble:** to be like or to look like

**run into:** meet by chance

**wander off:** to walk away from a place

# B FORM

## Imperatives

### Think Critically About Form

**A.** Read the sentences and complete the tasks below.

a. Bears are nervous animals.  c. Most bears do not attack cars.
b. Do not climb a tree.  d. Lie still and be quiet.

1. **IDENTIFY** Underline the verbs. Circle the subjects. Which sentences do not seem to have a subject? These are imperatives.

2. **RECOGNIZE** Look back at the webpage on page 19. Find five imperatives.

**B.** Discuss your answers with the class and read the Form charts to check them.

ONLINE
PRACTICE

| AFFIRMATIVE IMPERATIVES | |
| --- | --- |
| **BASE FORM OF VERB** | |
| **Open** | your books. |
| **Drive** | carefully. |
| **Be** | here at six. |

| NEGATIVE IMPERATIVES | | |
| --- | --- | --- |
| *DO + NOT* | **BASE FORM OF VERB** | |
| **Do not**<br>**Don't** | **open** | your books. |
| | **leave** | yet. |
| | **be** | late. |

- The subject of an imperative is *you* (singular or plural), even though we don't usually say or write the subject.
- The imperative has the same form whether we talk to one person or more than one.
  **Teacher to Student: Sit** down, please.      **Teacher to Class: Sit** down, please.
- In spoken English, *don't* is more common than *do not* in negative imperatives.

## B1 Listening for Form

CD1 T7  Listen to these sentences. Write the verb forms you hear.

1. _Don't leave._ It's early.

2. _____ right at the corner.

3. _____ in the kitchen.

4. _____ home before dinner.

5. _____ angry with me, please.

6. Please _____ off the light.

## B2 Forming Sentences with Imperatives

Use these words and phrases to form sentences with affirmative and negative imperatives. Punctuate your sentences correctly.

1. take/you/your/with/book _Take your book with you._

2. notebook/leave/your/home/at/don't _____

3. tomorrow/be/for/test/ready/the _____

4. questions/to/the/answer/all/try _____

5. not/the/during/talk/test/do _____

## B3 Working on Affirmative and Negative Imperatives

A. Read the tips below. Check ( ✓ ) the ones that you think are bad advice.

   _✓_ 1. Don't write English definitions for new words.

   ____ 2. Keep a vocabulary notebook.

   ____ 3. Don't try to use new words in conversation.

   ____ 4. Look up every new word you read.

   ____ 5. Try to guess the meaning of new words.

   ____ 6. Write a translation of every new word.

 B. Now change the bad advice to good advice. Compare answers with a partner.

   _Write English definitions for new words._

## B4 Building Sentences

Build ten imperative and simple present sentences. Use a word or phrase from each column, or from the second and third columns only. Punctuate **imperatives with an exclamation point.**

Imperative: _Listen to him!_       Simple Present: _She goes to class._

| she | goes | to class |
|------|--------|----------|
| don't | listen | gum |
| they | speak | late |
| | chew | to him |
| | is | Korean |

# Imperatives

## Think Critically About Meaning and Use

**A.** Read the sentences and answer the questions below.

    **a.** <u>Walk to the corner and turn left.</u> The post office is right there.

    **b.** <u>Watch out!</u> There's ice on the road.

    **c.** Are you getting coffee now? <u>Buy me a coffee, too, please.</u>

    **d.** <u>Talk to the teacher.</u> She can help you.

    **1. IDENTIFY** Which underlined sentence gives advice?

    **2. IDENTIFY** Which underlined sentence makes a request?

    **3. IDENTIFY** Which underlined sentence gives directions?

    **4. IDENTIFY** Which underlined sentence gives a warning?

**B.** Discuss your answers with the class and read the Meaning and Use Notes to check them.

## Meaning and Use Notes

ONLINE
PRACTICE

| **Common Uses of Imperatives** | |
|---|---|
| **▶ 1A** | An imperative tells someone to do something. Common uses include: |

        *Giving Commands:*   **Stop** the car!

        *Giving Advice:*   **Don't worry** about it.

        *Making Requests:*   Please **come** home early.

        *Giving Directions:*   **Turn** left. **Walk** three blocks.

        *Giving Instructions:*   First, **peel** the potatoes. Then, **boil** the water.

        *Giving Warnings:*   **Be** careful! The floor is wet.

        *Making Offers:*   Here. **Have** another piece of cake, Gina.

**▶ 1B**   Although we usually leave out the subject *you* (singular or plural), it is understood as the subject of an imperative.

**Boss to Employee**                 **Boss to Several Employees**

**Come** to my office, please.         **Come** to my office, please.

## Imperatives and Politeness

▶ **2A** Use *please* to make an imperative sound more polite or less authoritative. We often use imperatives with *please* in formal situations when we speak to strangers or to people in authority. In less formal situations, especially with friends and family members, *please* is often used to soften the tone of an imperative. If *please* comes at the end of a sentence, we put a comma before it.

| **Train Conductor to Passenger** | **Child to Parent** |
|---|---|
| <u>Please</u> **watch** your step. | Mom, **hand** me a towel, <u>please</u>. I spilled my drink. |

▶ **2B** You can also make an imperative sound more polite by using polite forms such as *sir, ma'am,* or *miss*. In written English, the polite form of address is separated from the rest of the sentence with a comma.

| <u>Sir</u>, **watch** your step! | **Stay** calm, <u>ma'am</u>. Help is on the way. |
|---|---|

## Using *You* or Names in Imperatives

▶ **3A** Although we usually leave out the subject *you*, we sometimes use it to make it clear who we are speaking to. We can also add the person's name with or without *you* as the stated subject.

**A Roommate to Two Other Roommates**

<u>You</u> **sweep** the hall, <u>you</u> **vacuum** the living room, and I'll clean the bathroom.

<u>Maria</u>, <u>you</u> **sweep** the hall. <u>Mei</u>, <u>you</u> **vacuum** the rug. I'll clean the bathroom.

# C1 Listening for Meaning and Use

▶ Notes 1–3

CD1 T8  Listen to each conversation. Who are the speakers? Choose the correct answer.

1.  a. a boss and an employee
    b. two co-workers
    c. two strangers

2.  a. a teacher and a student
    b. two family members
    c. two strangers

3.  a. two strangers
    b. two friends
    c. two family members

4.  a. two family members
    b. two strangers
    c. a boss and an employee

5.  a. a boss and an employee
    b. two family members
    c. two strangers

6.  a. a teacher and a student
    b. two friends
    c. two strangers

## C2 Giving Warnings and Commands

▶ Notes 1A, 1B, 2A

Look at the pictures. Match the warnings and commands to the pictures.

Stop! Police!    Please put your seat belt on.    Watch out for the ball!
Look out!    Don't step on the truck!    Sit down and be quiet.

1. _Look out!_

4. _____

2. _____

5. _____

3. _____

6. _____

## C3 Making Requests

▶ **Notes 1A, 1B, 2A, 2B**

Work with a partner. Write a request that you might hear in each place below.

1. (in a classroom) *Please give your papers to me.*

2. (in an office) _____

3. (in an airport) _____

4. (at the dinner table) _____

5. (at home) _____

6. (at a movie theater) _____

## C4 Giving Advice

▶ **Notes 1A, 1B**

Read each problem. In your notebook, write two sentences of advice: one with an affirmative imperative and one with a negative imperative. Then compare answers with a partner.

1. The light doesn't work.

   *Don't touch the lightbulb. Turn the light off first.*

2. My son is sick.

3. The gas tank is almost empty.

4. I can't sleep at night.

5. I don't have many friends.

6. I have a headache.

## C5 Giving Instructions

▶ **Note 1A, 1B, 2A**

Work with a partner. You are leaving on vacation, and a friend is going to stay in your apartment. Take turns telling your friend what to do while you are away. Use affirmative and negative imperatives.

| cat | mail | newspaper | rent | voice | mail |
|-----|------|-----------|------|-------|------|
| lights | neighbors | plants | trash | windows | |

*Don't forget to feed the cat.*
*Please leave the lights on at night.*

## C6 Understanding Uses of the Imperative

▶ Notes 1–3

A. Write an appropriate affirmative or negative imperative sentence for each situation.

1. Your friend is new in town. Tell him how to go to the post office:

   *Go down three blocks and turn left at the traffic light.*

2. You are a bus driver. A man is getting off the bus. Tell him to watch his step.

   _____

3. You are going on vacation with some friends. Your mother is worried. Reassure her.

   _____

4. You are a salesperson. Tell your customer to sign the credit card receipt.

   _____

5. You want your roommates to help you clean the apartment. Give each person a chore.

   _____

6. You dropped a glass on the floor. Warn your roommate.

   _____

7. Josh, a close friend, is visiting your home. Offer him something to eat.

   _____

8. Your uncle looks very tired. Give him some advice.

   _____

9. You are going out to dinner with some co-workers. Tell them to wait for you in the lobby.

   _____

10. You are crossing a busy street with your cousin. Give her a warning.

    _____

 B. Would you use *you* in any of the situations in part A? Why or why not? Discuss your ideas with a partner.

# WRITING   Write a Recipe

 **Think Critically About Meaning and Use**

A. Read what each person says. Is the imperative appropriate for the situation? If it is not appropriate, rewrite it.

1. (a police officer to a driver) Please pull over immediately. You're blocking the ambulance.

    _Pull over immediately! You're blocking the ambulance._

2. (a cook to his assistant) Bake the chicken at 375°F for one hour.

    _____

3. (one stranger to another on the street) Please look out! A car is coming!

    _____

4. (a young girl to her grandmother) Sit down!

    _____

5. (an adult to a child) Turn off the television, sir.

    _____

B. Discuss these questions in small groups.

1. **EVALUATE**  Why were the imperatives that you rewrote not appropriate?

2. **DRAW A CONCLUSION**  In what situation would the inappropriate imperative in 1 be appropriate?

## Edit

Some of these sentences have errors. Find the errors and correct them.

1. You ~~don't worrying~~ about your memory.
    ^Don't worry^

2. Be not noisy!

3. Don't to listen to her.

4. Megan, closes the door, please.

5. Study the vocabulary for tomorrow's test.

6. Leave not now!

## Write

**Write a recipe for a favorite food. Follow the steps below to write the recipe, including the ingredients and the steps for making the food. Use imperatives.**

1. **BRAINSTORM** Think about a favorite food that you know how to cook or bake. Think about how to prepare the food. Use these questions to help you.
   - What ingredients does this recipe use? How much of each ingredient? Make a list.
   - What is the first step in the recipe? What are the next steps? What is the last step? Write the steps in order.
   - Is there anything else people need to know about the recipe? Include that information.
   - Is there anything people should be careful *not* to do?

2. **WRITE A FIRST DRAFT** Before you write your draft, read the checklist below. Write your draft using imperatives.

3. **EDIT** Read your work and check it against the checklist below. Circle grammar, spelling, and punctuation errors.

| DO I ... | YES |
|---|---|
| give all the steps in the recipe? | ☐ |
| give all the ingredients and amounts? | ☐ |
| give clear directions? | ☐ |
| use imperatives correctly? | ☐ |

4. **PEER REVIEW** Work with a partner to decide how to fix your errors and improve the content.

5. **REWRITE YOUR DRAFT** Using the comments from your partner, write a final draft.

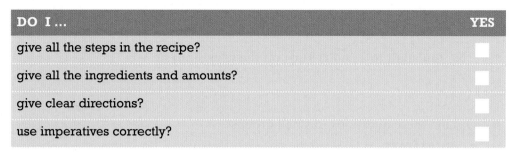

My favorite recipe is my mother's chocolate cake. First, beat two eggs in a bowl. Then, add a cup of milk and stir well. Next...

# CHAPTER

# 3

# The Present Continuous

# Long-Distance Voyager

## A1 Before You Read

 Discuss these questions.

Do you think exploring space is important? Why or why not? What do you think we can learn by exploring space?

## A2 Read

CD1 T9   Read the magazine article on the following page to find out about a famous spacecraft.

## A3 After You Read

Write *T* for true or *F* for false for each statement.

___T__ **1.** *Voyager* is a spacecraft.

_____ **2.** *Voyager* is traveling through space.

_____ **3.** *Voyager* is coming back to Earth soon.

_____ **4.** *Voyager* is reaching the end of the solar system.

_____ **5.** We aren't getting information from *Voyager* now.

_____ **6.** *Voyager* signals go to large antennas.

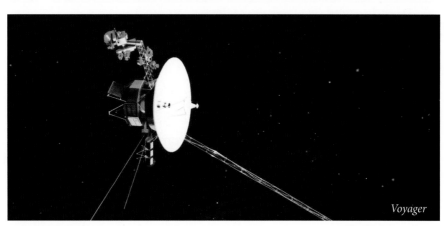
*Voyager*

## LONG-DISTANCE
# Voyager

    *Voyager 1* is a spacecraft that left Earth in 1977. Its purpose was to explore our solar system. Scientists expected to receive information about Jupiter and Saturn from *Voyager* for ten to fifteen years. They were wrong. They are still receiving messages from *Voyager* today. *Voyager* is currently moving away from
5  Earth at a speed of over 38,000 miles per hour (over 61,000 kilometers per hour). Now it is so far away that its messages take over fifteen hours to travel to Earth.

    How far away is *Voyager 1* now and what is it exploring? *Voyager* is many billions of miles from us. It is farther from Earth than any other human-made object. It is traveling in a part of our solar system beyond all the planets. In fact,
10  it is approaching the outer boundaries of our solar system. These days, *Voyager*'s messages are giving us information about this most distant part of our solar system. Large antennas on Earth are receiving its signals.

    Soon *Voyager* will leave our solar system. Then it will send us information about interstellar space—the space between our Sun and other stars. *Voyager* will
15  continue into interstellar space, and we will continue to learn from *Voyager*. Finally, sometime between about 2020 and 2025, *Voyager* will stop sending information and will travel silently through space.

---

**antenna:** equipment that receives signals

**outer boundaries:** far borders

**solar system:** the Sun and the planets that move around it

**spacecraft:** a vehicle that can travel in space

**voyager:** somebody or something that travels

# B FORM

# The Present Continuous

## Think Critically About Form

**A.** Read the sentences and complete the tasks below.

  **a.** *Voyager* is many billions of miles from us.
  **b.** It is traveling in a part of our solar system beyond all the planets.

  **1. IDENTIFY** Underline the verbs. Which is simple present? Which is present continuous?

  **2. DEFINE** How many words are necessary to form the present continuous? What ending is added to the base form of the verb?

  **3. RECOGNIZE** Look back at the article on page 31. Find three examples of the present continuous.

**B.** Discuss your answers with the class and read the Form charts to check them.

**ONLINE PRACTICE**

### AFFIRMATIVE STATEMENTS

| SUBJECT | BE | BASE FORM OF VERB + -ING | |
|---|---|---|---|
| I | am | | |
| You | are | | |
| He<br>She<br>It | is | working | today. |
| We<br>You<br>They | are | | |

| CONTRACTIONS | | |
|---|---|---|
| I'm | | |
| You're | working | today. |
| He's | | |
| They're | | |

### NEGATIVE STATEMENTS

| SUBJECT | BE | NOT | BASE FORM OF VERB + -ING | |
|---|---|---|---|---|
| I | am | | | |
| You | are | | | |
| He<br>She<br>It | is | not | working | today. |
| We<br>You<br>They | are | | | |

| CONTRACTIONS | | |
|---|---|---|
| I'm not | | |
| You're not<br>You aren't | | |
| He's not<br>He isn't | working | today. |
| They're not<br>They aren't | | |

| YES/NO QUESTIONS | | | |
|---|---|---|---|
| SUBJECT | SUBJECT | BASE FORM OF VERB + *-ING* | |
| Are | you | | |
| Is | it | **working** | now? |
| Are | they | | |

| SHORT ANSWERS | | | | | |
|---|---|---|---|---|---|
| YES | SUBJECT | BE | NO | SUBJECT + *BE* + *NOT* | |
| | I | am. | | I'm **not**. | |
| Yes, | it | is. | No, | it **isn't**. | |
| | they | are. | | they **aren't**. | |

| INFORMATION QUESTIONS | | | |
|---|---|---|---|
| *WH-* WORD | *BE* | SUBJECT | BASE FORM OF VERB + *-ING* |
| How | am | I | **doing**? |
| Who | are | you | **calling**? |
| What | is | he | **studying**? |
| Where | are | they | **working**? |
| Who | are | they | **visiting**? |

| *WH-* WORD (SUBJECT) | *BE* | | BASE FORM OF VERB + *-ING* |
|---|---|---|---|
| Who | is | | **laughing**? |
| What | is | | **happening**? |

- See Appendix 3 for the spelling of verbs ending in *-ing*.
- See Appendix 16 for more contractions with *be*.

> **!** Do not use contractions in affirmative short answers.
> Yes, I **am**.     **X** Yes, I'm. (INCORRECT)

> **!** Do not use a subject pronoun in information questions when *who* or *what* is the subject.
> **What** is happening?     **X** What is it happening? (INCORRECT)

## B1 Listening for Form

CD1 T10  Listen to each sentence. Choose the verb form you hear.

1. a. is living
   b. isn't living
   c. are living
   d. aren't living

2. a. am trying
   b. am not trying
   c. are trying
   d. are not trying

3. a. is meeting
   b. is not meeting
   c. are meeting
   d. are not meeting

4. a. am sleeping
   b. am not sleeping
   c. is sleeping
   d. is not sleeping

5. a. is working
   b. isn't working
   c. are working
   d. aren't working

6. a. am cooking
   b. am not cooking
   c. are cooking
   d. aren't cooking

## B2 Forming Statements and *Yes/No* Questions

A. Form sentences in the present continuous from these words and phrases. Use contractions where possible, and punctuate your sentences correctly.

1. in Canada/Maria and Hector/live

   Maria and Hector are living in Canada.

2. Hector/in a factory/work

3. not/Maria/in a factory/work

4. she/Spanish/teach

5. English/Hector/at night/study

6. not/live/they/in an apartment

7. rent/a small house/they

_____

8. learn/Maria and Hector/about life in Canada

_____

**B.** Work with a partner. Take turns asking and answering *Yes/No* questions about the sentences in part A.

A: *Are Maria and Hector living in Canada?*

B: *Yes, they are.* OR

A: *Are Maria and Hector living in the United States?*

B: *No, they're not. They're living in Canada.*

## B3 Writing Information Questions

Write an information question about each underlined word or phrase.

1. The rice is burning!

   What is burning?_____

2. Carol is talking on the telephone.

   _____

3. Ben is reading the newspaper.

   _____

4. Eric is studying at the library.

   _____

5. Their children are playing a game.

   _____

6. The children are yelling because they're excited.

   _____

7. He's feeling sad today.

   _____

8. They're doing their homework now.

   _____

## MEANING AND USE

# The Present Continuous

## Think Critically About Meaning and Use

**A.** Read the sentences and answer the questions below.

   **a.** The earth's climate is becoming warmer.

   **b.** I'm eating dinner now. Can I call you back?

   **c.** I'm taking a computer programming course this semester.

   **1. EVALUATE** Which sentence describes an activity that is happening at the exact moment the speaker is talking?

   **2. EVALUATE** Which sentence describes an activity that is in progress, but not happening at the exact moment the speaker is talking?

   **3. EVALUATE** Which sentence describes a changing situation?

**B.** Discuss your answers with the class and read the Meaning and Use Notes to check them.

## Meaning and Use Notes

ONLINE
PRACTICE

| Activities in Progress |
| --- |

▶ **1A**   Use the present continuous for activities that are in progress (or happening) at the exact moment the speaker is talking. You can use time expressions such as *now* or *right now* to emphasize that an action is happening currently (and may end soon).

**Activities in Progress at This Exact Moment**

Look! It**'s snowing**!

She**'s making** dinner <u>now</u>.

Steve can't come to the phone <u>right now</u>. He**'s taking** a bath.

▶ **1B**   Use the present continuous for activities that are in progress, but not happening at the exact moment the speaker is talking. You can use time expressions such as *this week* or *these days* to show when the action is happening.

**Activities in Progress, but Not Happening at This Exact Moment**

I**'m looking** for a cheap car. Do you have any ideas?

I**'m painting** my house <u>this week</u>. It**'s taking** a long time.

▶ **1C**  Use the present continuous for changing situations.

**Changing Situations**

My grades **are improving** this semester.

Computers **are getting** cheaper all the time.

## Stative Verbs and the Present Continuous

▶ **2A**  Many stative verbs are not generally used in the present continuous. They are usually used in the simple present. Some of these verbs are *know, mean, own, seem,* and *understand*. See Appendix 7 for a list of more stative verbs.

| **Simple Present** | **Present Continuous** |
|---|---|
| **Do** you **know** the answer? | X Are you knowing the answer? (INCORRECT) |
| What **does** *solar system* **mean**? | X What is *solar system* meaning? (INCORRECT) |
| We **don't own** a car. | X We're not owning a car. (INCORRECT) |

▶ **2B**  Some stative verbs can be used in the present continuous, but they are used as action verbs and have a different meaning from their simple present meaning. Some of these verbs are *have, look, see, taste, think,* and *weigh*.

| **Simple Present** | **Present Continuous** |
|---|---|
| They **have** a large house. (They own a large house.) | They**'re having** a good time. (They're experiencing a good time.) |
| Mark **looks** very unhappy. (Mark seems unhappy.) | Mark **is looking** for his car keys. (Mark is searching for his car keys.) |
| I **see** Lisa. She's behind Bob. (I'm looking at Lisa.) | I**'m seeing** a physical therapist for my back pain. (I'm going to a physical therapist.) |
| The soup **tastes** salty. (The soup has a salty taste.) | The chef **is tasting** the soup. (The chef is trying the soup.) |
| I **think** that's a great idea. (I believe that's a great idea.) | I**'m thinking** about Lisa. I'm worried about her. (Lisa is in my thoughts right now.) |
| The package **weighs** two pounds. (Its weight is two pounds.) | The postal worker **is weighing** the package. (The postal worker is using a scale.) |

▶ **2C**  Stative verbs that refer to physical conditions can occur in the simple present or present continuous with no difference in meaning. Some of these verbs are *ache, feel,* and *hurt*.

| **Simple Present** | **Present Continuous** |
|---|---|
| I **don't feel** well. | I**'m not feeling** well. |
| My throat **hurts**. | My throat **is hurting**. |

## C1 Listening for Meaning and Use

▶ Note 1A

CD1 T11   Listen to the announcements. Where would you hear each one?

in an airport       on an airplane       on a train
in a store          on a ship            on television or the radio

1. _on an airplane_      3. _____      5. _____

2. _____      4. _____      6. _____

## C2 Understanding Meaning and Use

▶ Notes 1A–1C

Read each conversation and look at the underlined verb form. Is the statement that follows true or false? Write *T* for true or *F* for false. Then discuss your answers with a partner.

1. **Carol:** Thanks for the ride, Marta. You seem really tired. Are you OK?

   **Marta:** Well, I'm working a lot of extra hours these days. I guess I am pretty tired.

   __F__ Marta is working in the office right now.

2. **Dan:** I need to find a cheap apartment, and it's not easy.

   **Lee:** I know. Rents here are getting higher every year.

   _____ The cost of renting an apartment is changing.

3. **Amy:** How's school this semester?

   **Emily:** Great! I'm studying physics, and I really like it.

   _____ Emily is studying physics at this exact moment.

4. **Nesha:** Please answer the phone, Nicole.

   **Nicole:** I'm sorry. I can't. I'm helping a customer.

   _____ Nicole is helping a customer right now.

5. **Steve:** How's your new kitten?

   **Jenny:** Don't ask! She's ruining everything in my apartment.

   _____ The kitten is ruining everything these days.

6. **Mei:** What's wrong, Hanna? You don't look happy.

   **Hanna:** I'm getting a cold.

   _____ Hanna woke up with a bad cold.

## C3 Describing Activities in Progress

▶ Note 1A

Look at the pictures. How are they different? In your notebook, write as many sentences as you can. Use the verbs below and the present continuous. (You can use some verbs more than once.)

chase    enter    help    look    run    shout    wait    walk

*In picture 1, the police officer is helping the woman.*

*In picture 2, he isn't helping the woman. He's chasing a thief.*

# Vocabulary Notes

## Adverbs and Time Expressions with the Present Continuous

**Still and the Present Continuous** *Still* is an adverb that is often used with the present continuous. *Still* emphasizes that the activity or state is in progress. It often suggests surprise that the activity or state has not ended. Place *still* after *be* in affirmative statements, before *be* in negative statements, and after the subject in questions.

| **Affirmative Statement** | **Negative Statement** |
| --- | --- |
| He is **still** living with his parents. | He **still** isn't living on his own. |

| ***Yes/No* Question** | **Information Question** |
| --- | --- |
| Is he **still** living with his parents? | Why is he **still** living with his parents? |

**Time Expressions with the Present Continuous** Time expressions are also commonly used with the present continuous. Some time expressions refer to an exact moment in the present. These include *now, right now,* and *at the moment.*

Others refer to a longer time period that includes the present moment. These include *this morning, this afternoon, this evening, this week, this month, this semester, this year, these days,* and *nowadays.*

Time expressions can occur at the beginning or end of a sentence.

| **Exact Moment** | **Longer Time Period** |
| --- | --- |
| **Now** I'm making dinner. | She's working hard **this morning**. |
| He's sleeping **right now**. | **This week** I'm doing research at the library. |
| He's taking a shower **at the moment**. | |
| | She's feeling much better **these days**. |

## C4 Using Adverbs and Time Expressions with the Present Continuous

In your notebook, write sentences about yourself and people you know. Use the present continuous and these subjects and time expressions.

1. I/right now
   *I am studying English right now.*

2. My best friend/these days

3. Some of my friends/still

4. My English class/right now

5. My family/nowadays

6. I/still

7. I/this year

8. My neighbor/still

## C5 Contrasting Routines with Activities in Progress ▶ Note 1A

Look at the pictures. In your notebook, use these words and phrases to write sentences about the people's jobs and what they are doing now.

**1.** Tom/drive a taxi/watch TV

*Tom drives a taxi. Now he's watching TV.*

**4.** Greg/teach math/play the violin

**2.** Celia/teach filmmaking/shop for food

**5.** David/cook in a restaurant/fish

**3.** Linda and Kendra/wait on tables/go to the movies

**6.** Ed and Riku/work in a hospital/bowl

## C6 Distinguishing Between States and Actions

▶ Notes 2A–2C

A. Complete this conversation with the correct form of the verbs in parentheses. Use the simple present or present continuous. More than one answer is sometimes possible.

**Doctor:** What ___seems___ (seem) to be the problem?
1

**Rita:** I _____ (not/know). My head _____ (hurt),
2                     3

and my stomach _____ (ache).
4

**Doctor:** You _____ (look) pale. I _____ (think) it's probably the flu.
5                       6

**Rita:** Oh, no! I _____ (have) a hard time at work right now. I can't get
7

sick now!

**Doctor:** I _____ (think) about your health right now, not your work.
8

 B. Practice the conversation in part A with a partner.

## C7 Distinguishing Differences in Meaning

▶ Notes 2B–2C

A. Read each pair of sentences and look at the underlined verbs. Do the verbs have different meanings or the same meaning? Write *D* for different or *S* for same. Discuss your answers in small groups.

___D___ **1. a.** You <u>look</u> really nice today.

      **b.** We<u>'re looking</u> at some photos right now.

_____ **2. a.** I <u>weigh</u> 150 pounds.

      **b.** The clerk <u>is weighing</u> the bananas.

_____ **3. a.** I need to go home because I don't <u>feel</u> well.

      **b.** Paul says that he<u>'s not feeling</u> well.

_____ **4. a.** I <u>see</u> the boys. There they are!

      **b.** I<u>'m seeing</u> a doctor about my back pain. He's helping me a lot.

_____ **5. a.** Nicole <u>is thinking</u> about moving.

      **b.** I <u>don't think</u> that's a good plan.

_____ **6. a.** They<u>'re having</u> a good time on their vacation.

      **b.** We <u>have</u> a new TV.

## Think Critically About Meaning and Use

**A.** Complete each conversation.

**1.** A: Stop her! She _____ !

　　B: What's the matter?

　　　　a. leaves

　　　　(b.) is leaving

　　　　c. leave

**2.** A: Why _____ he _____ German?

　　B: He's not studying enough.

　　　　a. does/fail

　　　　b. is/failing

　　　　c. does/failing

**3.** A: How _____ the soup _____ ?

　　B: It's delicious.

　　　　a. is/tasting

　　　　b. is/taste

　　　　c. does/taste

**4.** A: What _____ ?

　　B: My parents. I'm worried about them.

　　　　a. do you think

　　　　b. do you think about

　　　　c. are you thinking about

**B.** Discuss these questions in small groups.

**1.** **EVALUATE** Which conversation uses a stative verb as an action verb? What is the verb?

**2.** **ANALYZE** Which two conversations use the present continuous for an activity in progress at the exact moment the speaker is talking? Which conversation uses the present continuous for an activity in progress that is not happening at the exact moment the speaker is talking?

## Edit

Find the errors in this email and correct them.

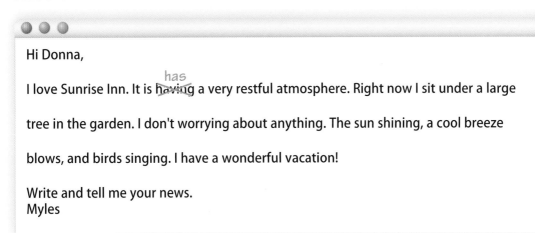

Hi Donna,

I love Sunrise Inn. It is ~~having~~ <sup>has</sup> a very restful atmosphere. Right now I sit under a large tree in the garden. I don't worrying about anything. The sun shining, a cool breeze blows, and birds singing. I have a wonderful vacation!

Write and tell me your news.
Myles

## Write

Imagine that you are updating your profile on a social-networking site. Follow the steps below to write a description of your current activities. Use the present continuous.

1. **BRAINSTORM** Make a list of things that you are doing these days. Include some details about each of these activities. Use these categories to help you.
   - classes and other school activities
   - work activities
   - activities with friends
   - activities with family members
   - other free-time activities
   - unexpected situations

2. **WRITE A FIRST DRAFT** Before you write your draft, read the checklist below. Write your draft using the present continuous.

3. **EDIT** Read your work and check it against the checklist below. Circle grammar, spelling, and punctuation errors.

| DO I... | YES |
|---|---|
| tell about various activities? | |
| use the present continuous? | |
| include at least one time expression? | |
| use the simple present for stative verbs? | |

4. **PEER REVIEW** Work with a partner to help you decide how to fix your errors and improve the content.

5. **REWRITE YOUR DRAFT** Using the comments from your partner, write a final draft.

Home  Profile  Account

**Current activities**

These days I'm studying a lot for my English exams.
I'm also cooking a lot of Italian food at home...

**Choose the correct word or words to complete each sentence.**

1. _____ write in the margins of your test booklet, class.

   **a.** Doesn't     **c.** Not

   **b.** Don't     **d.** No

2. Please _____ the bottom of this form, sir.

   **a.** sign     **c.** signing

   **b.** signs     **d.** to sign

3. Many economists believe the world economy _____ right now.

   **a.** am shrinking     **c.** are shrinking

   **b.** is shrinking     **d.** shrinking

4. Naomi and Emily _____ two brothers.

   **a.** are having     **c.** has

   **b.** having     **d.** have

5. If you lose something, _____ the lost and found.

   **a.** check     **c.** to check

   **b.** checks     **d.** be checking

6. _____ the vocabulary for tomorrow's test.

   **a.** Study     **c.** Studies

   **b.** Does study     **d.** Is studying

7. Solar energy _____ cause pollution. It is very clean.

   **a.** doesn't     **c.** isn't

   **b.** don't     **d.** aren't

8. How many people _____ in Moscow?

   **a.** lives     **c.** does live

   **b.** live     **d.** do live

9. Who _____ to right now?

   **a.** Diego and Carl are talking     **c.** Diego and Carl talk

   **b.** are Diego and Carl talking     **d.** Diego and Carl do talk

**10.** Mr. and Mrs. Warren _____ much money on electronics this year.

    **a.** not spending       **c.** aren't spending

    **b.** isn't spending      **d.** don't spend

**11.** When do _____ publish the economic reports for the quarter?

    **a.** it             **c.** they

    **b.** he            **d.** she

**Choose the correct word or words to complete each conversation.**

**12. A:** Is Irina coming to the meeting?

    **B:** (She's thinking / She thinks) about it.

**13. A:** What is Stefan doing this morning?

    **B:** He (is taking / takes) his car to the mechanic.

**14. A:** The weather doesn't look good at all.

    **B:** Don't forget your (glasses / umbrella).

**15. A:** Let's go to the movies tonight.

    **B:** (I'm thinking / I think) that's a great idea.

**16. A:** I'm going to the post office now.

    **B:** (Do you mail / Are you mailing) that card?

**Match the sentence parts.**

_____ **17.** Our instructor           **a.** ends next week.

_____ **18.** The word _humorous_     **b.** fly south for the winter.

_____ **19.** A lot of birds          **c.** are very interesting.

_____ **20.** College fees in the United States     **d.** means "funny."

                                       **e.** are very high.

                                       **f.** is an MP3 player.

                                       **g.** is always on time.

                                       **h.** usually stars in action films.

# The Simple Past

# The Decade That Made a Difference

## A1 Before You Read

Discuss these questions.

What do you know about the 1960s? What were some important events? Do you have a good opinion or a bad opinion about this decade?

## A2 Read

CD1 T12  Read the excerpt on the following page to find out about the 1960s.

## A3 After You Read

Write *T* for true or *F* for false for each statement.

___F___ **1.** John F. Kennedy led the Civil Rights movement in the United States in the 1960s.

_____ **2.** Hippies did not agree with the values of society.

_____ **3.** The peace symbol started with the hippies in San Francisco.

_____ **4.** In the 1960s, people became concerned about the environment.

_____ **5.** The changes of the 1960s happened only in North America and Europe.

_____ **6.** The "space race" involved the Soviet Union and the United States.

A hippie

# The Decade That Made A Difference

In the United States and other countries around the world, the 1960s was the decade that made a difference. It was a time of hope and, especially, of great change. When it ended, the world was a very different place than before.

Consider the 1960s in the United States. John F. Kennedy became president.
5　Martin Luther King, Jr., led the Civil Rights movement. Women's groups demanded equal rights. Young people listened to new kinds of music, including the music of the Beatles and other British bands. "Hippies" had long hair and wore strange, colorful clothes. They called for peace instead of war and questioned many of the values of American society, especially the focus on money.

10　　In many countries around the world, people wanted the freedom to be themselves and express themselves. They did not want to be limited because they were women or black or for any other reason. They wanted everyone to have the

15　same opportunities and they wanted to be able to explore different possibilities and ways of living. Cities such as London, Paris, Amsterdam, and San Francisco were centers of these new ideas. But many people in other cities and countries shared
20　these ideas, too.

*Britons march against nuclear weapons*

Around the world, people also felt growing concern for the planet Earth. In Britain, for example, one group argued for an end to nuclear weapons. This group created the most famous symbol of the 1960s—the peace symbol. People also became more and more concerned about the effects that humans have on the environment. In
25　fact, "Earth Day" first started in 1969.

The 1960s was also, of course, a time for technological advances. A symbol of these advances is the "space race" between the United States and the Soviet Union. At the start of the decade, in 1961, Russian astronaut Yuri Gagarin was the first person in outer space. At its end, in 1969, American astronauts Neil Armstrong and Buzz Aldrin
30　were the first people to walk on the moon. Over 500 million people watched the moon walk on TV—another symbol of technological change.

---

**Civil Rights movement:** political and social actions to gain equal rights for African Americans

**concern:** worry

**decade:** a period of ten years (for example, 1960–1969)

**opportunity:** chance

**technological:** applying science to discover and create useful things

**value:** a belief about what is right or wrong

# The Simple Past

 **Think Critically About Form**

**A.** Read the sentences and complete the tasks below.

  **a.** Young people questioned the values of American society.
  **b.** People wanted freedom.
  **c.** One group argued for an end to nuclear weapons.

  **1. IDENTIFY** Underline the verbs.

  **2. SUMMARIZE** All of these verbs are regular verbs in the simple past. How do we form the simple past of regular verbs?

  **3. COMPARE AND CONTRAST** Look back at the excerpt on page 49. Find the simple past of the irregular verbs below. How are they different from the verbs in sentences a, b, and c?
    make     become     have     lead     feel

**B.** Discuss your answers with the class and read the Form charts to check them.

**ONLINE PRACTICE**

| AFFIRMATIVE STATEMENTS | | |
|---|---|---|
| **SUBJECT** | **BASE FORM OF VERB + -D/-ED OR IRREGULAR FORM** | |
| I | | |
| You | | |
| He She It | arrived worked came | yesterday. |
| We | | |
| You | | |
| They | | |

| NEGATIVE STATEMENTS | | | |
|---|---|---|---|
| **SUBJECT** | ***DID + NOT*** | **BASE FORM OF VERB** | |
| I | | | |
| You | | | |
| He She It | did not didn't | arrive work leave | yesterday. |
| We | | | |
| You | | | |
| They | | | |

| YES/NO QUESTIONS | | | |
|---|---|---|---|
| *DID* | SUBJECT | BASE FORM OF VERB | |
| Did | you | arrive | yesterday? |
| | he | work | |
| | they | leave | |

| SHORT ANSWERS | | | | | | |
|---|---|---|---|---|---|---|
| *YES* | SUBJECT | *DID* | | *NO* | SUBJECT | *DID + NOT* |
| Yes, | I | did. | | No, | I | didn't. |
| | he | | | | he | |
| | they | | | | they | |

| INFORMATION QUESTIONS | | | | |
|---|---|---|---|---|
| *WH-* WORD | *DID* | SUBJECT | BASE FORM OF VERB | |
| Who | | you | see | |
| What | | he | do | |
| Where | did | she | go | yesterday? |
| When | | we | study | |
| Why | | you | leave | |
| How | | they | feel | |

| *WH-* WORD (SUBJECT) | | | VERB + *-D/-ED* OR IRREGULAR FORM | |
|---|---|---|---|---|
| Who | | | left | yesterday? |
| What | | | happened | |

- To form the simple past of most regular verbs, add *-ed* to the base form. If the base form of a regular verb ends in *e*, add *-d*. See Appendices 4 and 5 for the spelling and pronunciation of verbs ending in *-ed*. See also Pronunciation Notes on page 53.

- Some verbs are irregular in the simple past. See Appendix 6 for a list of irregular verbs and their simple past forms.

Do not use *did* in information questions when *who* or *what* is the subject.

What happened yesterday?

The verb *be* has two irregular simple past forms: *was* and *were*.

I **was** at the concert.     You **were** at the mall.     He **was** a musician.     They **were** home.

Do not use *did* in negative statements or questions with *was/were*.

I **wasn't there.**     Why **was** she late?     **We weren't** angry.     **Were** you at the concert?

## B1 Listening for Form

CD1 T13　Listen to these sentences. Write the simple past verb forms you hear.

1. Dan _____invited_____ us to the movies.

2. They _____ to the hockey game.

3. She _____ 20 dollars on the street.

4. They _____ the store at nine.

5. I _____ to work by car every day last week.

6. He _____ baseball for the New York Mets.

7. You _____ a haircut! It looks great!

8. We _____ chocolate cake at the restaurant.

## B2 Working on Regular Verb Forms

Complete this paragraph with the simple past form of the verbs below.

carry　　listen　　live　　talk　　study　　support　　want

I was a college student in the 1960s. I

___studied___ history at a university in Chicago.
　　　1

I _____ in an apartment near the
　　　2

university with four classmates. Like many other

students, we _____ about why war was bad,
　　　　　　　3

and we _____ signs that said "Peace."
　　　　　4

We _____ to change the world.
　　　5

We also _____ the Civil Rights
　　　　　6

movement and _____ to speeches by its
　　　　　　7

leader, Martin Luther King, Jr.

*Martin Luther King, Jr., 1963*

**Pronunciation Notes**

**Pronunciation of Verbs Ending in *-ed***

The regular simple past ending *-ed* is pronounced in three different ways, depending on the final sound of the base form of the verb.

1.  The *-ed* is pronounced /t/ if the verb ends with the sound /p/, /k/, /tʃ/, /f/, /s/, /ʃ/, or /ks/.

    work — worked /wərkt/     wash — washed /wɑʃt/     watch — watched /wɑtʃt/

2.  The *-ed* is pronounced /d/ if the verb ends with the sound /b/, /g/, /dʒ/, /v/, /ð/, /z/, /ʒ/, /m/, /n/, /ŋ/, /l/, or /r/.

    plan — planned /plænd/     judge — judged /dʒʌdʒd/     bang — banged /bæŋd/

    bathe — bathed /beɪðd/     massage — massaged /məˈsɑʒd/     rub — rubbed /rʌbd/

3.  The *-ed* is also pronounced /d/ if the verb ends with a vowel sound.

    play — played /pleɪd/     sigh — sighed /saɪd/     row — rowed /roʊd/

    bow — bowed /baʊd/     sue — sued /sud/     free — freed /frid/

4.  The *-ed* is pronounced as an extra syllable, /ɪd/, if the verb ends with the sound /d/ or /t/.

    guide — guided /ˈgaɪdɪd/     remind — reminded /ˌriˈmaɪndɪd/

    rent — rented /ˈrɛntɪd/     invite — invited /ˌinˈvaɪtɪd/

## B3 Pronouncing Verbs Ending in *-ed*

CD1 T14   Listen to the pronunciation of each verb. Which ending do you hear? Check ( ✓ ) the correct column.

|     |          | /t/ | /d/ | /ɪd/ |
| --- | -------- | --- | --- | ---- |
| 1.  | waited   |     |     | ✓    |
| 2.  | walked   |     |     |      |
| 3.  | rained   |     |     |      |
| 4.  | played   |     |     |      |
| 5.  | coughed  |     |     |      |
| 6.  | decided  |     |     |      |
| 7.  | jumped   |     |     |      |
| 8.  | answered |     |     |      |

## B4 Working on Irregular Verb Forms

**A.** Read about the first airplane flight by Wilbur and Orville Wright. Complete the paragraph with the verbs in parentheses and the simple past.

The first airplane flight

<u>took</u> (take) place in
_____
1

Kitty Hawk, North Carolina,

on December 17, 1903. Orville

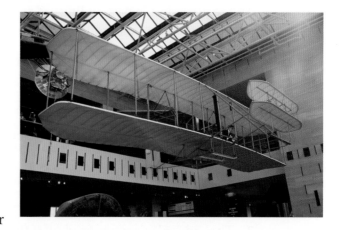

Wright _____ (lie) face
              2

down in the middle of the

airplane, and his brother, Wilbur

Wright, _____ (run) alongside it. Near the end of the runway, the plane
              3

_____ (rise) smoothly into the air. It _____ (fly) for several seconds,
        4                                                5

but then it _____ (fall) to the ground. This 12-second flight_____
              6                                                                  7

(make) history, but no one _____ (pay) attention to the Wright brothers at
                              8

first. However, after they _____ (give) many public demonstrations of their
                              9

flying machine, the Wright brothers _____ (become) famous.
                                      10

**B.** In your notebook, write three *Yes/No* and three *Wh-* questions about the paragraph in part A.

*Did the first airplane flight take place in North Carolina?*

OR

*Where did the first airplane flight take place?*

 **C.** Work with a partner. Take turns asking and answering your questions from part B.

*A: Did the first airplane flight take place in North Carolina?*
*B: Yes, it did.*
OR
*A: Where did the first airplane flight take place?*
*B: In North Carolina.*

## B5 Building *Yes/No* Questions in the Simple Past

Build eight logical *Yes/No* questions. Use a word or phrase from each column. Punctuate your sentences correctly.

*Did it rain yesterday?*

|  |  |  |
|---|---|---|
|  | it | rain yesterday |
|  | the concert | first |
| did | the test | nervous |
| was | Maria | fun |
| were | you | win |
|  | the children | leave |
|  | they | difficult |
|  | your team | start on time |

## B6 Working on *Yes/No* Questions and Short Answers in the Simple Past

A.  Complete this conversation with *did, didn't, was, wasn't, were,* or *weren't.*

**Lynn:** _Did_<sub>1</sub> you go to the basketball game last night?

**Gary:** Yes, I _____ <sub>2</sub>.

**Lynn:** _____ <sub>3</sub> it exciting?

**Gary:** Yes, it _____ <sub>4</sub> great. Maple Valley _____ <sub>5</sub> win until the last minute. What _____ <sub>6</sub> you and Bill do last night?

**Lynn:** We _____ <sub>7</sub> tired, so we _____ <sub>8</sub> go out.

**Gary:** _____ <sub>9</sub> you watch that new television show?

**Lynn:** Yes, we _____ <sub>10</sub> but we _____ <sub>11</sub> like it. It _____ <sub>12</sub> really boring!

B.  Practice the conversation in part A with a partner.

**Reduced Form of *Did You***

CD1 T15 Look at the cartoon and listen to the conversation. How is the underlined form in the cartoon different from what you hear?

> Did you forget my birthday? It was Saturday.

> Oh, no! I'm really sorry!

In informal speech, *Did you* is often pronounced /ˈdɪdʒə/.

| **Standard Form** | **What You Might Hear** |
|---|---|
| **Did you** work yesterday? | "/ˈdɪdʒə/ work yesterday?" |
| **Did you** eat yet? | "/ˈdɪdʒə/ eat yet?" |

## B7 Understanding Informal Speech

CD1 T16 Listen and write the standard form of the words you hear.

1. **A:** _Did you go_ _____ on the hike?
    <sub>1</sub>

   **B:** Yes, I did.

   **A:** _____ a good time?
    <sub>2</sub>

   **B:** Yes, but today I'm very tired.

2. **A:** _____ lunch yet?
    <sub>1</sub>

   **B:** Yes, I did.

   **A:** What _____?
    <sub>2</sub>

   **B:** A burger and fries.

3. **A:** _____ home last night? [1]

   **B:** No, I went to a movie.

   **A:** _____ it?
    <sub>2</sub>

   **B:** No, it wasn't very good.

4. **A:** Why _____ so late?
    <sub>1</sub>

   **B:** My boss needed help on a report.

   **A:** _____ it?
    <sub>2</sub>

   **B:** Yes, it wasn't difficult.

# The Simple Past

## Think Critically About Meaning and Use

**A.** Read the sentences and answer the questions below.

   **a.** I walk a mile every day.
   **b.** During my childhood we lived in Morocco.
   **c.** I went to Jake's house last night.

   **ANALYZE**  Which sentence talks about the present? Which sentences talk about situations that started and ended in the past? Which sentence talks about a situation that happened a short time ago? A long time ago?

**B.** Discuss your answers with the class and read the Meaning and Use Notes to check them.

## Meaning and Use Notes

**ONLINE PRACTICE**

| | **Actions or States Completed in the Past** |
|---|---|
| ▶ **1A** | Use the simple past for actions or states that started and ended in the past. Use time expressions to describe the time period.<br><br>I **lived** in Boston <u>in 2007</u>.      They **played** baseball <u>on Saturdays</u>.<br>We **went** shopping <u>yesterday</u>.    The garden **was** beautiful <u>last year</u>. |
| ▶ **1B** | The actions or states can happen in the recent past (a short time ago) or the distant past (a long time ago).<br><br>**Recent Past**                        **Distant Past**<br>He **called** five minutes ago.      They **got married** in 1983.<br>She **felt** tired yesterday.        He **was** very sick ten years ago. |
| ▶ **1C** | The actions or states can last for a long or short period of time.<br><br>**Long Period of Time**         **Short Period of Time**<br>I **worked** there for many years.  It **rained** hard all afternoon.<br>She **was** ill for six months.       He **seemed** happy to see me. |
| ▶ **1D** | The actions or states can happen once or repeatedly.<br><br>**Happened Once**                 **Happened Repeatedly**<br>I **graduated** on June 5, 2009.   He always **studied** hard before a test. |

## C1 Listening for Meaning and Use

CD1 T17 **A.** Listen to each conversation. Listen carefully for the phrases in the chart. Is the second speaker talking about the recent past or the distant past? Check ( ✓ ) the correct column.

| | | RECENT PAST | DISTANT PAST |
|---|---|---|---|
| 1. | grandmother died | ✓ | |
| 2. | walked to school | | |
| 3. | saw Kedra | | |
| 4. | bought the dress | | |
| 5. | studied French | | |

CD1 T18 **B.** Listen again. Is the second speaker referring to a situation that happened once or repeatedly? Check ( ✓ ) the correct column.

| | | HAPPENED ONCE | HAPPENED REPEATEDLY |
|---|---|---|---|
| 1. | grandmother died | ✓ | |
| 2. | walked to school | | |
| 3. | saw Kedra | | |
| 4. | bought the dress | | |
| 5. | studied French | | |

## C2 Making Excuses

▶ Notes 1A–1D

**A.** You were supposed to meet your friend for lunch yesterday, but you didn't. Use these words and phrases to make excuses.

1. go/the wrong restaurant

   *I'm sorry. I went to the wrong restaurant.*

2. forget/the name of the restaurant

3. have/an important meeting at work

4. my car/run out of gas

5. my watch/stop

6. have/a terrible headache

**B.** Now think of three more excuses. Use your imagination.

## C3 Guessing What Happened

▶ Notes 1A–1D

Work with a partner. Look at the pictures and guess what happened. Use *maybe* or *perhaps* and the simple past to make two sentences for each picture.

*Maybe she didn't study for the test.*
*Perhaps she forgot about the test.*

# Vocabulary Notes

## Time Expressions with the Simple Past

Time expressions are commonly used with the simple past. These words and phrases often refer to an exact point in time in the past or to a past time period. Time expressions can occur at the beginning or end of a sentence.

| | |
|---|---|
| yesterday | I saw Silvio **yesterday**. |
| the day before yesterday | We didn't go to school **the day before yesterday**. |
| this morning/afternoon | **This morning** she stayed home. |
| last night/week/month/year | Where did they go **last month**? |
| recently | Did you move **recently**? |
| a few/several/many years ago | **A few years ago** he lost his job. |
| a long time ago/a while ago | Rick graduated **a long time ago**. |

## C4 Using Time Expressions with the Simple Past

A. In your notebook, write sentences about yourself in the simple past with these time expressions and the phrases below. You can use a time expression more than once.

| | | |
|---|---|---|
| a while ago | recently | this … |
| last … | the day before yesterday | yesterday |

1. write a paper

   *I wrote a paper last night.*

2. wash the dishes

3. talk to a friend on the telephone

4. eat in a restaurant

5. speak English outside of class

6. go to a movie

7. receive a package

8. take a vacation

B. Work with a partner. Take turns asking and answering information questions about the sentences you wrote in part A.

A: *When was the last time you wrote a paper?*
B: *I wrote a paper last week.*

# Beyond the Sentence

## Using Time Expressions with Tense Changes

In stories and descriptions, we often use the simple past and the simple present to contrast situations in the past and present. We use time expressions to clarify the change of tenses.

Compare the paragraphs below. The paragraphs on the left are confusing because they do not use time expressions to show the change from the past to the present or the present to the past. The paragraphs on the right are clear because they use time expressions to clarify the tense change in each paragraph.

| **Without Time Expressions** | **With Time Expressions** |
|---|---|
| Sally **walked** home in the rain. She **feels** sick and **doesn't want** to go to work. | Sally **walked** home in the rain <u>yesterday</u>. <u>Now</u> she **feels** sick and **doesn't want** to go to work. |
| I usually take a **walk**. It **was** cold, and I **didn't want** to go outside. So I **stayed** home. | I usually take a **walk** <u>in the evening</u>. <u>This evening</u> it was cold, and I **didn't want** to go outside. So I **stayed** home. |

## C5 Using Time Expressions with Tense Changes

Complete these sentences with one of the time expressions below. There is more than one correct answer for each sentence.

| last night | now | recently | these days |
|---|---|---|---|
| last week | nowadays | the day before yesterday | this morning |

1. My parents rarely leave home, but _____*recently*_____ they decided to visit Washington, D.C.

2. A couple of weeks ago, I found a shorter way to go to school. _____ I go that way every time.

3. My two brothers don't always get along. _____ I found them arguing about something again.

4. My neighbors are very noisy. They often keep me up until late at night. _____ I finally called the police.

5. I was on my college swim team last year. However, _____ I don't have time for sports. I have too much homework.

6. I celebrated my birthday _____, and Jim didn't even send me a card.

# D FORM 2

## *Used To*

### Think Critically About Form

**A.** Read the sentences and complete the tasks below.

   **a.** He didn't use to visit his parents so often.
   **b.** Did she use to like the class?
   **c.** We used to swim every morning.
   **d.** Where did you use to live?

   **1. IDENTIFY** Underline *used to* or *use to* in each sentence. Circle all the examples of *did* or *didn't*.

   **2. APPLY** When do we use the form *used to*? When do we use the form *use to*?

**B.** Discuss your answers with the class and read the Form charts to check them.

**ONLINE PRACTICE**

### AFFIRMATIVE STATEMENTS

| SUBJECT | *USED TO* | BASE FORM OF VERB | |
|---|---|---|---|
| I | | | |
| You | | | |
| He She It | used to | arrive | late. |
| We | | | |
| You | | | |
| They | | | |

### NEGATIVE STATEMENTS

| SUBJECT | *DID + NOT* | *USE TO* | BASE FORM OF VERB | |
|---|---|---|---|---|
| I | | | | |
| You | | | | |
| He She It | did not didn't | use to | arrive | late. |
| We | | | | |
| You | | | | |
| They | | | | |

### *YES/NO* QUESTIONS

| *DID* | SUBJECT | *USE TO* | BASE FORM OF VERB | |
|---|---|---|---|---|
| Did | you he they | use to | arrive | late? |

### SHORT ANSWERS

| YES | SUBJECT | *DID* | | NO | SUBJECT | *DID + NOT* |
|---|---|---|---|---|---|---|
| Yes, | I he they | did. | | No, | I he they | didn't. |

## INFORMATION QUESTIONS

| WH- WORD | DID | SUBJECT | USE TO | BASE FORM OF VERB | |
|---|---|---|---|---|---|
| Why | | you | | arrive | early? |
| When | did | she | use to | go | to school here? |
| Where | | they | | live | in Chicago? |

| WH- WORD (SUBJECT) | | | USED TO | BASE FORM OF VERB | |
|---|---|---|---|---|---|
| Who | | | | live | across the street? |
| What | | | used to | happen | on New Year's Eve? |

- Use *used to* in affirmative statements.
- Use *use to* in negative statements with *didn't*, in *Yes/No* questions, and in information questions with *did*.
- The forms *used to* and *use to* have the same pronunciation: /ˈyustu/.

> **!** Do not use *did* in information questions when *who* or *what* is the subject. Use *used to* with these questions.
>
> Who used to take you to school?     **X** Who did used to take you to school? (INCORRECT)

## D1 Listening for Form

 CD1 T19   Listen to each sentence. Which form of *used to* does the speaker use? Check ( ✓ ) the correct column.

| | USED TO | DIDN'T USE TO | DID ... USE TO |
|---|---|---|---|
| 1. | ✓ | | |
| 2. | | | |
| 3. | | | |
| 4. | | | |
| 5. | | | |
| 6. | | | |
| 7. | | | |
| 8. | | | |

## D2 Rewriting Statements and Questions with *Used To*

Rewrite these simple past sentences and questions with the correct form of *used to*.

1. They walked to the park every Sunday.

   *They used to walk to the park every Sunday.*

2. Were you on a baseball team?

   _____

3. I didn't go to the movies very often.

   _____

4. He wasn't a good student in high school.

   _____

5. Did your family rent a beach house every summer?

   _____

6. We visited our parents on weekends.

   _____

## D3 Completing Conversations with *Used To*

Complete these conversations with the words in parentheses and the correct form of *used to*. Then practice the conversations with a partner.

*Conversation 1*

**A:** Where ___*did you use to live*___ (you/live)?
               1

**B:** In Chicago. _____ (we/have) an apartment on Lake
                        2
Shore Drive.

*Conversation 2*

**A:** _____ (Satomi/be) Eva's roommate?
            1

**B:** No, she didn't, but _____ (they/study) English together.
                              2

*Conversation 3*

**A:** _____ (I/not/like) Kevin.
            1

**B:** Yeah. _____ (he/not/be) nice to me, but now we are
                  2
good friends.

# The Habitual Past with *Used To*

## Think Critically About Meaning and Use

**A.** Read the sentences and answer the questions below. Then discuss your answers and read the Meaning and Use Notes to check them.

**1a.** We used to walk five miles to school.
**1b.** One morning the bus didn't come, and we walked five miles to school.
**2a.** Mary used to swim. Now she ice skates.
**2b.** Mary swam every day. She enjoyed it very much.

1. **EVALUATE** Look at 1a and 1b. Which one refers to a repeated action in the past?

2. **INTERPRET** Look at 2a and 2b. Which suggests that Mary's present situation is different from the past? Which doesn't suggest anything about Mary's present situation?

**B.** Discuss your answers with the class and read the Meaning and Use Notes to check them.

## Meaning and Use Notes

ONLINE
PRACTICE

| | Comparing the Past and the Present |
|---|---|

**▶ 1A** *Used to* suggests that a habit or situation was true in the past, but is not true now. Use *used to* for repeated (or habitual) actions or states that started and finished in the past. Do not use it for actions or states that happened only once. Adverbs of frequency and other time expressions with *used to* emphasize the repeated actions or states.

We <u>often</u> **used to visit** my grandparents <u>during summer vacation</u>. We don't <u>anymore</u>.

**Did** you **use to travel** a lot for work?

She **used to be** unfriendly. She <u>never</u> smiled.

This city **didn't use to have** a subway system <u>in the old days</u>.

**▶ 1B** You can use the simple present with time expressions to say how a present situation is different from the past.

I often **used to watch** TV after school. <u>Now</u> I <u>don't have</u> time to do that.

In the 1930s people **used to get** their news from newspapers or the radio. <u>These days</u> most people <u>get</u> their news from TV or the Internet.

## E1 Listening for Meaning and Use

▶ Notes 1A, 1B

 CD1 T20   Listen to each statement. Choose the sentence that best follows it.

1. **a.** Now I'm married and have a son.
   **b.** I enjoyed having a lot of people in the house.

2. **a.** We added two rooms last year.
   **b.** Now there isn't enough room.

3. **a.** Now we don't talk to each other.
   **b.** Now we see each other every day.

4. **a.** We always ate in restaurants together.
   **b.** Now we eat out twice a week.

5. **a.** Now they don't want to go.
   **b.** They always complained about their teachers.

6. **a.** I always did everything myself.
   **b.** We cleaned together every Saturday.

7. **a.** But we changed our minds.
   **b.** But we decided to have six.

## E2 Comparing the Past and the Present

▶ Notes 1A, 1B

 Work with a partner. Look at these facts about the past. How is the present different? Write two sentences for each fact. In the first, rewrite the fact using the correct form of *used to*. In the second, use the simple present with a time expression and the word or phrase in parentheses.

1. Few people had cars. (many)

   *In the past, few people used to have cars. Now many people have cars.*

2. Women didn't work outside the home. (have jobs)

3. Most people didn't go to college. (many)

4. Supermarkets didn't stay open late. (24 hours)

5. People didn't move away from their families. (live far away)

6. Most people got married very young. (many/in their thirties)

## E3 Remembering Your Past

▶ Note 1A

 Work with a partner. Talk about your past habits and routines. Use *used to* and other simple past verbs.

A: *I used to play basketball after school with my friends. We always had a lot of fun together, but we were extremely competitive.*

B: *I used to travel...*

## Think Critically About Meaning and Use

**A.** Choose the best answer to complete each conversation.

**1.** A: Did you go to school yesterday?

B: _____

    a. Yes, I go today.

    (b.) No, I was sick.

**2.** A: I went to the soccer game last night.

B: _____

    a. Who won?

    b. Is it fun?

**3.** A: When I was young, I used to climb trees.

B: _____

    a. Did you climb trees?

    b. Did you ever fall out of one?

**4.** A: Julie finished law school last year.

B: _____

    a. Is she still in school?

    b. Did she enjoy it?

**5.** A: It rained here last night.

B: Really? _____

    a. It didn't rain here.

    b. It isn't raining here.

**6.** A: She didn't use to live alone.

B: _____

    a. Did she like living with other people?

    b. Did she like living alone?

**B.** Discuss these questions in small groups.

  **1. EVALUATE**  Why are the wrong answers in 1, 2, 4, and 5 wrong?

  **2. DRAW A CONCLUSION**  In 3 and 6, why does speaker A use *used to*?

## Edit

**Some of these sentences have errors. Find the errors and correct them.**

1. I ~~used to graduate~~ *graduated* from high school in 1997.

2. We didn't needed any help.

3. Ana taked the cake to Milly.

4. Where did they went?

5. He failed his driving test three times!

6. Who give you a present?

7. When left he?

8. You didn't answer my question.

9. The test were on Saturday.

10. What did happened here?

## Write

Write a post for a history class blog. Write your post about a famous person from the past. Follow the steps below to write the blog post. Use the simple past, *used to*, and time expressions.

1.  **BRAINSTORM** Choose a famous person from the 1960s or another time in history. Research this person on the Internet. Take notes about what you want to say. Use these questions to help you.

    - Who is the person? When and where did he or she live?
    - What did he or she do?
    - What were some important events that he or she was involved in?
    - What changes did this person cause? Is anything different today than it was at that time because of this person? How?

2.  **WRITE A FIRST DRAFT** Before you write your draft, read the checklist below. Write your draft using the simple past, *used to*, and time expressions.

3.  **EDIT** Read your work and check it against the checklist below. Circle grammar, spelling, and punctuation errors.

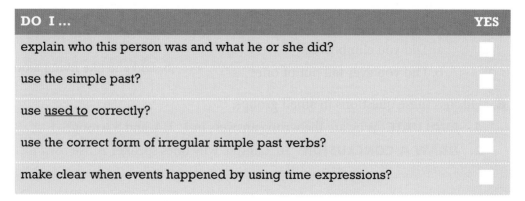

| DO I... | YES |
| --- | --- |
| explain who this person was and what he or she did? | ☐ |
| use the simple past? | ☐ |
| use <u>used to</u> correctly? | ☐ |
| use the correct form of irregular simple past verbs? | ☐ |
| make clear when events happened by using time expressions? | ☐ |

4.  **PEER REVIEW** Work with a partner to help you decide how to fix your errors and improve the content.

5.  **REWRITE YOUR DRAFT** Using the comments from your partner, write a final draft.

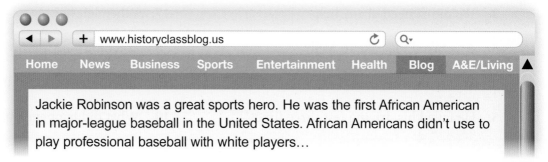

www.historyclassblog.us

| Home | News | Business | Sports | Entertainment | Health | Blog | A&E/Living |

Jackie Robinson was a great sports hero. He was the first African American in major-league baseball in the United States. African Americans didn't use to play professional baseball with white players…

# 5

# The Past Continuous and Past Time Clauses

# Galveston's Killer Hurricane

## A1 Before You Read

 Discuss these questions.

Do you have bad storms where you live? Do they cause a lot of damage? What do people in your city or town do to prepare for bad weather?

## A2 Read

 CD1 T21 Read this excerpt from a history textbook to find out about how much damage occurred during the worst storm in U.S. history.

# Galveston's Killer Hurricane

The worst weather disaster in the history of the United States was a hurricane that hit the city of Galveston on September 8, 1900.
5 Galveston is on an island near the Texas coast. At that time it was the richest city in Texas, and about 38,000 people <u>were living</u> there.

On the morning of Tuesday,
10 September 6, 1900, the head of the Galveston weather station, Isaac Cline, received a telegram about a storm. It was moving north over

*Galveston before the hurricane*

Cuba and coming toward Galveston. Cline didn't worry when he got the news.
15 Galveston often had bad storms. However, by the next afternoon Cline became concerned. The wind was getting stronger, the ocean waves were getting larger, and the tide was much higher than normal.

On the morning of September 8, Cline began to tell people to leave the island. However, few people listened. Most of them just went to friends' and
20 relatives' houses away from the water. By 4:00 that afternoon, the storm was much worse.

The tide was getting higher and higher when a four-foot wave went through the town. A twenty-foot wave followed it.

Cline was at his house with a lot of other people. While the storm was going
25 on, he was making careful notes of the water's height around his house. Suddenly, a huge wave hit the house and it collapsed. Everyone went into the water. For the next three hours, they floated on the waves. "While we were drifting," he later wrote, "we
30 had to protect ourselves from pieces of wood and other objects that were flying around."

After the storm ended, the city was in ruins. More than 7,000 people were dead. The storm also destroyed more than
35 3,600 buildings. As a result, the people of Galveston built a seawall. It was 3 miles long, 17 feet high, and 16 feet thick.

Today the people of Galveston depend on weather satellites and other technology to give them hurricane warnings, but they still talk about the great hurricane of 1900.

*Galveston after the hurricane*

---

**collapse:** to suddenly fall down
**concerned:** worried
**disaster:** an event that causes a lot of damage
**drift:** to be carried along by moving water

**satellite:** a man-made object that travels around the Earth and sends back information
**tide:** the regular rise and fall of the level of the ocean

## A3 After You Read

**Answer these questions in your notebook.**

1. What happened on September 8, 1900?

2. Where is Galveston?

3. What did most of the people of Galveston do before the storm hit?

4. Why did Isaac Cline's house collapse?

5. What did the people of Galveston do to protect themselves from other storms?

# B FORM 1

## The Past Continuous

### Think Critically About Form

A. Look back at the excerpt on page 70 and complete the tasks below.

1. **IDENTIFY** An example of the past continuous is underlined. Find four more examples.

2. **DEFINE** How many words are necessary to form the past continuous? What two forms of the verb *be* are used? What ending is added to the base form of the verb?

B. Discuss your answers with the class and read the Form charts to check them.

**ONLINE PRACTICE**

| AFFIRMATIVE STATEMENTS | | | |
|---|---|---|---|
| SUBJECT | *WAS/WERE* | BASE FORM OF VERB *-ING* | |
| I | was | | |
| You | were | | |
| He She It | was | living | there. |
| We | | | |
| You | were | | |
| They | | | |

| NEGATIVE STATEMENTS | | | |
|---|---|---|---|
| SUBJECT | *WAS/WERE* + *NOT* | BASE FORM OF VERB + *-ING* | |
| I | was not wasn't | | |
| You | were not weren't | | |
| He She It | was not wasn't | living | there. |
| We | | | |
| You | were not weren't | | |
| They | | | |

| *YES/NO* QUESTIONS | | | |
|---|---|---|---|
| *WAS/ WERE* | SUBJECT | BASE FORM OF VERB + *-ING* | |
| Were | you | | |
| Was | he | living | there? |
| Were | they | | |

| SHORT ANSWERS | | | | | | |
|---|---|---|---|---|---|---|
| YES | SUBJECT | *WAS/ WERE* | NO | SUBJECT | *WAS/WERE* + *NOT* | |
| Yes, | I | was. | No, | I | wasn't. | |
| | he | | | he | | |
| | they | were. | | they | weren't. | |

| INFORMATION QUESTIONS | | | |
|---|---|---|---|
| **WH-** WORD | **WAS/WERE** | **SUBJECT** | **BASE FORM OF VERB + -ING** |
| Who | were | you | watching? |
| What | was | she | |
| When | | | |
| Where | were | they | traveling? |
| Why | | | |
| How | | | |

| **WH-** WORD (SUBJECT) | **WAS/WERE** | | **BASE FORM OF VERB + -ING** |
|---|---|---|---|
| Who | was | | leaving? |
| What | | | happening? |

• See Appendix 3 for the spelling of verbs ending in *-ing*.

>   Do not use a subject pronoun when *who* or *what* is the subject of an information question.
>
> What was happening?      **X** What was it happening? (INCORRECT)

## B1 Listening for Form

**CD1 T22**   Listen to these sentences. Choose the verb forms you hear.

1.  **a.** are living
    **b.** were living ⟵
    **c.** was living

2.  **a.** wasn't raining
    **b.** was raining
    **c.** isn't raining

3.  **a.** were leaving
    **b.** weren't leaving
    **c.** are leaving

4.  **a.** aren't going
    **b.** were going
    **c.** weren't going

5.  **a.** are … going
    **b.** were … going
    **c.** was … going

6.  **a.** was … crying
    **b.** is … crying
    **c.** wasn't … crying

## B2 Forming Statements and *Yes/No* Questions in the Past Continuous

A. Look at the picture. Write sentences about what the people were doing at Kevin and Kim's house last night.

1. Paulo and Dan ___were playing music._____

2. Alex _____

3. Myles and Reiko _____

4. Kevin _____

5. Kalin and Kim _____

6. Nicole and Linda _____

B. Work with a partner. Take turns asking and answering *Yes/No* questions about the people in the picture.

A: *Was Paulo playing the guitar?*

B: *No, he wasn't. He was playing the drums.*

## B3 Forming Information Questions in the Past Continuous

In your notebook, form information questions from these words and phrases. Punctuate your sentences correctly.

1. four o'clock/happening/what/was/yesterday afternoon/at

   *What was happening at four o'clock yesterday afternoon?*

2. feeling/how/your/was/grandfather/last night

3. the/this morning/leading/meeting/who/was

4. was/what/Mr. Gonzalez/last semester/teaching

5. you/living/five years ago/were/where

6. Dan and Ben/were/on Saturday/fighting/why

## B4 Asking and Answering Information Questions in the Past Continuous

Work with a partner. Take turns asking and answering questions with these time expressions and the past continuous.

1. two hours ago

   *A: What were you doing two hours ago?*
   *B: I was making dinner.*

2. at three o'clock yesterday afternoon

3. last night at midnight

4. at seven o'clock this morning

5. at six o'clock yesterday evening

6. ten minutes ago

## B5 Building Past Continuous and Simple Past Sentences

Build as many logical sentences as you can in the past continuous or simple past. Use a word or phrase from each column. Punctuate your sentences correctly.

Past Continuous: *Carlos was sleeping.*     Simple Past: *Carlos had a cold.*

| Carlos | was | sleeping |
|---|---|---|
| you | had | call |
| Ana and Rose | didn't | studying |
| | weren't | a cold |
| | | early |

## MEANING AND USE 1

# The Past Continuous

### Think Critically About Meaning and Use

**A.** Read the sentences and answer the questions below.

  **a.** This morning I took a walk and then I ate breakfast.

  **b.** At seven o'clock this morning, I was taking a walk and my sister was making breakfast.

  **1. EVALUATE** Which sentence shows two past activities in progress at the same time?

  **2. EVALUATE** Which sentence shows two completed past activities?

**B.** Discuss your answers with the class and read the Meaning and Use Notes to check them.

## Meaning and Use Notes

ONLINE
PRACTICE

| **Activities in Progress in the Past** |
|---|
| ▶ **1A** Use the past continuous to talk about activities that were in progress (happening) at a specific time in the past. This may be an exact moment in the past or a longer period of time in the past. <br><br> It **wasn't raining** <u>at lunchtime</u>. It **was snowing**. <br><br> You **were acting** strangely <u>last night</u>. <br><br> I **was studying** at Tokyo University <u>in 2010</u>. |
| ▶ **1B** The past continuous is often used to talk about several activities that were in progress at the same time. <br><br> <u>At six o'clock</u> she **was making** a phone call, and we **were eating** dinner. |
| ▶ **1C** The past continuous expresses an ongoing past activity that may or may not be completed. In contrast, the simple past usually expresses a completed past activity. |

| **Past Continuous** | **Simple Past** |
|---|---|
| At 5:45 Greg **was making** dinner in the kitchen. (He was in the middle of making dinner.) | At 5:45 Greg was in the kitchen. He **made** dinner. Then he washed the dishes. (He completed dinner preparations.) |

## Stative Verbs and the Past Continuous

▶ **2A**  Many stative verbs are used in the simple past but not in the past continuous. Some of these verbs are *know*, *own*, *mean*, *seem*, and *understand*.

**Simple Past**

I **knew** all the answers.           X I was knowing all the answers. (INCORRECT)

They **owned** three cars in 2008.    X They were owning three cars in 2008. (INCORRECT)

▶ **2B**  Some stative verbs are used in the past continuous, but they are used as action verbs with a different meaning. Some of these verbs are *have*, *think*, *taste*, and *weigh*.

| **Simple Past** | **Past Continuous** |
|---|---|
| Did you **have** a car? | We **were having** a good time at the basketball game. |
| (Did you own a car?) | (We were experiencing a good time.) |
| I **thought** it was a great idea. | I **was thinking** about Jenny recently. |
| (I believed it was a good idea.) | (Jenny was in my thoughts.) |

## C1 Listening for Meaning and Use

▶ Notes 1A–1C

CD1 T23  Listen to each statement. Look at the phrases in the chart. Is the speaker talking about an ongoing past activity or a completed past activity? Check ( ✓ ) the correct column.

|   |   | **ONGOING** | **COMPLETED** |
|---|---|---|---|
| 1. | live in Japan | | ✓ |
| 2. | write a book | | |
| 3. | paint the house | | |
| 4. | fix the air conditioner | | |
| 5. | write a paper | | |
| 6. | take flying lessons | | |

## C2 Describing Activities in Progress at the Same Time

▶ Notes 1A–1C

Think about a time when you arrived late for an event. In your notebook, write about what was happening when you arrived. Then read your description to the class.

I arrived at the soccer game late. My favorite team was winning. The crowd was standing and everyone was cheering...

## C3 Describing Past Situations

▶ Notes 1A–C, 2A, 2B

A. Complete these conversations with the correct form of the verbs in parentheses. Use the past continuous or the simple past where appropriate.

*Conversation 1*

**Chris:** Where were you during the summer of 2007?

**Matt:** I ____was traveling____ (travel) around the United States.
1

**Chris:** How? By plane?

**Matt:** No, by car. I _____ (own) a car then.
2

*Conversation 2*

**Paul:** How well _____ you _____ (know)
1                                          2
Takeshi before this year?

**Eric:** Not very well. I _____ (arrive) at school in the middle
3
of the year. Takeshi _____ (take) several courses at that
4
time, but we _____ (not/be) in the same classes.
5

*Conversation 3*

**Josh:** You _____ (miss) the turn! Now we're on the
1
wrong road.

**Amy:** Oops. I'm sorry. I _____ (not/pay) attention. I
2
_____ (think) about something else.
3

*Conversation 4*

**Celia:** I _____ (see) Susan at the library yesterday.
1

**Maria:** What _____ she _____ (do) there?
2                              3

**Celia:** She _____ (look) for information for her English
4
project.

 B. Practice the conversations in part A with a partner.

## Beyond the Sentence

### Introducing Background Information with the Past Continuous

The past continuous and simple past often occur together in the same story. The past continuous is used at the beginning of a story to describe background activities that are happening at the same time as the main events of the story. The simple past is used for main events.

> Yesterday <u>was</u> beautiful. The sun **was shining**, the birds **were singing**, and I **was walking** in a valley. Suddenly, the sky <u>became</u> dark. From nowhere, a storm <u>arrived</u>. The rain <u>fell</u> harder and harder. And there <u>were</u> no buildings nearby.

### C4 Introducing Background Information with the Past Continuous

A. Work with a partner. Imagine that each sentence is the beginning of a story. Write two sentences in the past continuous to give background information.

1. The beach was gorgeous. _The sun was shining on the water. The waves were moving quickly._

2. The bank was full of customers. _____

   _____

3. The students were late to class. _____

   _____

4. My boss was very angry. _____

   _____

5. The cafeteria was crowded and noisy. _____

   _____

6. The sky looked cloudy and dark. _____

   _____

B. Complete one of the story beginnings in part A. Use the past continuous to add more background information, and use the simple past for main events.

> The beach was gorgeous. The sun was shining on the water. The waves were moving quickly. Suddenly, a swimmer yelled for help. A lifeguard dove into the water...

# D

## Past Time Clauses

### Think Critically About Form

**A.** Read the sentences and complete the tasks below.

    **a.** At that time, Galveston was the richest city in Texas.
    **b.** Cline didn't worry when he got the news.
    **c.** After the storm ended, the city was in ruins.

    **1. IDENTIFY** Underline the verbs. Which sentences have two verbs?

    **2. RECOGNIZE** Look at the sentences with two verbs. Each verb is part of a clause. There is a main clause and a past time clause. A past time clause begins with a word such as *before, when, while,* or *after*. Circle the past time clauses.

**B.** Discuss your answers with the class and read the Form charts to check them.

**ONLINE PRACTICE**

### SENTENCES WITH PAST TIME CLAUSES

| PAST TIME CLAUSE | | | MAIN CLAUSE | |
|---|---|---|---|---|
| | SUBJECT | VERB | SUBJECT | VERB |
| Before | the storm | hit, | everyone | was sleeping. |
| When | the house | collapsed, | I | was eating dinner. |
| While | I | was sleeping, | the phone | rang. |
| After | the play | ended, | everyone | clapped. |

### POSITION OF PAST TIME CLAUSES

| PAST TIME CLAUSE | MAIN CLAUSE |
|---|---|
| When the house collapsed, | I was eating dinner. |
| After the play ended, | everyone clapped. |

| MAIN CLAUSE | PAST TIME CLAUSE |
|---|---|
| I was eating dinner | when the house collapsed. |
| Everyone clapped | after the play ended. |

**Overview**

- A clause is a group of words that has a subject and a verb.
- A main clause can stand alone as a complete sentence.
- A dependent clause cannot stand alone and must be used with a main clause.

**Past Time Clauses**

- Past time clauses are dependent clauses. They begin with words such as *before, when, while,* and *after.*
- The verbs in a past time clause and main clause can be in the simple past or in the past continuous.
- A past time clause can come before or after the main clause with no change in meaning. If the past time clause comes first, it is separated from the main clause by a comma.

## D1 Listening for Form

CD1 T24  **Listen to these sentences. Write the past time clauses you hear.**

1. Some people left town _____before the storm began_____.

2. The weather forecaster warned us about the storm _____.

3. _____, the tornado hit the house.

4. _____, we went into the basement.

5. The river overflowed _____.

6. The sky was beautiful _____.

## D2 Forming Sentences with Past Time Clauses

**Match the clauses to make logical sentences. Pay attention to punctuation.**

__f__ 1. He went to bed

_____ 2. When the storm hit,

_____ 3. After we visited Chicago,

_____ 4. I made a phone call

_____ 5. Before Steve gave Alan the award,

_____ 6. She closed her eyes

a. several people were still outside.

b. while I was waiting for the train.

c. he made a speech.

d. when he was taking her picture.

e. we went to Cleveland.

f. before I came home.

## D3 Practicing Punctuation with Past Time Clauses

Read this paragraph. Underline the time clauses. Add commas where necessary.

A terrible storm hit last night <u>while my friend was staying at my house</u>. All the lights went out when lightning struck the house. While I was looking for matches I tripped over a rug. I heard a knock on the door. I went to the door and answered it. A strange man was standing outside. He was wearing a hood. The wind was blowing the trees back and forth while the storm was raging. When I saw the stranger I became nervous. Then, when he began to speak I recognized his voice. It was my friend's father.

## D4 Changing the Position of Past Time Clauses

Change the order of the clauses in these sentences. Add or delete commas where necessary.

1. Alex saw Maria when he went to the laundromat.

   When Alex went to the laundromat, he saw Maria.

2. While Reiko was swimming, she got a cramp in her leg.

   _____

3. When my sister woke up this morning, she ate pizza for breakfast.

   _____

4. It started to rain while I was driving to work.

   _____

5. Eva became a lawyer after she finished high school.

   _____

# Past Time Clauses

 **Think Critically About Meaning and Use**

**A.** Read the sentences and complete the tasks below.

**a.** I was taking a nap when the mailman knocked on the door.
**b.** I put on suntan lotion before I went to the beach.
**c.** We were playing soccer while Josh was studying for an exam.

1. **EVALUATE** Which sentence shows that two events were happening at exactly the same time?

2. **EVALUATE** Which sentence shows that one event interrupted the other?

3. **EVALUATE** Which sentence shows that one event happened after the other?

**B.** Discuss your answers with the class and read the Meaning and Use Notes to check them.

## Meaning and Use Notes

 **ONLINE PRACTICE**

### Simultaneous Events

▶ 1  Sentences with past time clauses describe the order in which two past events occurred. When the verbs in both the time clause and the main clause are in the past continuous, the events were simultaneous (happening at exactly the same time). *When* or *while* introduces the time clause.

| **Past Continuous** | **Past Continuous** |
|---|---|
| **When I was sleeping,** | the children <u>were watching</u> TV. |
| I <u>was sleeping</u> | **while the children were watching TV.** |

### Interrupted Events

▶ 2  When one verb is in the simple past and the other is in the past continuous, it shows that one event interrupted the other. The event in the past continuous started first and was interrupted by the simple past event. *When* or *while* begins the time clause, which uses the past continuous.

| **Past Continuous (First Event)** | **Simple Past (Second Event)** |
|---|---|
| **When I was sleeping,** | the telephone rang. |
| **While I was sleeping,** | the telephone rang. |

*(Continued on page 84)*

| Events in Sequence |
|---|

▶ **3**  When the verbs in both the time clause and the main clause are in the simple past, one event happened after the other (in sequence). *Before, when,* or *after* introduces the time clause and indicates the order of events.

| Simple Past (First Event) | Simple Past (Second Event) |
|---|---|
| I <u>walked</u> past my sister | **before I recognized her**. |
| **When the phone rang,** | I <u>answered</u> it. |
| **After he gave me the diploma,** | I <u>shook</u> his hand. |

## E1 Listening for Meaning and Use

▶ Notes 1–3

 CD1 T25   Listen to each conversation. Is the second speaker talking about simultaneous events, an interrupted event, or events in sequence? Check ( ✓ ) the correct column.

|  | SIMULTANEOUS | INTERRUPTED | IN SEQUENCE |
|---|---|---|---|
| 1. |  | ✓ |  |
| 2. |  |  |  |
| 3. |  |  |  |
| 4. |  |  |  |
| 5. |  |  |  |

## E2 Understanding Time Clauses

▶ Notes 2, 3

Work with a partner. Discuss why these sentences are not logical. Then change the time clause in each sentence to make it logical.

1. Before Carlos threw the ball, I caught it.

   *A: Sentence 1 isn't logical. You can't catch a ball before someone throws it.*
   *B: It should be "After Carlos threw the ball, I caught it."*

2. While Ben found his car keys, he drove away.

3. When the sun came up, it was very dark.

4. Everyone listened before he began to talk.

5. After we went swimming, they filled the pool with water.

## E3 Writing About Events in Sequence

▶ Note 3

Read each situation. Then complete each sentence with a clause in the simple past.

1. Silvio and Maria bought a new house last month.

   Before they bought the house, _they saved a lot of money._

   When they saw the house for the first time, _____

   After they moved in, _____

2. Megan went to a great concert last night.

   Before she went to the concert, _____

   When she arrived at the concert, _____

   After she left the concert, _____

3. Paul traveled to Europe last summer for his vacation.

   Before _____

   When _____

   After _____

## E4 Expressing Simultaneous, Interrupted, and Sequential Events

▶ Notes 1–3

Complete the time clauses. Use the simple past or the past continuous.

1. Donna and I made dinner together last night. While Donna was

   chopping the vegetables, _I was baking a cake for dessert._

2. We were watching the movie when _____

3. I'm sorry I didn't answer the phone this morning. It rang while _____

   _____

4. Last night while I was watching TV, _____

5. At first Lauren wasn't a good student. After _____

   _____, her grades improved.

6. Why did you leave class so early? It was so interesting! After you left,

   _____

# WRITING   Write About a Natural Disaster

 **Think Critically About Meaning and Use**

**A.** Read each sentence and answer the questions that follow with *Yes, No,* or *It's not clear*.

1. We ran out of the building when the fire alarm started to ring.
   - _____Yes_____ a. Were they in the building before the fire alarm started to ring?
   - _____No_____ b. After the fire alarm rang, did they stay in the building for a long time?

2. Lynn was sleeping while Holly was cleaning the house.
   - _____ a. Did Lynn help Holly clean the house?
   - _____ b. Did Lynn fall asleep before Holly started cleaning the house?

3. Luis saw Jake this morning. He was walking down the street.
   - _____ a. Did Luis walk down the street with Jake?
   - _____ b. Did Jake continue walking after Luis saw him?

4. Jake was working on the roof when he fell off.
   - _____ a. Did he hurt himself badly?
   - _____ b. Did he work after he fell?

5. When he left the house, he wasn't carrying his umbrella.
   - _____ a. Did he take his umbrella with him?
   - _____ b. Was it raining when he left the house?

6. The fire started after we left the building.
   - _____ a. Were we in danger?
   - _____ b. Did we start the fire?

7. She was unlocking the door when she heard a loud noise.
   - _____ a. Did she hear the noise before she unlocked the door?
   - _____ b. Did she hear the noise at the same time as she was unlocking the door?

8. Don was waiting in the car while Helen was buying stamps.
   - _____ a. Did Don go into the post office?
   - _____ b. Did Don and Helen both buy stamps?

**9.** Mike left before the game ended.

_____ a. Did Mike see the end of the game?

_____ b. Did the game end after Mike left?

**B.** Discuss these questions in small groups.

**1.** **ANALYZE** If we change both verbs in 7 to the simple past, how does the meaning of this sentence change?

**2.** **GENERATE** Create a sentence with two past continuous verbs and a sentence with one past continuous and one simple past verb.

## Edit

**Some of these sentences have errors. Find the errors and correct them.**

**1.** I feel terrible. I ~~was breaking~~ *broke* my favorite necklace when I put it on this morning.

**2.** I'm so sorry about your mug. I was dropping it.

**3.** They were owning a house before they had children.

**4.** It snowing when we went to school.

**5.** While we were shopping, they were cleaning the house.

**6.** After he was throwing the ball, it hit the window.

**7.** What did he say to you while you watched the movie?

**8.** Where were you going when I was seeing you yesterday?

**9.** She was reading after she fell asleep.

**10.** He hit his head when he had the car accident.

## Write

Write a paragraph about a hurricane, flood, or other natural disaster. Follow the steps below to write the paragraph. Use the simple past and the past continuous.

1. **BRAINSTORM** Think of some recent and past natural disasters. Research one of these disasters. Take notes. Use these questions to help you.
   - What was the disaster? When and where did it occur?
   - What, if anything, did people do to prepare for the disaster?
   - What did they do when the disaster struck?
   - What damage occurred during the disaster?
   - What happened after the disaster?

2. **WRITE A FIRST DRAFT** Before you write your draft, read the checklist below and look at the reading on page 70. Write your draft using the simple past and the past continuous.

3. **EDIT** Read your work and check it against the checklist below. Circle grammar, spelling, and punctuation errors.

| DO I ... | YES |
|---|---|
| give the basic information and some details about the disaster? | ☐ |
| use the simple past? | ☐ |
| use the past continuous? | ☐ |
| use the simple past for stative verbs? | ☐ |
| include at least one sentence with a time clause? | ☐ |
| use correct punctuation in sentences with time clauses? | ☐ |

4. **PEER REVIEW** Work with a partner to decide how to fix your errors and improve the content.

5. **REWRITE YOUR DRAFT** Using comments from your partner, write a final draft.

> *A terrible earthquake hit my country last year. When it hit, people were working at their jobs and children were studying at school. It seemed like a normal day...*

# The Present Perfect

*Gramática en el discurso.*

*Cuentos*

# Tales of a World Traveler

## A1 Before You Read

Discuss these questions.

Do you like to travel? What are some good and bad things about traveling? Name some countries you have visited. Where else do you want to go?

## A2 Read

CD1 T26 **Read this online magazine article to find out about world traveler Charles Veley.**

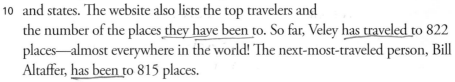

Travel

# The World's Most-Traveled Man

Charles Veley is only in his mid-40s, but he has been to more places than anyone else in the world. You can see this on the website of the group
5    he started, Most Traveled People. Members of this group have listed the world's places—872 of them, including all the countries plus islands, territories, regions,
10   and states. The website also lists the top travelers and the number of the places they have been to. So far, Veley has traveled to 822 places—almost everywhere in the world! The next-most-traveled person, Bill Altaffer, has been to 815 places.

When Veley was a boy, he wanted to travel, but he never left the United
15   States—his family didn't have much money. But things changed. As a young man, he started a software company and became a millionaire. When he was 25, he got married, and he and his wife Kimberly decided to travel around the world for a year. They had a great time, so one year became four. And Veley has traveled ever since.

*P. P*

20    Veley has experienced it all! He's traveled 1,686,953 miles. He's traveled to remote places. For example, he went to Bouvet Island, near Antarctica. Very few people have ever been there. He's faced danger.

For example, his canoe tipped over in the Zambezi River. The river was filled with hippopotamuses.

25 Where hasn't Veley been? The very few places include Navassa Island, a small island in the Caribbean; Oeno Island, a small island in the South Pacific; and Jan Mayen, in the Arctic.

Not surprisingly, Veley has many favorite places, all over the world. These include Lord Howe Island, Australia; Kauai, Hawaii; and the Lauterbrunnen 30 Valley, in Switzerland.

How has he done it? Having the money to travel, of course, is part of the answer. Veley has spent a little over $1 million just for plane tickets! Another part, he says, is being patient and having a good attitude. Veley has learned a lot from his travels, and he has this advice for other travelers:

35 • "Travel light—pack only the basics." Many of Veley's best experiences (and souvenirs) have come because he needed something."
• "Each place has its own beauty. You need to go there and discover it."
• "Go everywhere at least twice." Veley follows his own advice. He has returned to places again and again to make new discoveries.

---

**canoe:** a light, narrow kind of boat

**hippopotamus:** a large, heavy African animal, often in water

**patience:** the quality of being able to deal with delays and problems in a calm way

**remote:** very far from other places

**territory:** an area of land that belongs to a country

## A3 After You Read

A. Circle the places that Charles Veley has *not* visited.

| Bouvet Island | Lauterbrunnen Valley | Oeno Island |
|---|---|---|
| Jan Mayen | Lord Howe Island | Navassa Island |

B. Match each number with the correct description.

_a_ **1.** 872

_d_ **2.** a little over 1 million

_e_ **3.** 822

_b_ **4.** 815

_c_ **5.** 1,686,953

**a.** the number of places Most Traveled People has listed on its website

**b.** the number of places Bill Altaffer has visited

**c.** the number of miles Charles Veley has traveled

**d.** the amount of money Charles Veley has spent on plane tickets

**e.** the number of places Charles Veley has visited

# B FORM

## The Present Perfect

 **Think Critically About Form**

**A.** Read the sentences and complete the tasks below.      *P. P.*

**1a.** He <u>has</u> crossed the Atlantic many times.      *Past tense*

**1b.** He <u>crossed</u> the Atlantic in 2009.

**2a.** They <u>flew</u> to Paris last night.      *Simple Past*

**2b.** They <u>have</u> flown to Paris many times.

1. **IDENTIFY** Which two sentences are in the simple past? Which two sentences are in the present perfect? How many words are necessary to form the present perfect?

2. **RECOGNIZE** Underline the verb forms that follow *has* and *have*. These are past participles. Which form resembles the simple past? Which form is irregular?

3. **LABEL** Look back at the article on page 90. Find five examples of the present perfect.

**B.** Discuss your answers with the class and read the Form charts to check them.

| AFFIRMATIVE STATEMENTS | | | |
|---|---|---|---|
| **SUBJECT** | **HAVE/HAS** | **PAST PARTICIPLE** | |
| I | **have** | | |
| You | | | |
| He | **has** | traveled *viajó* | to Paris. |
| She | | flown *volado* | |
| It | | | |
| We | | | |
| You | **have** | | |
| They | | | |

| NEGATIVE STATEMENTS | | | | |
|---|---|---|---|---|
| **SUBJECT** | **HAVE/HAS** | **NOT** | **PAST PARTICIPLE** | |
| I | **have** | | | |
| You | | | | |
| He | **has** | **not** | traveled | to Paris. |
| She | | | flown | |
| It | | | | |
| We | | | | |
| You | **have** | | | |
| They | | | | |

| CONTRACTIONS | | |
|---|---|---|
| I've | | |
| She's | **traveled** | to Paris. |
| They've | | |

| CONTRACTIONS | | |
|---|---|---|
| I | **haven't** | |
| She | **hasn't** | **traveled** | to Paris. |
| They | **haven't** | |

| YES/NO QUESTIONS | | | |
|---|---|---|---|
| **HAVE/ HAS** | **SUBJECT** | **PAST PARTICIPLE** | |
| Have | you | | |
| Has | he | **traveled flown** | to Paris? |
| Have | they | | |

| SHORT ANSWERS | | | | | |
|---|---|---|---|---|---|
| **YES** | **SUBJECT** | **HAVE/ HAS** | **NO** | **SUBJECT** | **HAVE/HAS + NOT** |
| | I | have. | | I | haven't. |
| Yes, | he | has. | No, | he | hasn't. |
| | they | have. | | they | haven't. |

| INFORMATION QUESTIONS | | | | |
|---|---|---|---|---|
| **WH- WORD** | **HAVE/HAS** | **SUBJECT** | **PAST PARTICIPLE** | |
| Who | have | you | seen? | |
| What | | | | |
| Why | has | she | been | in the hospital? |
| How long | have | they | | |

| **WH- WORD (SUBJECT)** | **HAS** | **SUBJECT** | **PAST PARTICIPLE** | |
|---|---|---|---|---|
| Who | has | | traveled | to Paris? |
| What | | | happened? | |

- The past participle of a regular verb has the same form as the simple past (verb + -d/ -ed). See Appendices 4 and 5 for the spelling and pronunciation of verbs ending in -ed.
- Irregular verbs have special past participle forms. See Appendix 6 for a list of irregular verbs and their past participles.

---

**!** Do not confuse the contraction of *is* with the contraction of *has* in the present perfect.

He**'s traveling** a lot = He is traveling a lot.

He**'s traveled** a lot = He has traveled a lot.

- See Appendix 16 for more contractions with *have*.

---

**!** Do not use a subject pronoun in information questions when the *wh-* word is the subject.

**What** has happened?     X What has it happened? (INCORRECT)

## B1 Listening for Form

CD1 T27 Listen to these sentences. Write the present perfect verb forms you hear. You will hear both contracted and full forms.

1. I ____have worked____ here for three years.

2. We __haven't seen__ Yuji since August.

3. I'm sorry. Mr. O'Neill __has gone__ for the day.

4. Our class __hasn't taken__ the exam yet.

5. It __has rained__ every day this week!

6. Don't leave yet. You __haven't eaten__ your breakfast.

*Present Perfect Tense*

## B2 Working on Irregular Past Verb Forms

Complete the chart. See Appendix 6 if you need help.

| | BASE FORM | SIMPLE PAST | PAST PARTICIPLE |
|---|---|---|---|
| 1. | know | knew | known |
| 2. | get | got | gotten |
| 3. | take | taked | taken |
| 4. | buy | bought | |
| 5. | leave | left | left |
| 6. | cost | cost | cost |
| 7. | show | showed | |
| 8. | be | was were | been |
| 9. | go | went | gone |
| 10. | eat | eated | eaten |
| 11. | make | maked | made |
| 12. | do | did | done |
| 13. | see | saw | seen |
| 14. | think | thought | thought |
| 15. | grow | grew | grown |
| 16. | spend | spent | spent |

*See Pag A-5 A-6*

**Reduced Forms of *Have* and *Has***

CD1 T28 Look at the cartoon and listen to the conversation. How is the underlined form in the cartoon different from what you hear?

*Sandra Change* [handwritten]

Wow... <u>Sandra has</u> changed a lot!

She's gotten her hair cut. She looks great!

In informal speech, we often reduce *have* and *has* with names and other nouns.

| Standard Form | What You Might Hear |
|---|---|
| Mark **has** changed. | "/mɑrks/ changed." |
| The cities **have** grown. | "The /ˈsɪtizəv/ grown." |

We also often reduce *have* and *has* with *wh-* words in informal speech.

| Standard Form | What You Might Hear |
|---|---|
| Why **has** he left? | "/waɪz/ he left?" |
| Where **have** you been? | "/ˈwɛrəv/ you been?" |

## B3 Understanding Informal Speech

CD1 T29 Listen and complete these sentences with the standard form of the words you hear.

1. John _____has been_____ here for a long time.
2. Kendra and Rick _____have seen_____ the movie already.
3. Paul's _____has got_____ a new racing bicycle.
4. The guests _____have gone_____ home.
5. The police _____have caught_____ the thief.
6. Where _____has_____ she _____been_____?
7. Fresno _____has grown_____ bigger since the 1930s.
8. Why _____has_____ it _____taken_____ so long?

*Where's she going? Present continuo* [handwritten]
*where is she going?* [handwritten]

## B4 Completing Conversations with the Present Perfect

**A.** Complete these conversations with the words in parentheses and the present perfect. Use contractions where possible.

*Conversation 1*

**Silvio:** How long _____ have _____ you _____ lived _____ (live) here?

**Victor:** Five years. _____ have _____ you _____ been _____ (be) here long?

**Silvio:** No, I _____ haven't _____ (not). I _____ has _____ only _____ been _____ (be) here for six months.

*Conversation 2*

**Gina:** Hi, Julie. I _____ haven't see _____ (not/see) you for a long time.

**Julie:** Hi, Gina. I think it _____ has been _____ (be) almost three years since we last met. How _____ has _____ your family _____ been _____ (be)?

**Gina:** Oh, there _____ been _____ (be) a lot of changes. My older brother, Chris, _____ has got _____ (get) married, and Tony and his wife, Marta, _____ have had _____ (have) two children.

**B.** Practice the conversations in part A with a partner.

## B5 Building Sentences

**A.** Build eight logical sentences: four in the present perfect and four in the simple past. Punctuate your sentences correctly.

Present Perfect: *She has been a good friend.*
Simple Past: *She went to a restaurant.*

| she | have | been | for a long time |
|---|---|---|---|
| they | has | waited | to a restaurant |
| | | learned | a good friend |
| | | went | English |

**B.** Rewrite your sentences as negative statements.

# Continuing Time Up to Now

## Think Critically About Meaning and Use

**A.** Read the sentences and answer the questions below.

**1a.** Hiro has lived in New York since 1989.  **2a.** Rosa has been a teacher for ten years.

**1b.** Hiro lived in Chicago for three years.  **2b.** Rosa was a nurse for one year.

1. **ANALYZE** Which sentences show situations that began and ended in the past? What tense do they use? 1b 2b

2. **ANALYZE** Which sentences show situations that began in the past and have continued up to the present time. What tense do they use? 1a 2a

**B.** Discuss your answers with the class and read the Meaning and Use Notes to check them.

## Meaning and Use Notes

ONLINE
PRACTICE

| | **Continuing Time Up to Now** |
|---|---|
| ▶ 1 | The present perfect connects the past with the present. Use the present perfect for actions or states that began in the past and have continued up to the present time. These actions or states may continue into the future. |
| | He**'s worked** here for five years.    She**'s lived** in the same town since 2001. |

P.P                   P.P

| | ***For* and *Since*** |
|---|---|
| | Sentences expressing continuing time up to now often use *for* and *since*. |
| ▶ 2A | *For* + a length of time tells how long an action or state has continued up to the present time. |
| | I've worked here **for** <u>a long time</u>.    I've lived here **for** <u>ten years</u>. |
| ▶ 2B | *Since* + a point in time tells when an action or state began. |
| | I've worked here **since** <u>2000</u>.    I've been here **since** <u>Tuesday</u>. |
| | *Since* can also introduce a time clause. When it does, the verb in the time clause is usually in the simple past. |
| | I've lived here **since** <u>I was 20</u>.    I've worked here **since** <u>I left home</u>. |

Simple past

## C1 Listening for Meaning and Use ▶ Note 1

CD1 T30  Listen to each sentence. Is the speaker talking about a past situation that continues to the present, or a situation that began and ended in the past? Check (✓) the correct column.

| | PAST SITUATION THAT CONTINUES TO THE PRESENT | SITUATION THAT BEGAN AND ENDED IN THE PAST |
|---|---|---|
| 1. | ✓ | |
| 2. | | |
| 3. | | |
| 4. | | |
| 5. | | |
| 6. | | |
| 7. | | |
| 8. | | |

## C2 Contrasting *For* and *Since* ▶ Note 2

A. Complete these sentences with *for* or *since*.

1. Alex has climbed mountains ___since___ he was 15 years old.

2. They've been out of town ___since___ Saturday.

3. My boss has been in a meeting ___for___ a long time.

4. He has worked in Brazil ___since___ last September.

5. That restaurant has been closed ___for___ a week now.

6. I've known Matt ___since___ we were in high school.

7. They've studied French ___for___ a few months.

8. Lisa has lived in New York ___for___ ten years.

9. Keiko has liked winter sports ___since___ she was a child.

10. We've been here ___for___ half an hour.

B. Use these words and phrases to write sentences. Use the present perfect with *for* or *since*.

1. Sue/live/Rome/2009

   <u>Sue has lived in Rome since 2009.</u>

2. Betty/work/at Happy Systems/ten years

   <u>Betty has worked at Happy Systems for ten years.</u>

3. Paul/study/French/two semesters

   <u>Paul has studied French for two semesters.</u>

4. I/be married/to Kalin/last August

   <u>I has been married to Kalin since last August.</u>

5. Liz and Sheryl/know/Celia/many years

   <u>Liz and Sheryl have known Celia for many years.</u>

## C3 Talking About How Long ▶ Notes 1–2

 A. Work with a partner. Look at the timeline. Use the phrases below and the present perfect to ask and answer questions about Gary's life. Use contractions where possible.

| **be a U.S. citizen** | **have a business** | **live in the U.S.** |
| **be married** | **know his best friend** | **own a house** |

A: *How long has he been a U.S. citizen?*

B: *He's been a U.S. citizen since 2003.* OR *He's been a U.S. citizen for . . . years*

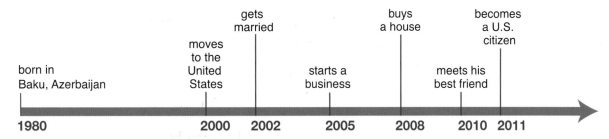

 B. Make a list of questions about your partner's life. Use the present perfect with *for* and *since*. Take turns asking and answering each other's questions. Use contractions where possible.

A: *How long have you studied English?*

B: *I've studied English for five years.*

B: *How long have you lived in this city?*

A: *I've lived here since 2010.*

## Indefinite Past Time

### Think Critically About Meaning and Use

Read the sentences and answer the questions below.

**1a.** I've flown in an airplane.
**1b.** I flew to Rome last month.
**2a.** There have been many car accidents on this road.
**2b.** There <u>was</u> an accident here yesterday.

1. **EVALUATE** Which sentences talk about an indefinite (not exact) time in the past? Which form of the verb is used in these sentences? *1a 2a*

2. **EVALUATE** Which sentences talk about a definite (exact) time in the past? Which form of the verb is used in these sentences? *1b - 2b*

**B.** Discuss your answers with the class and read the Meaning and Use Notes to check them.

## Meaning and Use Notes

ONLINE
PRACTICE

| | **Indefinite Past Time** |
|---|---|
| ▶ **1A** | Use the present perfect to talk about actions or states that happened at an indefinite (not exact) time in the past.<br><br>A: Have you met Bob?<br><br>B: Yes, I**'ve met** him. He's really nice. |
| ▶ **1B** | Actions or states in the present perfect can happen once or repeatedly.<br><br>He**'s visited** Hawaii <u>once</u>.<br><br>I**'ve tried** <u>three times</u> to pass my driver's license exam. |
| ▶ **1C** | Do not use the present perfect with time expressions that express a definite (exact) time in the past. When you mention the definite time an event happened, use the simple past.<br><br>I **went** to Europe in 2009.   x I've gone to Europe in 2009. (INCORRECT) |

## Using *Ever* with Indefinite Past Time

▶ 2  The adverb *ever* means "at any time." Use *ever* in present perfect questions to ask if an action took place at any time in the past.

A: **Have** you **ever been** in a helicopter?

B: Yes, I have. OR
   No, I haven't.

> **!** We usually do not use *ever* in present perfect affirmative statements.
>
> I have been in a helicopter.     **X** I have ever been in a helicopter. (INCORRECT)

## D1 Listening for Meaning and Use

▶ Notes 1A, 1C

 CD1 T31   Listen to each sentence. Does it refer to a definite time in the past or an indefinite time in the past? Check (✓) the correct column.

| | DEFINITE TIME IN THE PAST | INDEFINITE TIME IN THE PAST |
|---|---|---|
| 1. | | ✓ |
| 2. | | |
| 3. | | |
| 4. | | |
| 5. | | |
| 6. | | |
| 7. | | |
| 8. | | |
| 9. | | |
| 10. | | |

# D2 Contrasting Definite and Indefinite Past Time ▶ Notes 1A–1C

A. Each of these situations begins with a sentence about the indefinite past.
Complete the second sentence with an example expressing the definite past.

1. I've met a lot of famous people. For example, last year I _spoke to_
   _Bill Gates in an elevator at the Plaza Hotel._

2. I've met some interesting people since I moved here. For example, this year
   I _met Karyme Lozano at the club._

3. My friend has done a lot of crazy things. Last month _he went_
   _to México with no money._

4. My parents have helped me a lot. When I was younger, they _worked_
   _hard to save money and I go to the University._

5. I had a difficult professor a while ago. For example, once _maked me_
   _repeat all my homework in class._

B. Now write sentences about an indefinite time in the past. Use the present perfect
to introduce each situation.

1. _My parents have traveled a lot_ . Last summer they went to Thailand
   and South Korea, and they visited Brazil and Peru in October.

2. _He has had many jobs_. He worked in a restaurant for
   one year, he sold cars for six months, and he worked as a bank teller for
   only one month!

3. _She has. performed on Broadway and Chicago_. She danced in a Broadway
   musical last December, and she sang in another show in Chicago this year.

4. _I've been very busy_ . This morning I cleaned the
   _I've been very energetic_
   house, washed the clothes, and even worked in the garden!

5. _They have lived in several diferent places_. They lived in Venezuela for two
   years, they stayed in Mexico for six months, they lived in Seattle for one
   OR year, and now they live in Tucson, Arizona.
   _They have moved a lott in the past few years_

*[handwritten top margin: Present Perfect Tense Has + past participle / Have regular / irregular]*

## D3 Asking Questions About Indefinite Past Time
▶ Notes 1A, 2

*[handwritten: A-5]*

Write two *Yes/No* questions for each of these situations. Use the present perfect.

1. Your friends have traveled a lot. You want to find out about their trips.

   Have you ever been to Egypt? Have you seen the pyramids?

2. You are thinking about buying a used car. You meet a woman who is trying to sell her car.

   *[handwritten: Have you driven this car a lot?]*
   *[handwritten: Have you had any trouble with this car?]*

3. You want to hire a babysitter. You are interviewing a teenager for the job.

   *[handwritten: Have you worked as a babysitter before?]*
   *[handwritten: Have you had little brothers?]*

4. You are looking for a new roommate. Someone comes to see your apartment.

   *[handwritten: Have you ever lived with a roomate before?]*
   *[handwritten: have you had any problems with roomate before?]*

5. Your friend, Lee, has moved to a new town. You want to find out about his experiences.

   *[handwritten: Have you been to the local library?]*
   *[handwritten: Have you found a job yet?]*
   *[handwritten: have you made any new friends?]*

## D4 Describing Progress
▶ Notes 1A, 1B

Paul has made a list of things to do before he moves to his new apartment. Look at the list and make statements about his progress so far. *[handwritten: Use Pres Perofc Tense]*

*He's called the moving company.*

*He hasn't cleaned the apartment.*

TO DO

✔ Call the moving company

Clean apartment

✔ Disconnect computer

Pack clothes

Throw away trash

Contact the post office

✔ Call mom and give her new address

Say goodbye to neighbors

Leave key with superintendent

# Vocabulary Notes

## More Adverbs with the Present Perfect

*Never* means "not ever" or "not at any time." We can use *never* instead of *not* in negative statements. Do not use *never* with *not*. *Never* comes before the past participle.

> She has **never** been to Greece.

*Already* means "at some time before now." Use *already* with questions and affirmative statements. It comes before the past participle or at the end of a sentence.

> She has **already** left.   Have they **already** eaten?   What has he **already** done?
>
> She has left **already**.   Have they eaten **already**?   What has he done **already**?

*Yet* means "up to now." Use *yet* with negative statements and *Yes/No* questions. It comes at the end of a sentence.

> They haven't arrived **yet**.   Have you met him **yet**?

*Still* also means "up to now." It has a similar meaning to *yet*, but with the present perfect is used only in negative statements. It comes before *have* or *has*.

> She **still** hasn't called. (= She hasn't called **yet**.)

*So far* means "at any time up to now." Use *so far* in affirmative and negative statements and in questions. It comes at the beginning or end of a sentence.

> **So far** he's spent $500.        How much money have you spent **so far**?
> **So far** I haven't had a good time.    Have you had a good time **so far**?

## D5 Using Adverbs with the Present Perfect

A. Rewrite these sentences. Place the word or words in parentheses in an appropriate position in each sentence. Use contractions where possible.

*Conversation 1*

**A:** Have you asked Sheryl to help you (yet)?

Have you asked Sheryl to help you yet?
1

**B:** No, I haven't asked her (still).

No, I still haven't ask her.
2

*Conversation 2*

**A:** Have you played golf (ever)?

_Have you ever played golf?_ [1]

**B:** No, I've played golf (never).

_I, I've never played golf._ [2]

*Conversation 3*

**A:** Has she bought the tickets (yet)?

_Has she bought the tickets yet?_ [1]

**B:** No. She's made the reservations (already), but I don't think that she has paid for the tickets (yet).

_No, she's already made reservations, but I don't think she's paid for the tickets yet._

*Conversation 4*

**A:** How's the fund drive going? Have you raised any money (yet)?

_Have you raised any money yet?_ [1]

**B:** Yes. We've raised $2,000 (so far). We haven't finished (still).

_Yes, we've raised $200 so far. We still haven't finished_ [2]

*Conversation 5*

**A:** Has Rick left (yet)?

_Has Rick left yet?_ [1]

**B:** Yes, he has left (already).

_Yes, he's already left._ [2]

*Conversation 6*

**A:** Have you made any friends at school (yet)?

_Have you made any friends at school yet?_ [1]

**B:** No, I've been too busy (so far).

_No, I've been too busy so far._ [2]

**B.** Practice the conversations in part A with a partner.

## Think Critically About Meaning and Use

**A.** Choose the best answer to complete each conversation.

**1.** A: He visited Sweden four years ago.

   B: _____

   a. Where is he staying?
   b. Did he have a good time?

**2.** A: Emily has worked for the school for a long time.

   B: _____

   a. Is she going to retire soon?
   b. Why did she leave?

*Up to now*

**3.** A: I've already cooked dinner.

   B: _____

   a. Can I help you?
   b. What did you cook?

**4.** A: It has rained only once this month.

   B: _____

   a. Does it usually rain more?
   b. Has it rained a lot?

**5.** A: I haven't been to Europe yet.

   B: _____

   a. Do you want to go sometime?
   b. When did you go?

**6.** A: Have you ever flown a plane?

   B: _____

   a. No, I didn't.
   b. No, not yet.

**7.** A: So far I've spent $100 on course books.

   B: _____

   a. Do you think you'll need to buy more?
   b. You're lucky you don't need any more.

**B.** Discuss these questions in small groups.

    **1. EVALUATE**   In 2 and 3, can speaker A use the simple past instead of the present perfect? If so, does the meaning change?

    **2. EXPLAIN**   Look at 2, 3, 5, and 7. How does Speaker A use the present perfect: for time up to now or the indefinite past?

## Edit

**Find the errors in this paragraph and correct them. Use the simple present, the simple past, and the present perfect.**

Rita and Bob have been the most- *[are]*

traveled people I know. They went almost *[has been]*

everywhere. Rita has been a photographer, *[is]*

and Bob has been a travel writer, so they *[is]*

often travel for work. They been to many *[have]*

countries, such as Nepal and India. They

have also travel to Turkey, Greece, and *[been]*

Bulgaria. They have see some places yet, *[haven't seen]*

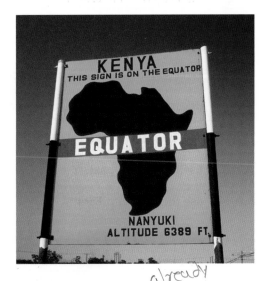

though. For example, they still haven't visited New Zealand. This year they've been *[already]*

already away from home a total of three months, and it has been only June. In January *[so far] [is]*

Rita has gone to Kenya while Bob has toured Indonesia. Then they both have traveled to *[Went]*

Argentina and Norway. Right now they're at home. They were here for two weeks already. *[i've been]*

Two weeks at home is like a vacation for Rita and Bob.

## Write

Write a paragraph about someone you admire. Follow the steps below. Use the present perfect.

1. **BRAINSTORM** Think about a person you admire. This person must still be alive. He or she can be someone you know or someone you know about. Take notes about what you want to say. Use these questions to help you.
   - Who is this person and why do you admire him or her?
   - What are some basic facts of this person's life? For example, where has this person lived and worked?
   - What has the person done that seems special to you? For example, has he or she worked somewhere special or helped other people?
   - How has the person influenced you?

2. **WRITE A FIRST DRAFT** Before you write your draft, read the checklist below. Write your draft using the present perfect, the simple past, and simple present.

3. **EDIT** Read your work and check it against the checklist below. Circle grammar, spelling, and punctuation errors.

| DO I ... | YES |
|---|---|
| describe what this person has done and show why I admire him or her? | ☐ |
| use the present perfect? | ☐ |
| use the simple past? | ☐ |
| use the simple present? | ☐ |
| include *for, since,* and adverbs with the present perfect? | ☐ |

4. **PEER REVIEW** Work with a partner to help you decide how to fix your errors and improve the content.

5. **REWRITE YOUR DRAFT** Using the comments from your partner, write a final draft.

> I admire my Uncle Tomás. He is a doctor. He has worked
> with poor people since he graduated from college twenty
> years ago...

**Choose the correct word or words to complete each sentence.**

1. Who ___won___ the Nobel Peace Prize in 2001?

   **a.** win       **(b.)** won       **c.** used to win       **d.** use to win

2. Did New York ___Used to___ be the capital of the United States?

   **(a.)** used to       **b.** use to       **c.** did       **d.** was

3. My aunt and uncle ___bought___ a new house near the beach last year.

   **a.** has bought       **(b.)** bought       **c.** buys       **d.** is buying

4. Have you ___wrote___ your report yet?

   **a.** wrote       **b.** written       **c.** write       **d.** have written

5. It's 3:00, and we ___haven't eaten___ lunch yet.

   **a.** not eaten       **b.** don't eat       **c.** haven't eaten       **d.** didn't use to eat

6. The city ___used to own___ this building and the land around it.

   **a.** use to own       **b.** owning       **c.** used to own       **d.** didn't use to

7. Chris was standing near the telephone when he ___heard___ it ring.

   **a.** was hearing       **b.** were hearing       **c.** heard       **d.** has heard

8. Joon-ho ___wasn't studying___ when I called.

   **a.** not studying       **b.** wasn't studying       **c.** hasn't studied       **d.** isn't studying

**Choose the correct word or words to complete each conversation.**

9. **A:** How many fish have you caught (yet / so far)?
   **B:** I haven't caught any. yet

10. **A:** I've already mowed the lawn.
    **B:** (How long did it take? / Can I help you do it?)

11. **A:** He's worked at the high school for 20 years.
    **B:** (I guess he likes it. / Why did he leave?)

12. **A:** She didn't use to live alone.

   **B:** Did she like living (with other people / <u>alone</u>)?

13. **A:** Bob (starts his new job tomorrow / <u>started his new job last week</u>).

   **B:** He seems to like it.

14. **A:** I'm sorry. I didn't know you (<u>were using</u> / used) the computer.

   **B:** That's okay. I'll be done soon.

15. **A:** What (did you do last night / <u>were you doing at 3:00 yesterday</u>)?

   **B:** I was sleeping. I was feeling sick.

16. **A:** Have you traveled a lot?

   **B:** Yes, I (have / <u>did</u>).

**Complete each sentence with the affirmative or negative past continuous form of the word or words in parentheses. Use contractions for the negative past continuous form.**

17. Tim and Frank _____plays_____ (play) baseball on Sunday. Their team won.

18. It was cold and cloudy yesterday. The sun ___wasn't shine___ (not/shine).

19. Why did you wake me? I _____had_____ (have) a great dream.

20. I _____talked_____ (talk) to Elsa after class. She's really nice.

CHAPTER

7

# Future Time:
# *Be Going To, Will,* and the Present Continuous

# The Election

## A1 Before You Read

Discuss these questions.

Are you interested in politics? Do you vote? Why or why not?

## A2 Read

 CD1 T32 Read this feature article from an online news website to find out about four people's opinions of candidates in an election for governor.

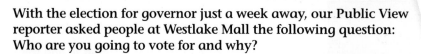

# THE ELECTION

With the election for governor just a week away, our Public View reporter asked people at Westlake Mall the following question: Who are you going to vote for and why?

5 I'm voting for Greta Monroe. She's the best candidate. She's honest, hardworking, and intelligent. Just think, we are going to
10 have our first woman governor! I am sure that she'll do a great job. For one thing, she's fair. She wants to help poor people, but she isn't going to raise taxes for the rest of us. She's also
15 very interested in education, and that's important to me.

***Diane Marshall, 67***
*retired teacher*

I'm not voting. I used to vote in every election and nothing changed. I'm not going to waste
20 my time anymore. In fact, I am leaving for Chicago the day before the election, so I'm not even going to be here. Besides, I'm sure Overmeyer
25 is going to win. He's not a politician; he's a businessman. He started his own company and now it's one of the state's largest employers. All the business people will vote for him. The others don't have
30 a chance.

***Richard Chen, 26***
*accountant*

I'm undecided. I'm not voting for Monroe, that's for sure. So I still have to decide between either Overmeyer or Kelly. Overmeyer has made a lot of promises, but will he keep them? He says that he is going to help bring jobs to the state. But how is he going to do that? And what kind of jobs will they be? Are they going to be jobs for skilled workers at good salaries, or will they be minimum-wage jobs for teenagers? And Kelly? Well, I'm not sure about him, either. He's done a good job as mayor, but running a state is a lot more difficult than running a city.

**Steve Corum, 38**
*unemployed mechanic*

I'm new here and I don't know enough about the candidates to make a decision. People say that Kelly will probably raise taxes, Monroe won't be able to do the job, and Overmeyer will only help businesses. I've received a lot of information in the mail about all three. I'm going to sit down this weekend and read it. I hope I can make a decision after that.

**Marcy Willis, 28**
*chef*

---

**governor:** the head of a state government
**candidate:** a person who people can vote for in an election
**running:** managing, directing

**mayor:** the head of a city government
**skilled:** trained
**minimum wage:** the lowest amount an employer can pay a worker for an hour's work

## A3 After You Read

Look at the questions in the chart. Check ( ✓ ) the correct column.

| | WHICH CANDIDATE . . . | MONROE | OVERMEYER | KELLY |
|---|---|---|---|---|
| 1. | isn't going to raise taxes? | ✓ | | |
| 2. | is a woman? | | | |
| 3. | runs a large company? | | | |
| 4. | promises to bring jobs to the state? | | | |
| 5. | is a mayor? | | | |
| 6. | wants to raise taxes? | | | |

**FORM 1**

# The Future with *Be Going To* and the Present Continuous

 ## Think Critically About Form

**A.** Look back at the article on page 112 and complete the tasks below.

1. **IDENTIFY** An example of *be going to* + verb is underlined. Find three more affirmative examples.

2. **RECOGNIZE** What form of *be going to* is used with *we*? with *he*? with *I*?

3. **LABEL** An example of the present continuous as future (*be* + verb + *-ing*) is circled. Find one more affirmative example.

**B.** Discuss your answers with the class and read the Form charts to check them.

▶ ## The Future with *Be Going To*

ONLINE
PRACTICE

### AFFIRMATIVE STATEMENTS

| SUBJECT | BE | GOING TO | BASE FORM OF VERB | |
|---|---|---|---|---|
| I | am | | | |
| You | are | | | |
| He She It | is | going to | help | later. |
| We | | | | |
| You | are | | | |
| They | | | | |

### NEGATIVE STATEMENTS

| SUBJECT | BE | NOT | GOING TO | BASE FORM OF VERB | |
|---|---|---|---|---|---|
| I | am | | | | |
| You | are | | | | |
| He She It | is | not | going to | help | later. |
| We | | | | | |
| You | are | | | | |
| They | | | | | |

### YES/NO QUESTIONS

| BE | SUBJECT | GOING TO | BASE FORM OF VERB | |
|---|---|---|---|---|
| Are | you | | | |
| Is | she | going to | help | later? |
| Are | they | | | |

### SHORT ANSWERS

| YES | SUBJECT | BE | NO | SUBJECT + BE + NOT |
|---|---|---|---|---|
| | I | am. | | I'm not. |
| Yes, | she | is. | No, | she isn't. |
| | they | are. | | they aren't. |

| INFORMATION QUESTIONS | | | | | |
|---|---|---|---|---|---|
| *WH-* WORD | *BE* | SUBJECT | *GOING TO* | BASE FORM OF VERB | |
| Who | are | you | | call | later? |
| What | is | she | going to | do | tomorrow? |
| When | are | they | | study | at the library? |

| *WH-* WORD (SUBJECT) | BE | | *GOING TO* | BASE FORM OF VERB | |
|---|---|---|---|---|---|
| Who | is | | going to | win | the election? |
| What | | | | happen | next? |

- See Appendix 16 for contractions with *be going to*.

 Do not use contractions with affirmative short answers.

Yes, I **am**   ✗ Yes, I'm. (INCORRECT)

## ▶ The Present Continuous as Future

| AFFIRMATIVE STATEMENTS | | | |
|---|---|---|---|
| SUBJECT | *BE* | BASE FORM OF VERB + *-ING* | |
| She | is | helping | later. |

| NEGATIVE STATEMENTS | | | | |
|---|---|---|---|---|
| SUBJECT | *BE* | *NOT* | BASE FORM OF VERB + *-ING* | |
| She | is | not | helping | later. |

| *YES/NO* QUESTIONS | | | |
|---|---|---|---|
| *BE* | SUBJECT | BASE FORM OF VERB + *-ING* | |
| Are | they | helping | later? |

| INFORMATION QUESTIONS | | | | |
|---|---|---|---|---|
| *WH-* WORD | *BE* | SUBJECT | BASE FORM OF VERB + *-ING* | |
| When | are | they | helping? | |

- See Chapter 3 for more information on the present continuous.

## B1 Listening for Form

A. **Listen to these sentences. Write the subjects and future verb forms you hear.**

1. _She's going to start_ school next year.

2. _____ home tonight. The airline canceled our flight.

3. Where _____ tonight?

4. Take your umbrella. _____.

5. _____ TV tonight?

6. They hate that hotel so _____ there again.

7. _____ on vacation tomorrow.

8. _____ to the office next week. I'm on vacation.

9. Study hard, or _____ the test.

10. I'm really excited. _____ on a business trip to Brazil next month.

B. **Work with a partner. Look at each sentence again. Which future form is used: *be going to* or the present continuous as future?**

## B2 Working on *Be Going To*

**Complete these sentences with the correct forms of *be going to* and the words in parentheses. Use contractions where possible.**

1. Soo-jin _is going to study_ (study) in the United States next year.

2. She and her classmates _____ (take) language exams in December.

3. She _____ (not/apply) to many schools—just a few in Boston.

4. She knows that it _____ (be) difficult to study abroad.

5. Her parents aren't worried, because she _____ (not/be) alone.

6. She _____ (stay) with relatives there.

7. She _____ (live) with her aunt and uncle.

8. Soo-jin and her relatives are very close so they _____ (enjoy) living together.

## B3 Building Present Continuous Sentences

Build six logical sentences with the present continuous as future. Use a word or phrase from each column. Punctuate your sentences correctly.

*I am taking a test tomorrow.*

| I | am | giving | a test | next summer |
|---|---|---|---|---|
| my friends | is | taking | to Europe | tomorrow |
| our teacher | are | going | to a restaurant | tonight |

## B4 Forming Questions with *Be Going To*

Complete each conversation with a *Yes/No* question or information question. Use *be going to* and the words and phrases in parentheses.

1. **A:** Is he going to study tonight? _____ (study/tonight)

   **B:** Yes, he is.

2. **A:** _____ (call/tomorrow)

   **B:** No, they aren't.

3. **A:** _____ (graduate/this semester)

   **B:** No, I'm not.

4. **A:** _____ (move/to Canada)

   **B:** No, I'm not.

5. **A:** _____ (he/study/tonight)

   **B:** In the library.

6. **A:** _____ (they/call)

   **B:** Tonight.

7. **A:** _____ (you/graduate)

   **B:** Next semester.

8. **A:** _____ (you/move)

   **B:** To Japan.

### Reduced Form of *Going To*

CD1 T34 Look at the cartoon and listen to the conversation. How are the underlined forms in the cartoon different from what you hear?

Are you <u>going to</u> see Mary tonight?

No, I'm <u>going to</u> study. I have a lot of homework.

In informal speech, *going to* is often pronounced /ɡənə/.

| Standard Form | What You Might Hear |
|---|---|
| They are **going to** call. | "They're /ɡənə/ call." |
| He is **going to** buy a new phone. | "He's /ɡənə/ buy a new phone." |
| I am **going to** stay home. | "I'm /ɡənə/ stay home." |

## B5 Understanding Informal Speech

CD1 T35 Listen and write the standard form of the words you hear.

1. We _____are going to make_____ dinner soon.

2. I _____ to the beach.

3. We _____ him in Seattle.

4. Our class _____ next Wednesday.

5. The store _____ in five minutes.

6. Mark _____ at Lincoln University.

7. The children _____ happy about this.

8. They _____ the test tomorrow.

# *Be Going To* and the Present Continuous as Future

## Think Critically About Meaning and Use

**A.** Read the sentences and answer the questions below.

   **a.** I'm going to buy my father a book for his birthday.

   **b.** I think we're going to have a storm tonight.

   **c.** We're taking a trip next month.

   **1. EVALUATE** Which two sentences talk about an intention (something you're thinking about doing) or a plan?

   **2. EVALUATE** Which sentence makes a prediction (a guess about the future)?

**B.** Discuss your answers with the class and read the Meaning and Use Notes to check them.

## Meaning and Use Notes

**ONLINE PRACTICE**

| Intentions and Plans with *Be Going To* and the Present |
|---|
| ▶ **1A** Use *be going to* to talk about intentions or future plans.<br><br>**I'm going to study** hard for the test.<br><br>**I'm going to visit** Greece this summer.<br><br>A: What **is** Josh **going to study** at college?<br><br>B: He**'s going to study** chemistry. |
| ▶ **1B** You can also use the present continuous to talk about intentions or future plans. A future time expression is usually used with the present continuous to show that the sentence refers to the future (and not something happening right now). The verbs *go, come, do,* and *have,* as well as verbs related to travel, are especially common with the present continuous as future.<br><br>When **are** you **coming** to see me?<br><br>**I'm visiting** Greece <u>this summer</u>.<br><br>My flight **is arriving** <u>in the afternoon</u>. My father **is meeting** me at the airport.<br><br>A: What **are** you **doing** <u>tomorrow</u>?<br><br>B: **I'm having** lunch with friends. Then we**'re going** to a movie. |

*(Continued on page 120)*

▶ **1C** The present continuous often refers to more definite plans than *be going to*. With *be going to*, the speaker often has not decided on the details.

**Present Continuous as Future (Details Definite)**

I'**m taking** a 3:00 flight to Chicago. In Chicago, I'**m changing** planes and **flying** on to Miami.

***Be Going To* (Details Not Definite)**

A: I'**m going to buy** a car.

B: What kind **are** you **going to get**?

A: I don't know yet.

---

### Predictions with *Be Going To*

▶ **2** Use *be going* to for predictions (guesses about the future), especially when there is evidence that something is just about to happen. The present continuous is not used to make predictions.

Be careful! That glass **is going to fall**!

It's cloudy. I think it'**s going to rain** tonight.

x It's cloudy. I think it's raining tonight. (INCORRECT)

---

## C1 Listening for Meaning and Use

▶ Notes 1A,1B, 2

CD1 T36  Listen to each sentence. Is the speaker talking about an intention or plan, or making a prediction? Check (✓) the correct column.

| | INTENTION/PLAN | PREDICTION |
|---|---|---|
| 1. | | ✓ |
| 2. | | |
| 3. | | |
| 4. | | |
| 5. | | |
| 6. | | |
| 7. | | |
| 8. | | |

## C2 Making Predictions with *Be Going To*

▶ Note 2

 Work with a partner. Look at the pictures and make two predictions about what is going to happen in each situation. Use *be going to*.

*I think she's going to take a trip.*
*I think she's going to travel to a cold place.*

# Vocabulary Notes

## Future Time Expressions

The future time expressions below are commonly used in sentences about the future.

| Today/Tonight/Tomorrow | This + Time Period | Next + Time Period |
|---|---|---|
| today | this afternoon | next Sunday |
| tonight | this Sunday | next week |
| tomorrow | this week | next August |
| the day after tomorrow | this year | next month |
| tomorrow morning/ afternoon/night | this spring | next year |
| They're arriving **tomorrow**. | I'm leaving **this week**. | **Next week** I'm visiting Ana. |

| IN + QUANTITY OF TIME | THE + TIME PERIOD + AFTER NEXT |
|---|---|
| in five minutes | the week after next |
| in a few days | the weekend after next |
| in a few weeks | the month after next |
| in a few months | the year after next |
| He's going to call **in a few hours**. | We're having a test **the week after next**. |

## C3 Using Future Time Expressions

Work with a partner. Take turns asking and answering questions with *when* and *be going to* or the present continuous as future. Use *be going to* for intentions and the present continuous as future for more definite plans. Use future time expressions in your answers.

1. you/study

   A: *When are you going to study?*

   B: *I'm going to study tonight.*

   OR

   A: *When are you studying?*

   B: *I'm studying this afternoon.*

2. your best friend/visit you

3. you/finish your homework

4. your friends/moving to Rio

5. you/check your email

6. your history teacher/give a test

7. your family/take a vacation

8. you/clean your apartment

## C4 Talking About Intentions and Plans

▶ Notes 1A–1C

A. Write sentences about what you intend or plan to do at the future times in parentheses. Use *be going to* for intentions and the present continuous as future for more definite plans.

1. (next weekend)  *Next weekend I'm going to visit my parents.*

2. (the day after tomorrow) _____

3. (next spring) _____

4. (in six months) _____

5. (next year) _____

6. (in an hour) _____

B. Work with a partner. Ask your partner about his or her intentions or plans. Use future time expressions in your questions.

A: *What are you doing next weekend?*

B: *I'm visiting my parents.*

## C5 Thinking About Intentions and Plans

▶ Notes 1A–1C

A. Think about these possible events. Check ( ✓ ) the events that you can plan.

✓ 1. learn to drive a car     _____ 7. look for a job

_____ 2. have bad weather     _____ 8. go camping

_____ 3. shop for clothes     _____ 9. have an eye exam

_____ 4. go to college     _____ 10. get married

_____ 5. get sick     _____ 11. win the lottery

_____ 6. have a car accident     _____ 12. watch a movie

B. Work with a partner. Talk about the things you plan to do. You can use the events you checked in part A or others. Use *be going to* for intentions or the present continuous as future for more definite plans. Use future time expressions.

A: *I'm going to learn to drive this summer. My brother is going to teach me.*

B: *I'm watching a movie with some friends tonight. My friend Silvia is renting a video, and everyone is coming to my house at 7:00.*

## C6 Planning a Meeting

▶ Notes 1B–1C

A. Fill in the chart below with your schedule for the next week.

|  | Monday | Tuesday | Wednesday | Thursday | Friday |
|---|---|---|---|---|---|
| 8:00 A.M. |  |  |  |  |  |
| 9:00 A.M. |  |  |  |  |  |
| 10:00 A.M. |  |  |  |  |  |
| 11:00 A.M. |  |  |  |  |  |
| 12:00 P.M. |  |  |  |  |  |
| 1:00 P.M. |  |  |  |  |  |
| 2:00 P.M. |  |  |  |  |  |
| 3:00 P.M. |  |  |  |  |  |
| 4:00 P.M. |  |  |  |  |  |
| 5:00 P.M. |  |  |  |  |  |

B. Now work with three other students to find a time for a two-hour meeting, a lunch date, and a one-hour work-out at the gym. Use the present continuous as future and time expressions to talk about your future plans.

A: *What is the easiest subject you have ever studied?*

B: *I'm free next Tuesday at 9 A.M.*

C: *I'm not. I'm working all morning.*

D: *What are you doing next Thursday at one?*

C: *I'm not doing anything until three.*

# D FORM 2

# The Future with *Will*

 **Think Critically About Form**

**A.** Read the sentences and complete the tasks below.

    **a.** I will decide in a few weeks.    **c.** They will vote for him.

    **b.** He will probably raise taxes.    **d.** Will Overmeyer keep his promises?

  **1. IDENTIFY** Underline *will* + verb in each sentence. Circle the subjects.

  **2. APPLY** Does the form of *will* change with different subjects?

  **3. APPLY** Does *will* go before or after the subject in a question?

**B.** Discuss your answers with the class and read the Form charts to check them.

**ONLINE PRACTICE**

| AFFIRMATIVE STATEMENTS | | | |
|---|---|---|---|
| **SUBJECT** | **WILL** | **BASE FORM OF VERB** | |
| I | | | |
| You | | | |
| He She It | will | leave | tomorrow. |
| We | | | |
| You | | | |
| They | | | |

| NEGATIVE STATEMENTS | | | | |
|---|---|---|---|---|
| **SUBJECT** | **WILL** | **NOT** | **BASE FORM OF VERB** | |
| I | | | | |
| You | | | | |
| He She It | will | not | leave | tomorrow. |
| We | | | | |
| You | | | | |
| They | | | | |

| CONTRACTIONS | | |
|---|---|---|
| I'll | | |
| She'll | leave | tomorrow. |
| They'll | | |

| CONTRACTIONS | | |
|---|---|---|
| I | | |
| She | won't | leave | tomorrow. |
| They | | |

*(Continued on page 126)*

| YES/NO QUESTIONS | | | |
|---|---|---|---|
| *WILL* | SUBJECT | BASE FORM OF VERB | |
| Will | you<br>she<br>they | leave | tomorrow? |

| SHORT ANSWERS | | | | | |
|---|---|---|---|---|---|
| *YES* | SUBJECT | *WILL* | *NO* | SUBJECT | *WILL + NOT* |
| Yes, | I<br>she<br>they | will. | No, | I<br>she<br>they | won't. |

| INFORMATION QUESTIONS | | | | |
|---|---|---|---|---|
| *WH-* WORD | *WILL* | SUBJECT | BASE FORM OF VERB | |
| Who | will | he | see | at the wedding tomorrow? |
| What | | they | do | later? |

| *WH-* WORD (SUBJECT) | *WILL* | | BASE FORM OF VERB | |
|---|---|---|---|---|
| Who | will | | leave | first? |
| What | | | happen | next? |

- Use the same form of *will* with every subject. See Appendix 16 for contractions with *will*.

> **!** Do not use contractions with affirmative short answers.
>
> Yes, I **will**.  **X** Yes, I'll. (INCORRECT)

## D1 Listening for Form

CD1 T37  Listen to each sentence. Which form is used to talk about the future: *be going to*, the present continuous, or *will*? Check ( ✓ ) the correct column.

| | *BE GOING TO* | PRESENT CONTINUOUS | *WILL* |
|---|---|---|---|
| 1. | | ✓ | |
| 2. | | | |
| 3. | | | |
| 4. | | | |
| 5. | | | |
| 6. | | | |
| 7. | | | |

## D2 Completing Conversations with *Will*

 Complete these conversations with the words in parentheses and *will* or *won't*. Use contractions where possible. Then practice the conversations with a partner.

*Conversation 1*

**Susan:** I don't believe all these predictions. In the next ten years

_____*we won't have*_____ (we/not/have) hydrogen-powered cars.
<br>1

**Bob:** Oh, I think _____ (we).
<br>2

*Conversation 2*

**Jenny:** _____ (we/be) friends in five years?
<br>1

**Keiko:** Of course, _____ (we/be) friends.
<br>2

*Conversation 3*

**Lauren:** Take your jacket or _____ (you/be) cold.
<br>1

**Dan:** No, _____ (I/not). It's not cold outside.
<br>2

*Conversation 4*

**Paul:** _____ (I/do) my homework in the morning. I
<br>1

promise, Mom.

**Mom:** No, _____ (you/not). You're always too tired in
<br>2

the morning. Do it now.

*Conversation 5*

**Carol:** _____ (I/never/learn) how to download files to
<br>1

my new MP3 player.

**Betty:** I have the same one. _____ (I/show) you.
<br>2

*Conversation 6*

**Robin:** Do you think _____ (you/find) an apartment in
<br>1

San Francisco?

**Kedra:** That's a good question. _____ (it/be) difficult.
<br>2

Maybe _____ (I/try) Oakland, too.
<br>3

## D3 Asking *Yes/No* Questions with *Will*

A. Imagine that this is the first day of your new English class. You are feeling very nervous. Use these phrases to write *Yes/No* questions to ask your teacher. Use *will* in your questions.

1. (get homework every night) <u>Will we get homework every night?</u>

2. (have a final exam) _____

3. (get grades for class participation) _____

4. (use a textbook) _____

5. (have a lot of tests) _____

6. (use the language lab) _____

B. Work with a partner. Think of two more questions to ask your teacher.

*Will we use the Internet in class?*

C. Take turns asking and answering the questions in parts A and B.

*A: Will we get homework every night?*

*B: Yes, you will. It will help you a lot.*

## D4 Building Sentences

Build six logical information questions with *will*. Use each *wh-* word at least once. Remember that *wh-* (subject) questions do not need an item from the third column. Punctuate your sentences correctly.

*What will you talk about at the meeting?*

| what | will | dinner | talk about | from college |
|------|------|--------|-----------|--------------|
| when | | you | be | after class today |
| where | | your boss | go | at the meeting |
| who | | | graduate | ready |

## Informally Speaking

### Reduced Form of *Will*

CD1 T38  Look at the cartoon and listen to the conversation. How are the underlined forms in the cartoon different from what you hear?

> Who will pick up the kids from school?

> I will. My boss will let me leave early.

In informal speech, *will* is often contracted with nouns and *wh-* words.

| Standard Form | What You Might Hear |
|---|---|
| **Jake will** be late. | "/ˈdʒeɪkəl/ be late." |
| The **children will** be here soon. | "The /ˈtʃɪldrənəl/ be here." |
| **How will** you get to Boston? | "/ˈhaʊəl/ you get to Boston?" |
| **Where will** you live? | "/ˈwɛrəl/ you live?" |

## D5 Understanding Informal Speech

CD1 T39  Listen and write the standard form of the words you hear.

1.  _What will_____ you say to him tonight?

2.  _____ Tony be home?

3.  The _____ need paper and pencils for the test.

4.  _____ help me carry these bags?

5.  _____ help you with your homework.

6.  After the test, the _____ grade our papers.

7.  _____ get the job. He's so qualified.

8.  The _____ be over at ten o'clock.

# *Will* vs. *Be Going To*

 **Think Critically About Meaning and Use**

**A.** Read the conversations and answer the questions below.

a. **Waiter:** Our special today is chicken salad.
   **Customer:** I think I'll have a tuna sandwich instead, please.

b. **Father:** I'm very angry with you.
   **Daughter:** I'm sorry. I'll never lie to you again.

c. **Wife:** What time are your parents arriving?
   **Husband:** They'll probably be here by six.

1. **ANALYZE** In which conversation is the second person making a prediction?

2. **ANALYZE** In which conversation is the second person making a quick decision?

3. **ANALYZE** In which conversation is the second person making a promise?

**B.** Discuss your answers with the class and read the Meaning and Use Notes to check them.

## Meaning and Use Notes

**ONLINE
PRACTICE**

| **Predictions with *Will* and *Be Going To*** |
|---|
| ▶ **1A** Use *will* or *be going to* to make predictions (guesses about the future). You can also use *probably* and other adverbs with *will* and *be going to* to express certainty or uncertainty. |

| *Will* | *Be Going To* |
|---|---|
| Electric cars **will become** popular in the next ten years. | Electric cars **are going to become** popular in the next ten years. |
| They**'ll** <u>probably</u> **win** the championship. | They**'re** <u>probably</u> **going to win** the championship. |

▶ **1B** With predictions, the meanings of *will* and *be going* to are not exactly the same. Use *be going to* when you are more certain that an event will happen because there is evidence. Do not use *will* in this situation.

    She**'s going to have** a baby!      X She'll have a baby! (INCORRECT)

## Quick Decisions vs. Advance Plans

▶ **2**  In statements with *I*, *will*, and *be going to* have different meanings. *Will* is often used to express a quick decision made at the time of speaking (such as an offer to help). *Be going to*, however, shows that you have thought about something in advance. Do not use *be going to* for quick decisions.

| *Will* for Quick Decisions | *Be Going To* for Advance Plans |
|---|---|
| A: I don't have a fork. | A: Do we have plastic forks for the picnic? |
| B: **I'll ask** the waiter to bring you one. | B: No. **I'm going to ask** Lisa to bring some. |
| A: Someone is at the door. | A: Have you decided to buy the car? |
| B: **I'll get** it. | B: Yes. **I'm going to get** it tomorrow. |

## Promises with *Will*

▶ **3**  In statements with *I*, *will* is often used to express a promise.

A: Chris, please clean your room.
B: **I'll do** it later, Mom. I promise.

## E1 Listening for Meaning and Use ▶ Notes 1A, 1B, 2, 3

CD1 T40  Listen to each sentence. Is the speaker making a promise, a prediction, or a quick decision? Check ( ✓ ) the correct column.

|    | PROMISE | PREDICTION | QUICK DECISION |
|----|---------|------------|----------------|
| 1. |         | ✓          |                |
| 2. |         |            |                |
| 3. |         |            |                |
| 4. |         |            |                |
| 5. |         |            |                |
| 6. |         |            |                |

## E2 Contrasting *Be Going* To and *Will*

▶ Notes 1B, 2

Complete each conversation with the words in parentheses and the correct form of *be going to* or *will*. Use contractions where possible.

*Conversation 1*

**A:** <u>Are you going</u> (you/go) to Jake's soccer practice?
  1

**B:** I can't. _____ (I/visit) my grandmother this weekend.
  2

*Conversation 2*

**A:** Did you hear? _____ (Maria/have) a baby in February!
  1

**B:** That's great news!

*Conversation 3*

**A:** Oh, there's the doorbell.

**B:** Don't worry. _____ (I/answer) it.
  1

*Conversation 4*

**A:** Maria, I have to ask you something important.

_____ (you/marry) me?
  1

**B:** Yes, of course, _____ (I), Luis.
  2

## E3 Making Quick Decisions

▶ Note 2

Complete each conversation with an offer of help. Use *will* and a contraction.

*Conversation 1*

**A:** My cat is stuck in the tree again! I'll never get it down.

**B:** <u>Don't worry! I'll get it down for you.</u>

*Conversation 2*

**A:** I can't open the door. I'm carrying too many groceries.

**B:** _____

*Conversation 3*

**A:** Oh no! I don't have enough money to pay for dinner.

**B:** _____

*Conversation 4*

**A:** I'll never have time to clean this apartment before my mom comes over.

**B:** ————————————————————————————————

*Conversation 5*

**A:** I lost my math notes and I need them to study for the quiz.

**B:** ————————————————————————————————

## E4 Making Promises ▶ Note 3

**Read the situations. Write promises *with* will or *won't*.**

1. Tony got bad grades this semester. His parents are angry. What does he promise them?

   *I'll study much harder next semester.*

2. Derek went away on vacation. He forgot to lock his house. Thieves came in and stole everything. What does he promise himself?

   ————————————————————————————————

3. Pedro forgot his essay. What does he promise his professor?

   ————————————————————————————————

4. Dr. Smith is about to give Sara an injection. What does he promise her?

   ————————————————————————————————

5. Eve is on the telephone with the manager of the local telephone company. She hasn't paid her bill for three months. What does she promise?

   ————————————————————————————————

## E5 Making Predictions ▶ Note 1A

**Work in small groups. Look at these topics. Make predictions using *be going to* and *will*. Then discuss your predictions with the rest of the class.**

1. medicine

   *Medical care is going to become more expensive, but more people will have health insurance.*

2. space travel

3. technology

4. cars and planes

5. education

6. wealth and poverty

## Think Critically About Meaning and Use

**A.** Complete each conversation.

**1.** A: _____

B: I'm getting up early, packing a lunch, and taking a bus to the beach.

   a. What are you doing now?

   (b.) What are you going to do tomorrow?

**2.** A: I don't need an umbrella. It's not raining.

B: _____

   a. But it's raining this afternoon.

   b. But it's going to rain this afternoon.

**3.** A: Tomorrow's election is going to be close.

B: _____

   a. Yes, but I think O'Casey's winning.

   b. Yes, but I think O'Casey will win.

**4.** A: Next Monday is Pat's birthday.

B: _____

   a. Yes. We're going to invite her to dinner.

   b. Yes. We'll invite her to dinner.

**5.** A: This box is very heavy. I can't carry it any longer.

B: _____

   a. Don't worry. I'm going to carry it.

   b. I'll carry it. You carry the lighter one.

**6.** A: We're going on a Caribbean cruise.

B: _____

   a. Wow! You're having a great time.

   b. Wow! You're going to have a great time.

**7.** A: Does Lisa know whether she's going to have a boy or a girl?

B: _____

   a. Yes, the doctor told her. She will have a boy.

   b. Yes, the doctor told her. She's going to have a boy.

**B.** Discuss these questions in small groups.

**1.** **COMPARE AND CONTRAST** Compare the use of the present continuous in 1 and 2. What is the difference?

**2.** **GENERATE** In 3, how else could speaker B state the response?

## Edit

**Some of these sentences have errors. Find the errors and correct them.**

1. Betty $\overset{is}{\wedge}$ going to college this fall.

2. What she is going to study?

3. She is going to study cooking because

    she wants to be a chef.

4. Betty studying with some famous chefs next year.

5. Someday maybe Betty is being a famous chef, too.

6. Betty is also going to take some business classes.

7. After these classes she certainly wills know all

    about restaurant management.

8. Maybe in a few years Betty owns a restaurant.

9. What kind of food her restaurant will serve?

10. I predict it is serving Chinese.

## Write

Imagine that there is a problem in your school, and you have a plan to solve it. Follow the steps to write a comment about the problem to post on your school's website. Use *be going to*, the present continuous as future, and *will*.

1. **BRAINSTORM** Think about a problem at your school and how you (or others) can solve it. Use these questions to help you.
   - What is the problem?
   - What are you and/or others going to do to fix the problem?
   - What will the results be? How will the situation improve?

2. **WRITE A FIRST DRAFT** Before you write your draft, read the checklist below. Write your draft using different ways of expressing future time.

3. **EDIT** Read your work and check it against the checklist below. Circle grammar, spelling, and punctuation errors.

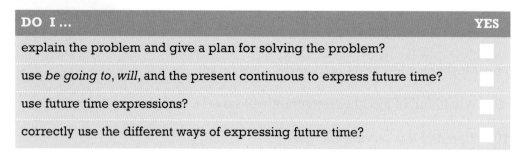

| DO I... | YES |
|---|---|
| explain the problem and give a plan for solving the problem? | ☐ |
| use *be going to*, *will*, and the present continuous to express future time? | ☐ |
| use future time expressions? | ☐ |
| correctly use the different ways of expressing future time? | ☐ |

4. **PEER REVIEW** Work with a partner to help you decide how to fix your errors and improve the content.

5. **REWRITE YOUR DRAFT** Using the comments from your partner, write a final draft.

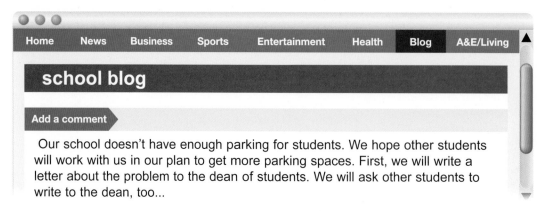

Home   News   Business   Sports   Entertainment   Health   Blog   A&E/Living

### school blog

Add a comment

Our school doesn't have enough parking for students. We hope other students will work with us in our plan to get more parking spaces. First, we will write a letter about the problem to the dean of students. We will ask other students to write to the dean, too...

CHAPTER

# 8

# Future Time Clauses and *If* Clauses

## What Will Happen in the Future?

### A1 Before You Read

Discuss these questions.

Do you think about life in the future? What will be different in the future? Will the world be a better or worse place than it is today? Why?

### A2 Read

 Read this magazine article to find out if your predictions about the future match one expert's predictions.

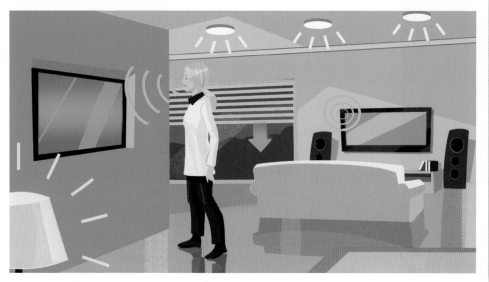

# What Will Happen in the Future?

**In the year 2020** our computers will be very good at communicating with us. Because they will understand everything we say, and we will
5 understand everything they say, we won't need a keyboard or mouse when we use them. At work, at school, and in stores, computers will be our assistants. With computers
10 really talking, many of life's tasks will become much easier for us.

Computers of the future will communicate with us.

In the year 2025 some people will live in "smart" houses. These houses will use less energy and will
15 be more environmentally friendly than the houses of today. If a room is empty, the lights and TV will go off. When the weather is cold, windows will shut automatically. They will
20 open when the weather is hot. The windows will also change the energy of the sun into electricity. Some people say that smart houses are not going to be very popular because
25 we will prefer our traditional houses. Others say that smart houses will change our way of life completely and everyone will love them.

In the year 2040 traveling by
30 car will also be easier and more environmentally friendly. Smart cars will do the driving themselves. And more cars will run on electricity instead of gasoline. Countries
35 will start to build underground automated highways (UAHs)— special roads under the ground for these smart cars. When we have these underground highways, we
40 will be able to travel quickly between large cities.

In the year 2045 humans will orbit Mars in a spaceship. Some years later, humans will land on
45 Mars and explore the planet.

---

**assistant:** helper
**environmentally friendly:** something that is good for the environment

**task:** job, something that needs to be done
**orbit:** go around

## A3 After You Read

Check ( ✓ ) the predictions that the writer makes in the article.

___✓___ **1.** In 2020 we will have computers that talk to us.

_____ **2.** In 2020 many people will have a computer for a boss.

_____ **3.** In 2030 underground roads will connect most cities.

_____ **4.** In 2025 smart houses will use energy from the sun.

_____ **5.** People in smart houses will not need electricity.

_____ **6.** People will orbit and explore Mars.

# B FORM

## Future Time Clauses and *If* Clauses

### Think Critically About Form

**A.** Read the sentences and complete the tasks below.

   **a.** I'll see him before I leave.
   **b.** When they graduate, they're going to look for work.
   **c.** We're going to have dessert after we finish dinner.

1. **IDENTIFY** Underline the main clause and circle the dependent clause in each sentence. What form of the verb is used in each main clause?

2. **RECOGNIZE** Look at each dependent clause. What is the first word? What form of the verb is used? These are future time clauses.

3. **RECOGNIZE** Look at this sentence. What is the first word of the dependent clause? This is an *if* clause.
   If I go to the store, I'll buy the groceries.

4. **LABEL** Look back at the article on page 138. Find two future time clauses and one *if* clause.

**B.** Discuss your answers with the class and read the Form charts to check them.

---

### ▶ Future Time Clauses

ONLINE
PRACTICE

| FUTURE TIME CLAUSE | SUBJECT | VERB | | MAIN CLAUSE |
|---|---|---|---|---|
| **Before** | I | **go** | to the movies, | I**'m going to do** my homework. |
| **When** | she | **gets** | to work, | she**'ll make** some phone calls. |
| **After** | we | **finish** | dinner, | we**'ll wash** the dishes. |

| MAIN CLAUSE | | FUTURE TIME CLAUSE | SUBJECT | VERB | |
|---|---|---|---|---|---|
| I**'m going to do** my homework | | before | I | **go** | to the movies. |
| She**'ll make** some phone calls | | when | she | **gets** | to work. |
| We**'ll wash** the dishes | | after | we | **finish** | dinner. |

## Overview

- A clause is a group of words that has a subject and a verb.
- A main clause can stand alone as a complete sentence.
- A dependent clause cannot stand alone and must be used with a main clause.

## Future Time Clauses

- Future time clauses are dependent time clauses. They begin with words such as *before*, *when*, *while*, and *after*.
- A future time clause can come before or after the main clause with no change in meaning. If the future time clause comes first, then it is separated from the main clause by a comma.
- Use *will* or *be going to* in the main clause.
- The verb in the future time clause is in the simple present even though it has a future meaning.

Do not use *be going to* or *will* in the future time clause.

After I **finish** my work, I'll watch TV.      **X** After I will finish my work, I'll watch TV. (INCORRECT)

## ▶ *If* Clauses

| | | IF CLAUSE | | | MAIN CLAUSE | |
|---|---|---|---|---|---|---|
| IF | SUBJECT | VERB | | (THEN) | | |
| | you | exercise | every day, | | you**'ll feel** better. | |
| If | it | rains | tomorrow, | (then) | they**'ll cancel** the picnic. | |
| | we | don't score | soon, | | we**'re going to lose** the game. | |

| MAIN CLAUSE | | IF CLAUSE | | | |
|---|---|---|---|---|---|
| | IF | SUBJECT | VERB | | |
| You**'ll feel** better | | you | exercise | every day. | |
| They**'ll cancel** the picnic | if | it | rains | tomorrow. | |
| We**'re going to lose** the game | | we | don't score | soon. | |

*(Continued on page 142)*

### *If* Clauses

- *If* clauses are dependent clauses. They must be used with a main clause.
- An *if* clause can come before or after the main clause with no change in meaning. When the *if* clause comes first, it is separated from the main clause by a comma.
- When the *if* clause comes first, *then* can be added before the main clause with no change in meaning.
- Use *will* or *be going to* in the main clause.
- The verb in the *if* clause is in the simple present even though it has a future meaning.

> **!** Do not use *be going to* or *will* in the *if* clause.
>
> If I **finish** my work, I'll watch TV.     **X** If I'll finish my work, I'll watch TV. (INCORRECT)

## B1 Listening for Form

CD1 T42 Listen to these sentences. Write the verb forms you hear.

1. When I _____see_____ Elena, I _____'ll give_____ her the message.

2. We _____ more time if the test _____ very difficult.

3. Marcus and Maria _____ to Budapest after they _____ Prague.

4. She _____ us when she _____ here.

5. If Matt _____ a loan from the bank, he _____ a new car.

## B2 Building Sentences

Build five logical sentences with future time clauses and *if* clauses. Use a clause from each column. Use the correct form of the verbs in parentheses. Punctuate your sentences correctly.

*After Megan finishes class, she'll have lunch.*

| after Megan (finish) class | we (get) a lot of money |
|---|---|
| before she (leave) the house | she (have) lunch |
| if we (win) the award | you (pass) the test |
| if you (study) hard | she (call) you |
| when we (get) to the movies | we (save) you a seat |

142 | **CHAPTER 8** Future Time Clauses and *If* Clauses

## B3 Working on Future Time Clauses and *If* Clauses

A. Complete each sentence with a future time clause or a main clause. Use the words and phrases in parentheses and the correct punctuation.

1. When I get a job *, I'll buy a car.* _____ (I/buy/a car)

2. _____ (after/she/graduate) she's going to move to L.A.

3. After we save some money _____ (we/look/for a house)

4. _____ (they/visit/the Eiffel Tower) before they leave Paris.

B. Complete each sentence with an *if* clause or a main clause. Use the words and phrases in parentheses and the correct punctuation.

1. We'll take her out to dinner *if she visits.* _____ (if/she/visit)

2. _____ (I/call) if I hear any news.

3. If I feel better _____ (I/go/to work)

4. _____ (if/you/not/study) you won't do well on the test.

## B4 Completing Sentences with Future Time Clauses and *If* Clauses

Complete this email with the correct form of the verb in parentheses.

From: George
To: Vinh
Subject: surprise party

Hi Vinh,

We're planning a surprise for Dan's graduation. Here are the plans.

Alex *will bring* (bring) me their house key after Dan _____ (leave)
                1                                                          2
for work on Friday. I _____ (cook) before I _____ (go) to class.
                           3                              4
I ordered a cake from the bakery. Stefan _____ (get) it when he
                                               5
_____ (go) shopping on Friday afternoon. But we need your help. If Dan
      6
_____ (come) home right after work, we _____ (not/be) ready.
      7                                            8
Will you ask him to drive you home after work? If you _____ (ask) him to
                                                            9
take you home, he _____ (not/be) suspicious. Then, when
                       10
everyone _____ (be) here, I _____ (call) you on your cell.
              11                       12
George

**C**

**MEANING AND USE 1**

# Using Future Time Clauses for Events in Sequence

 **Think Critically About Meaning and Use**

**A.** Read the sentences and complete the task below.

   **a.** We'll give you the information when we get the results.
   **b.** Before you take the test, the teacher will review the homework.
   **c.** He'll need help after he comes home from the hospital.

   **IDENTIFY** Look at each sentence. Underline the event that happens first. Which word or words in each sentence tell you the order of the events?

**B.** Discuss your answers with the class and read the Meaning and Use Notes to check them.

## Meaning and Use Notes

 **ONLINE PRACTICE**

| **Future Events in Sequence** |
| --- |

▶ **1**    Future time clauses show the time relationship between two events or situations in a sentence. When a time clause begins with *when* or *after*, the event in the time clause happens first. When a time clause begins with *before*, the event in the time clause happens second.

| **First Event** | **Second Event** |
| --- | --- |
| **When I get home,** | I'll call you. |
| **After they get married,** | they're going to move to California. |
| I'm going to water the plants | **before I go on vacation.** |

## C1 Listening for Meaning and Use

▶ Note 1

(») CD1 T43    Listen to each sentence. Which event happens first and which happens second? Write *1* next to the first event and *2* next to the second.

    <u>1</u> **1.** I look for a job.         <u>2</u> I graduate.

    _____ **2.** He gets here.         _____ We make dinner.

    _____ **3.** We go to the park.       _____ We go to the museum.

    _____ **4.** I call you.           _____ They leave.

    _____ **5.** I clean the house.      _____ I go shopping.

## C2 Talking About Two Future Events
▶ Note 1

A. Complete these sentences with future time clauses or main clauses.

1. _When I finish school_____, my family will be happy.

2. After I finish this English class, _____.

3. _____, I'll take a vacation.

4. I'll buy a new car _____.

5. _____, I'll speak English.

6. I'll be happy _____.

B. Work with a partner. In your notebook, write two main clauses and two future time clauses. Have your partner complete each one.

*I'll call you* _____.

*When my friend visits me,* _____.

## C3 Describing Future Events in Sequence
▶ Note 1

Think about your day tomorrow. Write two sentences for each part of the day. Use future time clauses with *before, when,* and *after.*

1. (tomorrow morning)

   _I'll get up when my alarm rings._

   _____

2. (tomorrow afternoon)

   _____

   _____

3. (tomorrow evening)

   _____

   _____

4. (tomorrow night)

   _____

   _____

# Expressing Future Possibility with *If* Clauses

## Think Critically About Meaning and Use

**A.** Read the sentences and complete the tasks below.

**1a.** If you take some aspirin, you'll feel better.
**1b.** I'll take you out to dinner if you help me with the housework.
**2a.** If Ben leaves, call me.
**2b.** When Ben leaves, call me.

1. **EVALUATE** Look at 1a and 1b. Underline the *if* clauses. Circle the main clauses. Which clause in each sentence describes a possible situation? Which clause in each sentence describes a possible result of that situation?

2. **INTERPRET** Look at 1a and 1b again. Which sentence gives advice? Which sentence makes a promise?

3. **APPLY** Look at 2a and 2b. In which sentence is it more certain that Ben will leave?

**B.** Discuss your answers with the class and read the Meaning and Use Notes to check them.

## Meaning and Use Notes

### Cause-and-Effect Relationships

▶ **1** Sentences with an *if* clause show a cause-and-effect relationship. The *if* clause introduces a possible situation (the cause). The main clause talks about the possible result (the effect) of that situation. The cause and effect can come in either order.

| *If* Clause (Cause) | Main Clause (Effect) |
|---|---|
| **If she gets that job,** | her salary will increase. |
| **If you press the red button,** | the elevator will stop. |

| Main Clause (Effect) | *If* Clause (Cause) |
|---|---|
| Her salary will increase | **if she gets that job.** |
| The elevator will stop | **if you press the red button.** |

## Expressing Advice, Warnings, Promises, and Predictions

▶ 2  Sentences with an *if* clause and a main clause with *be going to* or *will* have several common uses:

**Giving Advice:** If you rest now, you'll feel better later.

**Giving a Warning:** If you don't tell the truth, you're going to be sorry.

**Making a Promise:** If you elect me, I won't raise taxes.

**Making a Prediction:** If he moves to the city, he won't be happy.

## Possibility vs. Certainty

▶ 3  Use an *if* clause if you think something is possible, but you are not sure it will happen. Use a future time clause with *when* if you are certain something will happen.

| *If* Clause (Possible) | Future Time Clause (Certain) |
|---|---|
| **If it goes on sale,** I'll buy it. | **When it goes on sale,** I'll buy it. |
| I'll visit the Taj Mahal **if I go to India.** | I'll visit the Taj Mahal **when I go to India.** |

# D1 Listening for Meaning and Use

▶ Note 3

CD1 T44  Listen to each conversation. Does the second speaker think the situation is possible or certain? Check ( ✓ ) the correct column.

| | SITUATION | POSSIBLE | CERTAIN |
|---|---|---|---|
| 1. | She and Amy will see a movie. | ✓ | |
| 2. | He will go to the store. | | |
| 3. | It will snow this weekend. | | |
| 4. | He will go to Mexico. | | |
| 5. | Mark will ask Celia to marry him. | | |
| 6. | Jake will rent the apartment. | | |

## D2 Giving Warnings

▶ Notes 1, 2

Complete each warning with an *if* clause or a main clause.

1. If you don't stop at a red light, _____you'll get a ticket_____.

2. You'll burn your hand _____.

3. _____ if you don't pay your electric bill.

4. If you go swimming in cold weather, _____.

5. _____ if you don't eat breakfast.

6. _____ if you stay up all night.

7. You'll lose your job _____.

8. _____, you'll break your leg.

## D3 Giving Advice

▶ Notes 1, 2

Write two pieces of advice for the person in each situation. Each piece of advice should include an *if* clause and a main clause.

1. Your friend is always late for school.

   a. _If you leave home on time, you won't be late for school._____

   b. _____

2. Your brother wants to go to a good university.

   a. _____

   b. _____

3. Your sister doesn't get along with a co-worker.

   a. _____

   b. _____

4. Your cousin wants to move to a new apartment, but he doesn't have much money.

   a. _____

   b. _____

## D4 Making Promises

▶ Notes 1, 2

Work with a partner. Read these situations. Take turns making promises. Each promise should include an *if* clause and a main clause. Switch roles after each situation.

1. **Student A:** You are a student. You need help with your English homework.
   **Student B:** You are the student's best friend.

   *A: If you help me with my English homework, I'll help you with your math.*
   *B: I'll help you with your homework if you let me ride your motorcycle.*

2. **Student A:** You are a teenager. You want to borrow the family car.
   **Student B:** You are the teenager's parent.

3. **Student A:** You are a driver. You were speeding.
   **Student B:** You are a police officer.

4. **Student A:** You are an employee. You are often late for work.
   **Student B:** You are the employee's boss.

## D5 Making Predictions

▶ Notes 1, 2

Look at the picture. Write predictions about what will happen. Include an *if* clause and a main clause in each prediction.

*If the man trips over the telephone cord, he'll fall.*

# WRITING  Write a Campaign Flyer

## Think Critically About Meaning and Use

**A.** Read each sentence and the statements that follow. Check (✓) the statement that has the same meaning.

**1.** He'll come and get us when the program starts.

   ✓   a. The program will start, and then he'll come and get us.

   \_\_\_\_   b. He'll come and get us, and then the program will start.

**2.** Before you graduate, you'll need another math course.

   \_\_\_\_   a. You can't graduate without another math course.

   \_\_\_\_   b. You'll graduate, and then you'll take another math course.

**3.** He'll leave before I leave.

   \_\_\_\_   a. I'll leave when he leaves.

   \_\_\_\_   b. He'll leave, and then I'll leave.

**4.** He'll be happy if he gets the job.

   \_\_\_\_   a. He'll get the job, and then he'll be happy.

   \_\_\_\_   b. It's possible that he'll get the job. If he does, he'll be happy.

**5.** We're going to buy a house when we get married.

   \_\_\_\_   a. We feel certain that we'll buy a house after we marry.

   \_\_\_\_   b. We don't feel certain that we'll get married and buy a house.

**6.** If the store is open, I'll buy some milk.

   \_\_\_\_   a. The store will be open, so I'll buy some milk.

   \_\_\_\_   b. Maybe the store will be open, and I'll buy some milk.

**7.** I'll help you when I finish making lunch.

   \_\_\_\_   a. I'll make lunch. Then I'll help you.

   \_\_\_\_   b. I'll help you. At the same time, I'll make lunch.

**8.** She'll cook dinner when her husband comes home.

   \_\_\_\_   a. Dinner will not be ready when he arrives.

   \_\_\_\_   b. Dinner will be ready when he arrives.

9. I'll see Ben if I go to the café.

_____ a.  I'm not certain that I'm
going to the café.

_____ b.  Ben isn't certain that he's
going to the café.

**B.** Discuss these questions in small groups.

1.  **EVALUATE**  In 1, what change can you make to the time clause to make the other option correct?

2.  **COMPARE AND CONTRAST**  In 5, how does the meaning change if we use *if* instead of *when*?

## Edit

**Some of these sentences have errors. Find the errors and correct them. There may be more than one error in some sentences.**

1.  When I ~~will~~ see Debbie, I'll give her the book.

2.  If I won't feel better soon, I'll go to the doctor.

3.  If I get an A on the final, then I'll get an A for the course.

4.  I'm going to check the prices online before I'm going to buy a camera.

5.  We won't have time to see a movie after we go shopping.

6.  He's going to drive to Dallas if the weather will improve.

7.  When I'll get my paycheck, I'll pay my bills.

8.  They cancel the picnic if it will rain tomorrow.

9.  When the phone is going to ring, I'll answer it.

10.  She'll email her friends tonight if she has time.

## Write

Imagine you are running for election as mayor of your town or city. Follow the steps below to write a campaign flyer to tell voters why they should vote for you. Use future time clauses and *if* clauses.

1.  **BRAINSTORM** Think about the needs of your town or city and about the changes that you will make as mayor. Take notes about what you want to say. Use these questions to help you.

    • What will you do in your city or town if people elect you?
    • What will you NOT do if people elect you?
    • How will the town or city improve if you are mayor? How will people's lives change?
    • What bad things won't happen in the city or town if you are mayor?

2.  **WRITE A FIRST DRAFT** Before you write your draft, read the checklist below. Write your draft using future time clauses and *if* clauses.

3.  **EDIT** Read your work and check it against the checklist below. Circle grammar, spelling, and punctuation errors.

| DO I... | YES |
|---|---|
| explain why people should vote for me for mayor? | ☐ |
| make predictions and promises? | ☐ |
| use future time clauses for events in sequence? | ☐ |
| use *if* clauses to express future possibility? | ☐ |
| use correct verb forms in all clauses? | ☐ |

4.  **PEER REVIEW** Work with a partner to help you decide how to fix your errors and improve the content.

5.  **REWRITE YOUR DRAFT** Using the comments from your partner, write a final draft.

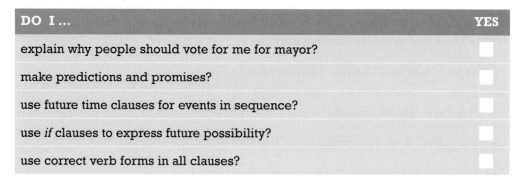

### On November 7, vote for Jenna Zabala for mayor!

*Ten good reasons to vote for me:*

• If you elect me, I will build new parks.

• When I am mayor, I won't raise city taxes.

• I will always be available if people want to talk to me.

**Choose the correct word or words to complete each sentence.**

1. We'll let you know about an interview _____ the manager reviews your résumé.

   **a.** while       **b.** before       **c.** after       **d.** until

2. The director isn't going to promote Amy if her evaluations _____ good.

   **a.** won't be       **b.** aren't       **c.** isn't       **d.** will be

3. Many reporters predict that the mayor _____ the election next year.

   **a.** is not winning   **b.** is not going to win   **c.** not win       **d.** doesn't win

4. _____ practicing with the team tomorrow?

   **a.** Is Jada       **b.** Will Jada       **c.** Is Jada going to   **d.** Won't Jada

5. If you eat that whole pizza, you _____ to walk!

   **a.** aren't able   **b.** won't be able   **c.** not able       **d.** isn't able

6. If the history class _____ full, I'm going to take Spanish.

   **a.** is       **b.** will be       **c.** is going to be   **d.** is being

7. When Hiro _____, we will start the dinner.

   **a.** will be coming   **b.** will come       **c.** comes       **d.** is going to come

8. The team _____ the game without Kedra.

   **a.** not winning   **b.** will not win   **c.** not win       **d.** win

9. Tomek _____ a lecture next month.

   **a.** give       **b.** is going to give   **c.** going to give   **d.** to give

10. Fumiko _____ to have dinner with Reiko on Friday night.

   **a.** go       **b.** are going       **c.** is going       **d.** will

**Choose the correct word or words to complete each conversation.**

11. **A:** We are (going to buy a new house some day / moving into our new house next week).
    **B:** Is it big?

12. **A:** I need to pay off my credit card debt.
    **B:** (I'll help you with a payment plan. / Will this purchase be cash or charge?)

13. **A:** So what is your prediction about the election tomorrow?
    **B:** Adams is (winning / going to win).

14. **A:** Why are they moving to a bigger apartment?
    **B:** Julia (is having / will have) a baby in a few months.

15. **A:** I can't carry all these shopping bags!
    **B:** (I'm going shopping for bags next week. / I'll help you. Give me that big one.)

16. **A:** If it rains, they'll cancel the game.
    **B:** I just heard the forecast. It's not (going to rain / raining).

17. **A:** I'm going to make dinner when you get home.
    **B:** Good. (I'm glad it'll be ready. / I'll have time for a shower.)

**Match the sentence parts.**

_____ 18. If you get more sleep,     **a.** if you leave it out.

_____ 19. The milk will spoil    **b.** if I find my checkbook.

_____ 20. I'll pay the rent    **c.** you won't be so tired.

   **d.** if the snow doesn't stop.

   **e.** your hands will be cold.

   **f.** I'll open the window.

   **g.** he'll miss his family.

   **h.** I'll cook dinner.

# Modals of Ability and Possibility

## Two Amazing People

### A1 Before You Read

Discuss these questions.

Who is someone you think is amazing? What makes this person amazing?

### A2 Read

CD1 T45   **Read this magazine article to find out about two amazing people and why they are so amazing.**

feature
**story**

Stephen Wiltshire

# Two Amazing People

Some people have exceptional abilities— they <u>can do</u> things that ordinary people cannot do. And for a very few people these abilities come with a lack of ability to do
5 some other things that ordinary people take for granted.

Think about Stephen Wiltshire. He is able to draw a city after flying over it for a half hour or so in a helicopter. He has
10 drawn huge pictures of cities including London, New York, Moscow, Tokyo, Rome, and Shanghai. In addition to drawing with great accuracy and detail from memory (such as the right number
15 of columns on the Pantheon in Rome), Stephen is able to show the feeling of each city. And yet Stephen has autism, a condition that affects various abilities, including language, intelligence, and the
20 ability to interact with other people.

As a young child in London, Stephen could not speak. But he <u>could draw</u> amazing pictures. At the special school he attended, his artistic ability was clear
25 by the time he was five years old. His first word was "paper"—he wanted drawing

paper. At 13, he published a book of drawings. He went on to study at the City and Guilds of London Art School. Since 30 then, he has published three other books and has drawn and shown his art in cities around the world.

Tony DeBlois is an exceptionally talented jazz pianist. And he's not just 35 a pianist. He also <u>can</u> play 21 other instruments, many of them very well. He can sing in 11 languages and is able to play over 8,000 pieces of music from memory.

Tony is autistic and has been blind 40 from birth. His musical ability emerged when he was two. He wasn't able to sit up, so his mother bought him a toy piano to encourage him. Music has been important to Tony in many ways. He learned to 45 brush his teeth by learning to play the violin, and he learned to brush his hair by learning to play drums. He couldn't button his clothes until he was 26, and he still can't buckle his belt or tie his shoes.

50 Nevertheless, after attending a school for the blind, Tony went on to the Berklee College of Music in Boston, Massachusetts. He graduated with honors, and ever since he has been playing 55 the piano—and inspiring audiences and other musicians.

---

**accuracy:** being correct
**condition:** illness
**emerge:** come out

**inspire:** give someone strong positive feelings
**interact:** to communicate and mix with, relate to
**take for granted:** to assume without thinking about

## A3 After You Read

**Write *T* for true or *F* for false for each statement.**

__T__ **1.** Stephen Wiltshire usually draws cities.

_____ **2.** Stephen Wiltshire draws cities after studying them for many days.

_____ **3.** As a young child, Stephen drew pictures before he learned to speak.

_____ **4.** Jazz pianist Tony DeBlois knows how to play only the piano.

_____ **5.** Both Stephen Wiltshire and Tony DeBlois are autistic.

# Modals of Ability: *Can* and *Could*; *Be Able To*

 **Think Critically About Form**

**A.** Look back at the article on page 156 and complete the tasks below.

1. **IDENTIFY** Look at the underlined examples of *can* + verb and *could* + verb. What form of the verb follows *can* and *could*?

2. **RECOGNIZE** Find the negative forms of *can* + verb and *could* + verb on the first page. What is unusual about the negative form of *can* + verb? What are the contracted negative forms of *can* and *could*?

**B.** Discuss your answers with the class and read the Form charts to check them.

## ▶ *Can* for Present and Future Ability

 **ONLINE PRACTICE**

| AFFIRMATIVE STATEMENTS | | | |
|---|---|---|---|
| SUBJECT | MODAL | BASE FORM OF VERB | |
| I | | play | the piano. |
| He | can | | |
| They | | work | tomorrow. |

| NEGATIVE STATEMENTS | | | |
|---|---|---|---|
| SUBJECT | MODAL + *NOT* | BASE FORM OF VERB | |
| I | | play | the piano. |
| He | cannot can't | | |
| They | | work | tomorrow. |

| *YES/NO* QUESTIONS | | | |
|---|---|---|---|
| MODAL | SUBJECT | BASE FORM OF VERB | |
| | you | play | the piano? |
| Can | he | | |
| | they | work | tomorrow? |

| SHORT ANSWERS | | | | | |
|---|---|---|---|---|---|
| *YES* | SUBJECT | MODAL | *NO* | SUBJECT | MODAL + *NOT* |
| | I | | | I | |
| Yes, | he | can. | No, | he | can't. |
| | they | | | they | |

## INFORMATION QUESTIONS

| WH- WORD | MODAL | SUBJECT | BASE FORM OF VERB | |
|---|---|---|---|---|
| What | can | you | play? | tomorrow? |
| How long | | he | work | |

| WH- WORD (SUBJECT) | MODAL | | BASE FORM OF VERB | |
|---|---|---|---|---|
| Who | can | | work | tomorrow? |
| What | | | fly? | |

- *Can* is a modal. Like all modals, it is followed by the base form of a verb and has the same form for all subjects.
- The negative form of *can* is *cannot*. Notice that *cannot* is written as one word.
- It is often difficult to hear the difference between *can* and *can't* because the final *t* in *can't* is not clearly pronounced. In sentences with *can* + verb, the vowel sound in *can* is very short and the stress is on the verb that follows *can*: I /kən/ g̊o. In sentences with *can't* + verb, the stress is on *can't* and the *a* is pronounced like the *a* in *ant*: I /kæn/ go.

## ▶ *Could* for Past Ability

### AFFIRMATIVE STATEMENTS

| SUBJECT | MODAL | BASE FORM OF VERB | |
|---|---|---|---|
| I | could | read | in kindergarten. |
| He | | | |
| They | | | |

### NEGATIVE STATEMENTS

| SUBJECT | MODAL + *NOT* | BASE FORM OF VERB | |
|---|---|---|---|
| I | could not couldn't | read | in kindergarten. |
| He | | | |
| They | | | |

### YES/NO QUESTIONS

| MODAL | SUBJECT | BASE FORM OF VERB | |
|---|---|---|---|
| Could | you | read | in kindergarten? |

### SHORT ANSWERS

| YES | SUBJECT | MODAL | NO | SUBJECT | MODAL + *NOT* |
|---|---|---|---|---|---|
| Yes, | I | could. | No, | I | couldn't. |

*(Continued on page 160)*

## INFORMATION QUESTIONS

| WH- WORD | MODAL | SUBJECT | BASE FORM OF VERB | |
|----------|-------|---------|-------------------|---|
| What | could | she | read | in kindergarten? |

| WH- WORD (SUBJECT) | MODAL | | BASE FORM OF VERB | |
|--------------------|-------|---|-------------------|---|
| Who | could | | read | in kindergarten? |

- *Could* is a modal. Like all modals, it is followed by the base form of a verb and has the same form for all subjects.

## ▶ *Be Able To* for Past, Present, and Future Ability

| AFFIRMATIVE STATEMENTS | | | |
|---|---|---|---|
| SUBJECT | *BE ABLE TO* | BASE FORM OF VERB | |
| He | was able to | work | yesterday. |
| | is able to | | today. |
| | will be able to | | tomorrow. |

| NEGATIVE STATEMENTS | | | |
|---|---|---|---|
| SUBJECT | *BE + NOT + ABLE TO* | BASE FORM OF VERB | |
| He | was not able to | work | yesterday. |
| | is not able to | | today. |
| | will not be able to | | tomorrow. |

- *Be able to* is not a modal, but it has the same meaning as *can* and *could*. The verb *be* in *be able to* changes form and agrees with the subject.
- See Appendix 16 for contractions with *be* and *will*.

## B1 Listening for Form

CD1 T46  Listen to this paragraph. Write *can* or *can't*.

Michael is blind. He ___can't___ see. He _____ do amazing things, however. He
                        1                              2
lives in Chicago, and he _____ walk around the city alone. Of course, he
                              3
_____ read the street signs, so sometimes he asks for help. After he has been
      4
somewhere with a friend, he _____ go there again by himself. Michael is good at
                                  5
sports, too. He's the best player on his bowling team, even though he _____ see
                                                                          6
the bowling pins.

## B2 Building Sentences with *Can* and *Can't*

Build three logical sentences with *can* and three logical sentences with *can't*. Use a word from each column.

*People can climb trees.*

| people | can | climb trees |
|--------|-----|-------------|
| fish | can't | bark |
| dogs | | swim |

## B3 Forming Statements and Questions with *Can* and *Could*

In your notebook, write a statement and a question for each set of words and phrases. Punctuate your sentences correctly.

1. Emily/house/can/our/come/to

   *Emily can come to our house.*
   *Can Emily come to our house?*

2. them/airport/could/we/the/take/to

3. his/languages/can/parents/speak/several

4. sister/your/can/Mandarin/speak

5. problem/us/can/she/this/with/help

## B4 Completing Conversations with *Be Able To*

Complete these conversations with the words in parentheses and the correct form of *be able to*. Use contractions where possible.

1. **A:** ___Were___ you ___able to finish___ (finish) the test yesterday?
      1                    2

   **B:** No, _____ (not), but I _____ (do) 45 out of the
                  3                          4
   50 questions.

2. **A:** Did David help you clean the attic?

   **B:** No, he _____ (not/come) on Saturday. But I think he
                        1
   _____ (help) me this weekend.
          2

3. **A:** _____ Susan _____ (practice) the piano at college last
              1                   2
   year?

   **B:** Well, not in the dorm, but she _____ (play) at the Student
                                                3
   Center.

4. **A:** _____ you _____ (call) me later?
              1              2

   **B:** No. I'm busy tonight, but I _____ (see) you tomorrow.
                                              3

# Past, Present, and Future Ability

## Think Critically About Meaning and Use

**A.** Read the sentences and answer the questions below.

   **a.** Carl can type 40 words a minute.

   **b.** Last year Carl could type 20 words a minute.

   **c.** When Carl's typing class ends, he will be able to type 60 words a minute.

   **1. EVALUATE** Which sentence talks about an ability that Carl has at the present time?

   **2. EVALUATE** Which sentence talks about an ability Carl doesn't have yet?

   **3. EVALUATE** Which sentence talks about an ability Carl had in the past?

**B.** Discuss your answers with the class and read the Meaning and Use Notes to check them.

## Meaning and Use Notes

ONLINE
PRACTICE

### Present Ability with *Can*

▶ **1A**   *Can* is used to talk about an ability in the present.

   The baby **can walk**, but she **can't talk** yet.

   Strong winds **can cause** a lot of damage.

▶ **1B**   *Be able to* also describes an ability in the present, but *can* is more commonly used.

| **Less Common** | **More Common** |
|---|---|
| He **is able** to speak French and Arabic. | He **can speak** French and Arabic. |

### Future Ability with *Be Able To* and *Can*

▶ **2A**   Use *will be able to* to talk about a skill or other ability that you don't have yet but will have in the future. Do not use *can* to describe an ability that you will have only in the future.

   After I complete this class, I'**ll be able to type** 60 words a minute.
   x After I complete this class, I can type 60 words a minute. (INCORRECT)

   I **will be able to see** better after I get new glasses.
   x I can see better after I get new glasses. (INCORRECT)

▶ **2B** Use *will be able to* or *can* to express ability that relates to decisions and arrangements for the future.

She $\left\{\begin{array}{l}\textbf{'ll be able to}\\\textbf{can}\end{array}\right\}$ **meet** you at the airport at 3:00.

I'm busy now, but I $\left\{\begin{array}{l}\textbf{'ll be able to}\\\textbf{can}\end{array}\right\}$ **help** you in ten minutes.

## Past Ability with *Could* and *Be Able To*

▶ **3A** Use *could* or *was/were able to* to talk about an ability that existed for a long period of time in the past.

**Long Period of Time**

When I was young, I $\left\{\begin{array}{l}\textbf{was able to}\\\textbf{could}\end{array}\right\}$ **eat** dessert every night, and I didn't gain weight.

▶ **3B** In affirmative statements with action verbs, do not use *could* to talk about an ability related to a single event. Use only *was/were able to*.

**Single Event with Action Verb (Affirmative)**

Yesterday I **was able to finish** my homework quickly.
x Yesterday I could finish my homework quickly. (INCORRECT)

▶ **3C** In affirmative statements with certain stative verbs such as *see, hear, feel, taste, understand*, and *remember*, use *could* or *was/were able to* to talk about ability related to a single event in the past.

**Single Event with Stative Verb (Affirmative)**

Last night the sky was clear and we $\left\{\begin{array}{l}\textbf{were able to}\\\textbf{could}\end{array}\right\}$ **see** for miles.

▶ **3D** In negative statements, use *couldn't* or *wasn't/weren't able to* for both ability during single events and ability over a long period of time.

**Single Event (Negative)**

Yesterday I $\left\{\begin{array}{l}\textbf{wasn't able to}\\\textbf{couldn't}\end{array}\right\}$ **finish** my homework quickly.

**Long Period of Time**

When I was younger, I $\left\{\begin{array}{l}\textbf{wasn't able to}\\\textbf{couldn't}\end{array}\right\}$ **finish** my homework quickly.

## C1 Listening for Meaning and Use ▶ Notes 1–3

CD1 T47 Listen to each speaker. Choose the correct response.

1. **a.** OK, let's go today.
   **b.** OK, we'll go tomorrow. *(circled)*

2. **a.** No, they can't. It's raining.
   **b.** Why not?

3. **a.** Were they very high?
   **b.** How disappointing!

4. **a.** Well, at least she tries.
   **b.** Of course she can. Her dad's a coach.

5. **a.** So what did they do?
   **b.** When did they learn?

6. **a.** Is she able to walk now?
   **b.** Will she be able to walk tomorrow?

## C2 Talking About Future Abilities ▶ Note 2A

Complete the sentences with *will/won't* + *be able to.* Use your own ideas.

1. Next year *I'll be able to drive.*

2. In 20 years people _____

3. In 50 years doctors _____

4. By 2030 scientists _____

5. In 10 years I _____

6. In 100 years humans _____

## C3 Distinguishing Between *Can* and *Be Able To* ▶ Notes 2A, 2B

In your notebook, rewrite these sentences with *can* where possible.

1. The teacher will be able to help you with your homework this afternoon.

   *The teacher can help you with your homework this afternoon.*

2. Paul will be able to drive us to school tomorrow morning.

3. Larry will be able to get a job when he learns how to create websites.

4. Will you be able to swim after you finish this swimming class?

5. The doctor will be able to see you at three o'clock this afternoon.

6. He will be able to walk again after the operation.

## C4 Talking About Past Abilities

▶ Notes 3A–3D

A. Work with a partner. Look at the topics below, and think about how people lived fifty years ago. Take turns making sentences with *could(n't)* and *was/were (not) able to.*

| | | | |
|---|---|---|---|
| education | food | housing | relationships |
| energy | health | leisure time | transportation |

A: *Fifty years ago many people weren't able to go to college.*

B: *Fifty years ago you could buy a house for ten thousand dollars.*

B. Share your ideas with your classmates.

## C5 Comparing Long Periods of Time and Single Events

▶ Notes 3A–3D

A. In your notebook, rewrite these sentences with *could* or *couldn't* where possible. Do not change the meaning.

1. For many years, we were able to take long vacations.

   *For many years, we could take long vacations.*

2. They were able to get tickets for the game this morning.

3. Before he hurt his knee, he was able to run five miles a day.

4. Even as a young child, she was able to swim well.

5. We weren't able to get to the concert on time last night.

6. Were you able to see the fireworks from your window the other night?

7. Matt wasn't able to find his keys this morning.

8. I was able to park the car in front of the restaurant this morning.

B. Look back at the sentences in part A. Which sentences cannot be rewritten? Why?

# Vocabulary Notes

### *Know How To*

You can use *know how to* instead of *can* to talk about a skill (a particular ability that you develop through training or practice).

| *Know How To* | *Can* |
|---|---|
| They **know how to** speak Portuguese. | They **can** speak Portuguese. |
| She **doesn't know how to** drive a car. | She **can't** drive a car. |

We do not use *know how to* to talk about abilities that do not require training or practice. We use *can* instead.

### *Can*

Hurricanes **can** cause damage.
x Hurricanes know how to cause damage. (INCORRECT)

The doctor **can** see you now.
x The doctor knows how to see you now. (INCORRECT)

## C6 Talking About Skills

A. Ask your classmates questions to find out who has the skills on the list. Ask four questions with *can* and four questions with *know how to*.

1. play chess
   *Can you play chess?* OR
   *Do you know how to play chess?*

2. change a tire

3. create a podcast

4. sew on a button

5. play the guitar
   (or other instrument)

6. ice skate

7. speak French

8. drive a motorcycle

B. Work in small groups. Talk about your classmates' abilities. Use *can* and *know how to*.
   *Carlos can play chess, but Mei Ling can't.* OR
   *Carlos knows how to play chess, but Mei Ling doesn't.*

# D FORM 2

# Modals of Future Possibility

## Think Critically About Form

**A.** Read the sentences and complete the tasks below.

   **a.** He might walk again.
   **b.** He has the strength of one hundred men.
   **c.** Researchers may find a cure.

   **1. IDENTIFY** Which sentences contain modals? Underline them. Which sentence contains a verb in the simple present?

   **2. COMPARE AND CONTRAST** Change all the sentences to negative statements. How are the negative statements with modals different from the negative statement in the simple present?

**B.** Discuss your answers with the class and read the Form charts to check them.

## ▶ *Can* for Present and Future Ability

**ONLINE PRACTICE**

| AFFIRMATIVE STATEMENTS | | | |
|---|---|---|---|
| SUBJECT | MODAL | BASE FORM OF VERB | |
| I | might may could will | leave | tomorrow. |
| You | | | |
| He | | | |
| They | | | |

| NEGATIVE STATEMENTS | | | |
|---|---|---|---|
| SUBJECT | MODAL + *NOT* | BASE FORM OF VERB | |
| I | might not may not won't | leave | tomorrow. |
| You | | | |
| He | | | |
| They | | | |

| *YES/NO* QUESTIONS |
|---|
| FUTURE FORM |
| Are you going to leave next weekend? |
| Will you leave next weekend? |
| Are you leaving next weekend? |

| SHORT ANSWERS | |
|---|---|
| AFFIRMATIVE | NEGATIVE |
| I may. | I may not. |
| I might. | I might not. |
| I could. | I may not. / I might not. |

*(Continued on page 168)*

- *Could not (couldn't)* is not usually used to express future possibility.

- *May not* and *might not* are not contracted in American English.

- *Yes/No* questions about future possibility are not usually formed with *may, might,* or *could.* Instead, they are formed with *be going to, will,* or the present continuous as future. You can use *may, might,* or *could* in short answers.

- Use modal + *be* in short answers to questions with *be.*

  A: Will you **be** home next weekend?
  B: I **might be.**

- Information questions about future possibility are also usually asked with future forms. You can answer with *may, might,* or *could.*

  A: When are you leaving?          A: When is he going to call?
  B: I'm not sure. I **may leave** next weekend.     B: He **might call** today.

## D1 Listening for Form

CD1 T48    **Listen to these conversations. Write the correct form of the modals you hear.**

1. **A:** What will you do when you finish college?

   **B:** I ___might___ look for a job, or I _____ go to graduate school instead.
         1                             2

2. **A:** The traffic is moving very slowly. We won't get to the theater on time.

   **B:** We _____. We still have plenty of time.
                   1

3. **A:** When is the package arriving?

   **B:** It _____ be here tomorrow, or it _____ arrive until the next day.
          1                         2

4. **A:** Will there be many people at the meeting?

   **B:** I don't know. There _____ be just a few of us.
                          1

5. **A:** What do you think? Is it going to snow tonight?

   **B:** Well, according to the weather report, there _____ be a lot of snow, but the storm _____ hit us at all.
                         1
                      2

## D2 Forming Affirmative and Negative Statements

A. **Form affirmative statements from these words and phrases. Punctuate your sentences correctly.**

1. fail/the/I/might/test

   *I might fail the test.*

2. game/you/win/next/could/the/Saturday

   _____

3. might/Bob and Carol/married/get/year/next

   _____

4. rain/could/tomorrow/it

   _____

5. tonight/cook/Sheryl/dinner/will

   _____

6. on/we/go/may/Sunday/beach/the/to

   _____

7. will/Yuji/at six o'clock/come

   _____

8. buy/Kim and Josh/a/house/might

   _____

9. Lynn/graduate/could/next semester

   _____

10. stay/may/home/Victor/next weekend

    _____

B. **In your notebook, rewrite the sentences as negative statements. Which three sentences cannot be made negative? Why? Discuss your answers with a partner.**

*I might not fail the test.*

# Future Possibility

## Think Critically About Meaning and Use

**A.** Read the sentences and answer the questions below.

    **a.** Ana could leave tomorrow, or she could leave today.

    **b.** Ana will leave tomorrow. She's ready to go.

    **c.** Ana may leave tomorrow. She's ready to go, but it depends on the weather.

    **d.** Maybe Ana will leave tomorrow. I'm not certain.

    **e.** Ana might leave tomorrow. I'm not sure.

    **ANALYZE** Which sentence is the most certain? Which sentences are less certain?

**B.** Discuss your answers with the class and read the Meaning and Use Notes to check them.

## Meaning and Use Notes

**ONLINE PRACTICE**

| **Expressing Future Possibility with *Could*, *Might*, and *May*** |
|---|
| ▶ **1A** *Could*, *might (not)*, and *may (not)* express possibility about the future. *Could* and *might* sometimes express more uncertainty than *may*.<br><br>I **could get** an A or a B in the course. It depends on my final paper.<br><br>I **may take** history next semester. It seems like a good idea. |
| ▶ **1B** You can talk about future possibility and future ability together with *might/may (not) + be able to*. You cannot use *might/may (not) + can*.<br><br>It's already April, but I **might be able to go** skiing one more time.<br><br>If I learn to speak Portuguese, I **may be able to get** a job in Brazil.<br>x If I learn to speak Portuguese, I may can get a job in Brazil. (INCORRECT) |
| ▶ **1C** Do not confuse *may be* and *maybe*. *May be* is the modal *may* and the verb *be*. *Maybe* is an adverb. It comes at the beginning of a sentence, and it is written as one word. *Maybe* can be used with *will* to express future possibility.<br><br>*May Be* (Modal + *Be*)           *Maybe* (Adverb)<br>We **may be** away next week.   =   **Maybe** we'll be away next week. |

▶ **1D**    Use *will* in *Yes/No* questions about future possibility. You can use *might*, but it will sound overly formal. Do not use *may*.

| *Will* | *Might/May* |
|---|---|
| **Will** he come home soon? | **Might** he come home soon? (OVERLY FORMAL) |
| | X May he come home soon? (INCORRECT) |

## Expressing Strong Certainty with *Will*

▶ **2**    Use *will* when you are certain about something. If you are not certain, you can weaken *will* by adding the adverbs *probably, maybe,* and *perhaps*.

| **Certain** | **Not Certain** |
|---|---|
| They**'ll move** in the summer. | They**'ll probably move** in the summer. |
| She**'ll find** a new job. | **Maybe** she**'ll find** a new job. |

## E1 Listening for Meaning and Use

▶ Notes 1A, 1B, 2

CD1 T49    **Listen to the conversation. Check ( ✓ ) the places that Mark and Dan are definitely going to see on their trip to Florida. Put a question mark (?) next to the places that they aren't sure about.**

   ✓ **1.** Disney World      _____ **4.** Miami Beach

   _____ **2.** Epcot Center      _____ **5.** the Everglades

   _____ **3.** Cape Canaveral      _____ **6.** Key West

The Colony Hotel, Miami Beach

## E2 Using Modals for Future Possibility ▶ Notes 1–2

Complete this conversation by choosing the appropriate word or phrase in parentheses.

**A:** So what's your daughter Lisa going to do this summer?

**B:** She's not sure, but she (could / 'll) probably work for an architect. What's your
                1
   son going to do? (Will / May) he have the same job as last summer?
                    2

**A:** He isn't sure. He (might / 'll) work in a movie theater again. But there aren't
                   3
   many jobs available, so he (couldn't / might not) find one.
                        4

**B:** They (can / might) be able to give him a job at my office. I'll speak to my boss.
            5
   (Maybe / May be) there will be an opening.
          6

**A:** Oh, thank you! That (maybe / may be) a better way for him to spend the
                   7
   summer. I (can / 'll) probably be able to convince him to apply.
        8

## E3 Contrasting *May Be* and *Maybe* ▶ Notes 1C, 2

Rewrite each sentence in your notebook. If the sentence uses *maybe*, rewrite it with *may be*. If it uses *may be*, rewrite it with *maybe*. Make all other necessary changes.

1. Lee's family may be in town next week.
   *Maybe Lee's family will be in town next week.*

2. Maybe the weather will be better on the weekend.

3. Maybe we'll be able to get tickets to the baseball game.

4. This may be an exciting game.

5. Maybe they won't be home this evening.

6. The final exam may not be very difficult.

7. He may be stuck in traffic.

8. Maybe they'll be able to help us clean the attic.

# E4 Expressing Future Possibility

▶ Notes 1A–2

A. Use your imagination to complete these conversations. Use a modal of future possibility and a verb.

*Conversation 1*

**A:** What are your roommates going to do tonight?

**B:** I don't know. They _____might go to the movies_____ , but they
1

_____may stay home and watch the game on TV_____ .
2

*Conversation 2*

**A:** Can you come to Europe with us this summer?

**B:** I don't have much money, but I _____.
1

*Conversation 3*

**A:** Tomorrow's Monday again! I don't want to go to school!

**B:** _____. Then we won't have to go to school.
1

*Conversation 4*

**A:** What are we having for dinner tonight?

**B:** We have a couple of choices. We _____, or we
1

_____.
2

*Conversation 5*

**A:** Where will you go on your next vacation?

**B:** I'm not sure. _____.
2

B. With a partner, write two more short conversations about these situations. Use *could, might (not), may (not), maybe, will, won't,* or *be able to.*

A student asks a teacher about finishing a paper late.

A reporter asks an athlete about the next Olympics.

## Think Critically About Meaning and Use

**A.** Choose the best answer to complete each conversation.

**1.** A: At that time, she could speak Japanese fluently.

   B: _____

   a. Maybe she can teach me.

   (b.) How did she learn it?

**2.** A: He won't be able to leave the hospital for a long time.

   B: _____

   a. Who's going to take care of him at home?

   b. I'll try to visit him every day.

**3.** A: The whole house is clean.

   B: _____

   a. It's amazing that you were able to do it by yourself.

   b. Who could help you?

**4.** A: We might go out to dinner tonight.

   B: _____

   a. OK. I was able to meet you there.

   b. Where do you think you'll go?

**5.** A: Do you know how to swim?

   B: _____

   a. Yes, but not very well.

   b. No, it's too cold today.

**6.** A: Were you able to go to the meeting last night?

   B: _____

   a. Yes, I could.

   b. Yes, I was.

**7.** A: What will you be able to do after this English class?

   B: _____

   a. I'll be able to speak English more fluently.

   b. I can speak English more fluently.

B. Discuss these questions in small groups.

1. **EVALUATE**  Why is the incorrect answer in 6 wrong?

2. **ANALYZE**  In 1, 2, 5, 6, and 7, is speaker A talking about past, present, or future ability?

## Edit

**Find the errors in this paragraph and correct them.**

My friend Jen might take̶s̶ us to the beach this weekend. The beach isn't far from her house. Jen can to walk there. She is a great swimmer. She could swim when she was three years old! My roommate Nicole doesn't know to swim, so I will probably teach

her this weekend. Nicole will able to swim by the end of the summer if she practices every day. May be we'll go sailing this weekend, too. Last Saturday Jen and I was able to go sailing because the weather was great. We could see dolphins near the boat. They were beautiful. Unfortunately, we couldn't touch them. If we're lucky, we can see some dolphins this weekend.

## Write

Imagine that you're going to graduate from college soon, and you want to write an email to a friend in another country talking about your plans for the future. Follow the steps below to write the email. Use modals of ability and possibility.

1. **BRAINSTORM** Think about your plans for the future. Take notes about what you want to say. Use these questions to help you.

   - What are you going to do when you finish college?
   - What things will you be able to do? What useful skills and abilities will you have?
   - What kind of work will you definitely do? What kind of work won't you do?
   - Where do you think you will live?
   - What do you think you'll probably do in your free time? What do you think you won't do?

2. **WRITE A FIRST DRAFT** Before you write your draft, read the checklist below. Write your draft using modals of ability and possibility.

3. **EDIT** Read your work and check it against the checklist below. Circle grammar, spelling, and punctuation errors.

| DO I... | YES |
|---|---|
| describe my definite and possible plans for the future? | ☐ |
| use the modal *be able to* to talk about future abilities? | ☐ |
| use the modals *might, may, could,* and *will* to talk about future possibilities? | ☐ |
| include at least one negative statement with a modal? | ☐ |
| use an adverb to weaken *will*? | ☐ |

4. **PEER REVIEW** Work with a partner to help you decide how to fix your errors and improve the content.

5. **REWRITE YOUR DRAFT** Using the comments from your partner, write a final draft.

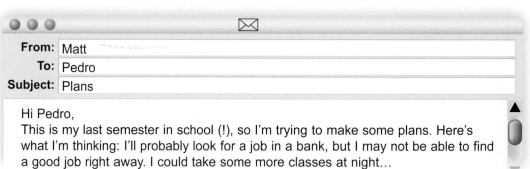

From: Matt
To: Pedro
Subject: Plans

Hi Pedro,
This is my last semester in school (!), so I'm trying to make some plans. Here's what I'm thinking: I'll probably look for a job in a bank, but I may not be able to find a good job right away. I could take some more classes at night...

# 10

# Modals and Phrases of Request, Permission, Desire, and Preference

# How *Not* to Ask for a Raise

## A1 Before You Read

Discuss these questions.

Have you ever asked for a raise (an increase in pay)? How did you ask? What did your boss say? What are some good ways to ask for a raise?

## A2 Read

 CD1 T50 Read this excerpt from an e-book to find out about good and bad ways to ask for a raise.

# How *Not* to Ask for a Raise
## A Case Study

As the manager of her own company, Rachel Franz has been asked for raises by many employees. Sometimes she has agreed and
5  sometimes she hasn't. Franz's decision is often influenced by how an employee asks. Here is a typical request for a raise. Find the mistakes that the employee makes
10  in this situation.

|  |  |
|---|---|
| **Robert:** | Ms. Franz, could I speak to you for a few minutes? |
| **Ms. Franz:** | Can we talk another time? It looks like we have a big problem with our computer system and... |
| **Robert:** | I would rather talk to you now, if possible. It will only take |
| 15 | a few minutes. |
| **Ms. Franz:** | Well, OK, come in. |
| **Robert:** | I don't know if you know this, but I'm getting married next month. |

|  | **Ms. Franz:** | No, I didn't know that, Robert. Congratulations! |
| 20 | **Robert:** | Thank you. Of course, getting married is quite expensive. <u>Would you consider</u> giving me a raise? |
|  | **Ms. Franz:** | Well, Robert, your performance review is coming up in six months. <u>I would like</u> to wait until your review. |
|  | **Robert:** | But six months is a long time. <u>Could we discuss a</u> raise sooner? |
| 25 | **Ms. Franz:** | We usually don't give raises between reviews, Robert. Now please excuse me. I have to find out about this computer problem. <u>Can you please ask</u> Kristen to come into my office when you leave? |

## Analysis

Robert made several errors. First of all, it is best to make an appointment with your boss in advance. Second, try to speak to your boss when things are going well, not badly. Listen when your boss says that it isn't a good time to talk, and arrange to speak to him or her later. Third, give your boss a good reason to give you a raise. Explain that you have more responsibilities at work now, or that you are working longer hours. Show your boss how important you are to the company, not how badly you need the money. Last, do your homework. Robert didn't know that the company doesn't give raises between reviews. Robert didn't get a raise, and he has probably hurt his chances of getting one in the future!

▼

Adapted from *Executive Female*

---

**consider:** to think about
**do your homework:** to prepare for something by finding out important information
**influence:** to have an effect on someone's behavior
*Comportamiento*

**performance review:** a meeting in which a boss and an employee discuss the employee's work
**responsibilities:** things that you must do as part of your job

## A3 After You Read

The writer says that Robert made several errors. Check ( ✓ ) the four errors that Robert made, according to the Analysis in the e-book excerpt.

___✓___ **1.** Robert didn't make an appointment with his boss in advance.

_____ **2.** Robert didn't speak politely to his boss.

___✓___ **3.** Robert chose a bad time to speak to his boss.

_____ **4.** Robert walked into his boss's office without her permission.

___✓___ **5.** Robert didn't have a good reason for his boss to give him a raise.

___✓___ **6.** Robert didn't know the company rules about raises before he spoke to his boss.

# Modals of Request; Modals of Permission;
# *Would Like*, *Would Prefer*, and *Would Rather*

*Its expression ITS not a verb*

## Think Critically About Form

**A.** Look back at the conversation in the e-book excerpt on page 178 and complete the tasks below.

    **1. IDENTIFY** Find questions with the modals *can*, *could*, and *would*. (An example is underlined.) What is the subject of each question? What form of the verb follows the subject?

    **2. CATEGORIZE** Find the expressions *would rather* and *would like*. Which one is followed by the base form of the verb? Which one is followed by an infinitive (*to* + verb)?

**B.** Discuss your answers with the class and read the Form charts to check them.

## ▶ Modals of Request

ONLINE
PRACTICE

| YES/NO QUESTIONS | | | |
|---|---|---|---|
| **MODAL** | **SUBJECT** | **BASE FORM OF VERB** | |
| Can | | close | the window? |
| Could | you | | |
| Will | | give | me a raise? |
| Would | | | |

| SHORT ANSWERS | | | | | |
|---|---|---|---|---|---|
| *YES* | **SUBJECT** | **MODAL** | *NO* | **SUBJECT** | **MODAL +** *NOT* |
| Yes, | I | can. | No, | I | can't. |
| | | will. | | | won't. |

- Modals of request are usually used in questions with *you*.
- We usually use *can* and *will* in affirmative short answers. *Could* and *would* are less common.
- We usually avoid using *won't* in negative short answers because it sounds very impolite and angry.

## ▶ Modals of Permission

<table>
<tr><th colspan="4">AFFIRMATIVE STATEMENTS</th></tr>
<tr><th>SUBJECT</th><th>MODAL</th><th>BASE FORM OF VERB</th><th></th></tr>
<tr><td rowspan="2">You</td><td>can</td><td rowspan="2">borrow</td><td rowspan="2">my car.</td></tr>
<tr><td>may</td></tr>
</table>

*Handwritten note above table:* Te Presto mi auto

*Handwritten note below table:* Usted puede tomar prestado mi coche.

<table>
<tr><th colspan="4">NEGATIVE STATEMENTS</th></tr>
<tr><th>SUBJECT</th><th>MODAL + NOT</th><th>BASE FORM OF VERB</th><th></th></tr>
<tr><td rowspan="2">You</td><td>cannot<br>can't</td><td rowspan="2">borrow</td><td rowspan="2">my car.</td></tr>
<tr><td>may not</td></tr>
</table>

<table>
<tr><th colspan="4">YES/NO QUESTIONS</th></tr>
<tr><th>MODAL</th><th>SUBJECT</th><th>BASE FORM OF VERB</th><th></th></tr>
<tr><td>Can</td><td rowspan="3">I<br>we</td><td rowspan="3">borrow</td><td rowspan="3">your car?</td></tr>
<tr><td>Could</td></tr>
<tr><td>May</td></tr>
</table>

<table>
<tr><th colspan="6">SHORT ANSWERS</th></tr>
<tr><th>YES</th><th>SUBJECT</th><th>MODAL</th><th>NO</th><th>SUBJECT</th><th>MODAL + NOT</th></tr>
<tr><td rowspan="2">Yes,</td><td rowspan="2">you</td><td>can.</td><td rowspan="2">No,</td><td rowspan="2">you</td><td>can't.</td></tr>
<tr><td>may.</td><td>may not.</td></tr>
</table>

<table>
<tr><th colspan="5">INFORMATION QUESTIONS</th></tr>
<tr><th>WH- WORD</th><th>MODAL</th><th>SUBJECT</th><th>BASE FORM OF VERB</th><th></th></tr>
<tr><td>What</td><td>can</td><td>I</td><td>call</td><td>you?</td></tr>
<tr><td>When</td><td>could</td><td>we</td><td>make</td><td>a reservation?</td></tr>
<tr><td>Where</td><td>may</td><td>I</td><td>put</td><td>my coat?</td></tr>
</table>

- Modals of permission are most often used in questions with *I* and *we* and in statements with *you*.
- Use *can* and *may* in statements and short answers. Do not use *could*.
- Use *can, could,* and *may* in Yes/No questions.
- There is no contracted form of *may not*.

*(Continued on page 182)*

# ▶ *Would Like, Would Prefer,* and *Would Rather*

| AFFIRMATIVE STATEMENTS | | |
|---|---|---|
| SUBJECT | *WOULD RATHER* | BASE FORM OF VERB |
| I | would rather | leave. |

| SUBJECT | *WOULD PREFER/ WOULD LIKE* | INFINITIVE OR NOUN PHRASE |
|---|---|---|
| I | would prefer | to leave. some tea. |
| | would like | |

| NEGATIVE STATEMENTS | | |
|---|---|---|
| SUBJECT | *WOULD RATHER + NOT* | BASE FORM OF VERB |
| I | would rather not | leave. |

| SUBJECT | *WOULD PREFER + NOT* | INFINITIVE |
|---|---|---|
| I | would prefer not | to leave. |

| *YES/NO* QUESTIONS | | | |
|---|---|---|---|
| *WOULD* | SUBJECT | *RATHER* | BASE FORM OF VERB |
| Would | you | rather | leave? |

| *WOULD* | SUBJECT | *PREFER/ LIKE* | INFINITIVE OR NOUN PHRASE |
|---|---|---|---|
| Would | you | prefer | to leave? some tea? |
| | | like | |

| SHORT ANSWERS | | | | | |
|---|---|---|---|---|---|
| *YES,* | SUBJECT | *WOULD* | *NO,* | SUBJECT | *WOULD + NOT* |
| Yes, | I | would. | No, | I | wouldn't. |

| *YES,* | SUBJECT | *WOULD* | *NO,* | SUBJECT | *WOULD + NOT* |
|---|---|---|---|---|---|
| Yes, | I | would. | No, | I | wouldn't. |

| INFORMATION QUESTIONS | | | | |
|---|---|---|---|---|
| *WH-* WORD | *WOULD* | SUBJECT | *RATHER* | BASE FORM OF VERB |
| What | would | you | rather | eat? |

| *WH-* WORD | *WOULD* | SUBJECT | *PREFER/LIKE* | INFINITIVE |
|---|---|---|---|---|
| What | would | you | prefer | to eat? |
| | | | like | |

- *Would rather* is similar to a modal verb. It is followed by the base form of the verb.
- Unlike modals, *would like* and *would prefer* are followed by the infinitive (*to* + verb). They can also be followed by a noun phrase.
- *Would like* is not usually used in negative statements. Use *don't/doesn't want* instead.

  I **don't want** to leave.     I **don't want** tea.
- For contractions with *would*, combine the subject pronoun + *'d*.

## B1 Listening for Form

CD1 T51 **Listen to these conversations. Write the form of the modals you hear.**

1. **A:** Kevin, _____will_____₁ you start dinner? I'm going shopping.

   **B:** Hmm… _Could_₂ you get some chocolate ice cream?

   **A:** I _would rather_ ~~prefer~~ ₃ buy more ice cream. You know we're both on a diet.

2. **A:** _Could_₁ I speak with Mrs. Thompson, please?

   **B:** No, I'm sorry. She's in a meeting. _Can_₂ you call back in an hour?

3. **A:** _would_₁ you _like_₂ a cup of coffee?

   **B:** No, thanks. I _would_₃ a cup of tea.

4. **A:** I _would_₁ to go to the beach with my friends this weekend, but I don't have any money. _Can_ / may ₂ I borrow $50?

   **B:** No, you _Can't_ / may not ₃. You already owe me $100!

## B2 Building Questions with Modals

**Build eight logical questions. Use a word or phrase from each column.**

*Can I come with you?*

| can | I | give | to leave now |
| could | you | come | with you |
| would | | prefer | me a ride |
| | | like | eat later |
| | | rather | some coffee |

## B3 Completing Conversations

 Complete these conversations using the words in parentheses. Use contractions where possible. Then practice the conversations with a partner.

1. **Guard:** Excuse me, sir. The sign says <u>visitors may not take</u>
   ₁
   (not/take/may/visitors) pictures inside the museum.

   **Visitor:** Oh, I'm sorry. I didn't see it. <u>where I can leave</u>
   ₂
   (leave/I/can/where) my camera?

2. **Salesclerk:** <u>May I help</u> (I/help/may) you?
   ₁

   **Customer:** Yes. I'm looking for a gift for my husband.
   <u>I would like to get</u> (like/I/get/would/to) him
   ₂
   something special.

3. **Visitor:** <u>Can I park</u> (I/park/can) here?
   ₁

   **Guard:** No, I'm sorry. <u>Visitors can not park</u> (can/visitors/park/not) in
   ₂
   this section.

4. **Husband:** <u>Will you answer</u> (you/will/answer) the phone, please?
   ₁
   My hands are wet.

   **Wife:** Sorry, <u>I can not</u> (I/not/can). I'm busy. They can
   ₂
   leave a message on the answering machine.

5. **Father:** <u>Would you like to go</u> (you/go/would/like/to) skiing with us
   ₁
   this weekend?

   **Daughter:** No, thanks. <u>I would rather stay</u> (rather/I/stay/would) home.
   ₂

6. **Waitress:** <u>Would you like to order</u> (order/like/you/would/to) now?
   ₁

   **Customer:** Yes, I'll have the broiled chicken.

   **Waitress:** <u>Would you prefer</u> (you/would/prefer) soup or salad as
   ₂
   an appetizer?

## B4 Working on Negative Sentences

Write the negative form of each sentence. Use contractions where possible. Remember to avoid the negative form of *would like.*

1. I would rather stay home tonight.

    *I'd rather not stay home tonight.*

2. We would prefer to exercise in the morning.

    *We would prefer not to exercise*

3. I would like to call you later.

    *I rather not call you later.*

4. They would rather live in the suburbs.

    *They rather not live in*

5. He would prefer to buy a new computer.

    *He prefer not to buy a new computer.*

6. He would like to finish his work now.

    *He rather not like to finish his*

## B4 Writing Short Conversations

In your notebook, write short conversations with information questions and answers using these words and phrases. Punctuate your sentences correctly.

1. where/would rather/live/in Hong Kong/in New York City

    A: *Where would you rather live, in Hong King or in New York City?*
    B: *I'd rather live in Hong Kong.*

2. who/would prefer/meet/a famous athlete/a famous writer

    *I would prefer*

3. where/would like/eat dinner tonight/at home/in a restaurant

4. what/would rather/do tonight/watch TV/go out

5. how/would rather/travel/by car/by plane

6. what/would like/buy/a laptop computer/desktop computer

7. what/would rather/eat/cookies/cake

8. where/would prefer/live/in a big city/in a small town

# C | MEANING AND USE 1

## Modals of Request

### Think Critically About Meaning and Use

**A.** Read the sentences and answer the questions below.

    **a.** Will you open the door?
    **b.** Would you open the door, please?
    **c.** Can you open the door, please?

    **EVALUATE** Which request is the most polite? Which request is the least polite?

**B.** Discuss your answers with the class and read the Meaning and Use Notes to check them.

## Meaning and Use Notes

ONLINE
PRACTICE

| | **Making Requests** |
|---|---|
| ▶ **1A** | Use *can, could, will,* and *would* to make requests. *Can* and *will* are less formal than *could* and *would*. We usually use *can* and *will* in informal conversations with friends and family. We use *could* and *would* to make polite requests in formal situations when we speak to strangers or to people in authority. |

| **Less Formal** | **More Formal** |
|---|---|
| To a Friend: **Can** you **tell** me the time? | To a Stranger: **Could** you **tell** me the time? |
| Mother to Child: **Will** you **be** quiet? | To a Boss: **Would** you **look** at my report? |

| | |
|---|---|
| ▶ **1B** | Add *please* to a request to make it more polite. |

| | |
|---|---|
| Can you tell me the time, **please**? | Would you **please** look over my report? |

| | **Agreeing to and Refusing Requests** |
|---|---|
| ▶ **2A** | Use *will* and *can* to agree to requests. Do not use *would* or *could*. We generally use *can't* to refuse a request. *Won't* is used for strong refusals, and sounds impolite. |

| **Agreeing to a Request** | **Refusing a Request** |
|---|---|
| A: **Will** you help me for a minute? | A: **Can** you **help** me with the laundry? |
| B: **Yes,** I **will**. | B: Sorry. I **can't** right now. (polite) |
| A: **Could** you **spell** your name for me? | A: Holly, will you clean up this room? |
| B: **Yes,** I **can**. It's C-L-A-R-K-E. | B: **No,** I **won't**. (impolite) |

▶ **2B** Instead of *can* or *will*, we often use expressions such as *OK, sure,* or *certainly* when agreeing to a request.

A: Will you help me for a minute?
B: **OK.**

A: Could you spell your name for me?
B: **Sure.** It's C-L-A-R-K-E.

▶ **2C** We often say *I'm sorry* and give a reason in order to make our refusal more polite.

A: Can you help me with the laundry?
B: **I'm sorry,** but I can't right now. **I have a doctor's appointment.**

## C1 Listening for Meaning and Use

▶ Notes 1A,1B

CD1 T52 **A. Listen to each conversation. Is the request you hear informal or formal? Check ( ✓ ) the correct column.**

|     | INFORMAL | FORMAL |
| --- | --- | --- |
| 1.  | ✓ |  |
| 2.  |  |  |
| 3.  |  |  |
| 4.  |  |  |
| 5.  |  |  |

CD1 T53 **B. Listen to the conversations again. Who are the speakers? Look at the choices, and write the correct letter for each conversation. Then discuss your answers with your classmates.**

1. __*a*__     a. mother and daughter

2. _____     b. two strangers

3. _____     c. two friends

4. _____     d. student and teacher

5. _____     e. employee and boss

## C2 Using the Telephone

▶ Notes 1–2

A. Choose the best response to complete each telephone conversation.

1.  **Student:** Could you connect me with Professor Hill's office?

    **Secretary:** ___b___

    a. No, I won't. He's busy.

    (b.) I'm sorry. He's not in right now. Would you like to leave a message?

2.  **Secretary:** Good morning, History Department.

    **Student:** I'd like to register for History 201. Is it still open?

    **Secretary:** ___b___

    a. Yes. Give me your name.

    b. Yes, it is. Could you give me your name, please?

3.  **Jenny's friend:** Will you please tell Jenny that I called?

    **Jenny's sister:** ___b___

    a. No, I won't. I'm going out.

    b. I won't be here when she gets home, but I'll leave her a note.

4.  **Mark's friend:** Hi. Is Mark there?

    **Mark's brother:** ___a___

    a. Sure. Can you hold on a minute?

    b. Certainly. Would you hold, please?

5.  **Client:** Would you please ask Ms. Banes to call me this afternoon?

    **Secretary:** ___a___

    a. I'm sorry, but she's out of the office until next week.

    b. Sorry, I can't.

6.  **Student:** Could you send me some information about scholarships?

    **Secretary:** ___a___

    a. Certainly.

    b. No, I can't. That's impossible right now.

B. Discuss your answers with a partner. Why did you choose each response? Why was the other response inappropriate?

C. Now practice the conversations with your partner.

## C3 Making Formal and Informal Requests

▶ Notes 1A, 1B

A   Work with a partner. Complete the requests with *can*, *will*, *could*, or *would*.
    (More than one answer is possible for each situation.)

1.   **Neighbor A:** _____Can_____ you take in our mail while we're away?
     **Neighbor B:** I'm sorry, but I can't. I'll be away then, too.

2. **Young Woman:** Excuse me, officer. _Could_ you please help me?
   **Police Officer:** Of course. What's the problem?

3.        **Parent:** _Can_ you help me for a minute?
        **Child:** OK.    *or would*

4.      **Customer:** _Could_ you put that in a box, please?
      **Salesclerk:** I'm sorry, ma'am. I don't have any boxes.

5.     **Employee:** When you get a chance, _Could o would_ you please show me how
                      to use this new computer program?
       **Manager:** Certainly. How about right now?

B.   Work with a different partner. Compare your answers. Be prepared to
     explain the modals you choose.

## C4 Agreeing to and Refusing Requests

▶ Notes 1, 2

Work with a partner. Read each situation. Then take turns making and
responding to requests. Use *can*, *will*, *could*, or *would* in your requests. Use
expressions such as *OK*, *sure*, *certainly*, and *I'm sorry* in your responses,
and give reasons for refusals.

1.   You are at a supermarket. You want the cashier to give you change for a dollar.

     *A: Could you give me change for a dollar, please?*
     *B: Certainly.*
     OR
     *I'm sorry. The manager doesn't allow us to make change.*

2.   You are moving to a new apartment. You want your friend to help you move.

3.   You would like your friend to lend you $50 until next week.

4.   You are on vacation. You want the hotel desk clerk to give you a larger room.

5.   You missed class yesterday, and you want your classmate to lend you her notes.

6.   You would like your mechanic to repair your car by the end of the week.

**MEANING AND USE 2**

# Modals of Permission

## Think Critically About Meaning and Use

**A.** Read the sentences and answer the questions below.

**1a.** Can I look at your book?    **2a.** May I borrow your book?

**1b.** Can you speak Russian?    **2b.** Can I borrow your book?

1. **EVALUATE** Look at 1a and 1b. Which question asks for permission to do something? Which question asks about ability?

2. **INTERPRET** Look at 2a and 2b. Which question is more formal?

**B.** Discuss your answers with the class and read the Meaning and Use Notes to check them.

## Meaning and Use Notes

**ONLINE
PRACTICE**

| **Asking for Permission** |
|---|
| ▶ **1A** Use *can, could,* and *may* to ask for permission. *Can* and *could* are less formal than *may*. We usually use *may* in formal situations when we speak to strangers or to people in authority. You can use *please* to make your request more polite. <br><br> **Less Formal** <br><br> *Child to Parent:* **Can I go** outside and play now? <br><br> *Friend to Friend:* **Could I borrow** your pen for a minute? <br><br> **More Formal** <br><br> *Business Call:* A: **May I speak** to Ms. Jones, **please**? <br>                  B: Certainly. **May I ask** who's calling? |
| ▶ **1B** Because *may* is more formal, it is often used in announcements and signs or other printed materials. <br><br> *Announcement:* Flight 26 has arrived. Passengers **may proceed** to Gate 2B <br>                           for boarding. <br><br> *Sign:* Visitors **may not park** in numbered spaces. |

## Giving and Refusing Permission

▶ **2A**   Use *may/may not* or *can/can't* to give or refuse permission. Do not use *could*.

| **Giving Permission** | **Refusing Permission** |
|---|---|
| A: Could I hand in my homework tomorrow? | A: Could I hand in my homework tomorrow? |
| B: **Yes, you may.** Just put it on my desk. | B: **No, you can't.** It's due today. |

▶ **2B**   Instead of answering with *can* or *may*, we often use expressions such as *sure, go (right) ahead,* or *certainly* when giving permission.

A: Can I use the computer now?          A: Could I turn on the radio?

B: **Sure.** I'm finished with it.          B: **Go right ahead.**

▶ **2C**   We often say *I'm sorry* and give a reason to make a refusal sound more polite.

A: Could I hand in my homework tomorrow?

B: **I'm sorry**, but you can't. **It's due today.**

## D1 Listening for Meaning and Use

▶ Notes 1A, 1B

CD1 T54   Listen to these conversations. In each, the first speaker is asking for permission. Who is the second speaker? Look at the choices and write the correct letter for each conversation.

1. ___d___          **a.** a boss

2. _____          **b.** a stranger

3. _____          **c.** a mother

4. _____          **d.** a friend

5. _____          **e.** a police officer

6. _____          **f.** a salesclerk

7. _____          **g.** a brother

8. _____          **h.** a teacher

## D2 Asking For Permission

▶ Note 1A

Look at the pictures. Make sentences to ask permission. Use informal and formal modals as appropriate.

*May I go in front of you?*

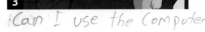
Can I use the computer?

Coud I Hold the baby?

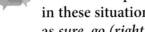
Can I open the window? Can I eat this piece a cake?

May I seat here?

## D3 Asking For and Giving or Refusing Permission

▶ Notes 1–2

Work with a partner. Take turns asking for and giving or refusing permission in these situations. Use *can*, *may*, or *could* in your questions. Use expressions such as *sure*, *go (right) ahead*, *certainly*, and *I'm sorry* in your responses.

1. You need to use your classmate's pencil.

   A: *Can I use your pencil for a minute?*

   B: *Sure. Here you are.*

2. You want to rent an apartment. The landlord shows it to you at night. You want to see it again in the daytime.

3. You want to borrow your friend's car this afternoon.

4. You are hungry, and your roommate has some leftover pizza in the refrigerator.

5. You are paying your bill at a restaurant. You want to pay with a credit card.

# *Would Like, Would Prefer,* and *Would Rather*

## Think Critically About Meaning and Use

**A.** Read the sentences and complete the tasks below.

**1a.** I want the check now.
**1b.** I'd like the check, please.

**2a.** Do you like ice cream?
**2b.** Would you like ice cream?

1. **EVALUATE** Compare 1a and 1b. Which sounds more polite?

2. **EVALUATE** Compare 2a and 2b. Which is an offer? Which asks about likes or dislikes?

**B.** Discuss your answers with the class and read the Meaning and Use Notes to check them.

## Meaning and Use Notes

**ONLINE PRACTICE**

| **Stating Desires and Making Requests with *Would Like*** |
| --- |

**▶ 1A** *Would like* has the same meaning as *want*. It is often used to talk about desires.

**Stating a Desire with *Would Like***
**I'd like** to go to China next year. (= I **want** to go to China next year.)

**▶ 1B** *Would like* is also used to make requests. In making requests, *would like* is more polite than *want*. Add *please* to make the request even more polite.

**Making a Request with *Would Like***
**I'd like** the check, please.          **X** I want the check. (NOT POLITE)

| **Making Offers with *Would Like*** |
| --- |

**▶ 2** Use *would like* in a question to make a polite offer.

A: **Would** you **like** some coffee?
B: Yes, please. With milk and sugar.

> Be careful not to confuse *would like* and *like*.
>
> | *Would Like* (to Make an Offer) | *Like* (to Ask About Likes and Dislikes) |
> | --- | --- |
> | A: **Would** you **like** some coffee? | A: Do you **like** coffee? |
> | B: Yes, please. With milk and sugar. | B: Yes, I do. I drink it every morning. |

*(Continued on page 194)*

## Accepting and Refusing Offers with *Thank You*

▶ 3  Use *thank you* to accept and refuse offers. We often give a reason to make our refusal more polite.

| Accepting an Offer | Refusing an Offer |
|---|---|
| A: Would you like a seat? | A: Would you like a seat? |
| B: Yes, **thank you.** | B: No, **thanks.** I'm getting off at the next stop. |

## Stating Preferences with *Would Like*, *Would Prefer*, and *Would Rather*

▶ 4A  Use *would like*, *would prefer*, or *would rather* to ask about and state preferences.

A: **Would** you ⎰ **like** to / **prefer** to / **rather** ⎱ walk home or take the bus?

B: **I'd like** to walk.

C: **I'd rather** take the bus. It's too far to walk.

▶ 4B  Use *would rather* with *than* to compare two actions.

**I'd rather** walk **than** take the bus.

**I'd rather** play basketball **than** (play) football.

# E1 Listening for Meaning and Use                ▶ Notes 1, 2, 4A, 4B

CD1 T55  Listen to each statement. Is the speaker making a request, making an offer, or stating a preference? Check ( ✓ ) the correct column.

|  | REQUEST | OFFER | PREFERENCE |
|---|---|---|---|
| 1. |  |  | ✓ |
| 2. |  |  |  |
| 3. |  |  |  |
| 4. |  |  |  |
| 5. |  |  |  |
| 6. |  |  |  |
| 7. |  |  |  |

Work with a partner. Look at the pictures and take turns making offers, asking about preferences, and responding appropriately. Use *would like*, *would prefer*, or *would rather*.

*doormen*

A: *Would you like some help?*

B: *Yes, thank you.* OR
   *No, thanks. I can carry them myself.*

*Would you like have some dessert,*
*Yes, please.*
*No, Thank you.*

*flattire*

*would you like some help?*

*Would you prefer the red or blue tie?*
*I would like to bay the blue tie.*

*Would you prefer to Paris or Rome?*
*I I rather go to Paris.*

*Would you like a room?*
*Yes, I would like a room*
*with some view.*

**E3** **Asking About and Stating Preferences** ▶ Notes 4A, 4B

**Work with a partner. Read each situation. Take turns asking and answering questions with *would prefer*, *would rather*, and *would like*.**

1.  You and your friend are making plans for the evening. You could see a movie, or you could go to a concert.

    *A: Would you rather see a movie or go to a concert?*

    *B: I'd rather see a movie.*

    OR

    *A: Would you prefer to see a movie or go to a concert?*

    *B: I'd prefer to go to a concert.*

2.  You and your roommate are trying to decide what to eat for dinner: chicken or fish.

3.  You need to finish a project by tomorrow. Your boss asks if you want to stay late today or come in early tomorrow.

4.  You are making arrangements to travel from Paris to Rome. The travel agent asks you if you want to fly or go by train.

5.  You want your roommate to help with the housework. You give her a choice: do the dishes or vacuum.

**E4** **Discussing Preferences** ▶ Notes 4A–4C

**Work with a small group. Look at these winter vacation ideas and choose where you would like to go. Then discuss your preferences by explaining what you would like to do. Use *would prefer*, *would rather*, and *would like*.**

1.  Mountain resort — watch ski competitions, go downhill skiing, go cross-country skiing, hike, watch birds, visit nearby towns

2.  Caribbean cruise — swim, play volleyball, play tennis, sunbathe, go scuba diving, visit islands, eat fancy buffet dinners

3.  Trip to Europe — shop, visit art museums, try foreign foods, speak foreign languages, visit cities, see famous buildings, take photographs

*I'd prefer to go on a Caribbean cruise because I'd rather be in the tropics than in the mountains. Once I get there, I'd rather play tennis than volleyball. I'd also like to go scuba diving, but I prefer not to eat fancy buffet dinners. I'm on a diet!*

## Think Critically About Meaning and Use

**A.** Choose the best answer to complete each conversation.

**1.** A: Could you help me?

B: I'm sorry. _b_

  a. I didn't have the time.

  (b.) I'm busy right now.

**2.** A: Could I borrow your car later?

B: No, I'm sorry, but _a_ .

  a. you can't.

  b. you couldn't.

**3.** A: Would you help me choose a present for my wife?

B: _a_

  a. Yes, I may.

  (b.) Certainly.

**4.** A: Do you like to play soccer?

B: _a_

  (a.) Not really.

  b. Yes. I'd love to.

**5.** A: Could you give me a ride to work?

B: Sure, _a_ .

  (a.) no problem.

  b. no way.

**6.** A: Would you rather go to the art museum or stay home?

B: _b_

  a. Yes, I would.

  (b.) I'd rather stay home tonight.

**B.** Discuss these questions in small groups.

**1. COMPARE AND CONTRAST** How are the questions in 1, 2, 3, and 5 different from the questions in 4 and 6?

**2. ANALYZE** Why is the correct response in 1 a little more polite than the correct response in 2?

## Edit

**Some of these sentences have errors. Find the errors and correct them.**

**1.** I would rather ~have~ an apple.

**2.** You ~Can~ could not borrow my van next week.

**3.** May we leave now?

**4.** You ~mayn't~ *(may not / can't)* leave until the exam is over.

**5.** Where ~would like~ you prefer to go this weekend?

**6.** I'd rather not ~to~ go now.

**7.** She'd like ~to~ learn to drive.

**8.** What would you rather do tonight?

## Write

Imagine that you want to ask your professor for an extension on a paper. Write an email asking for permission. Follow the steps below. Use modals and phrases of request, permission, and desire.

1. **BRAINSTORM** Think about what you will say in your email. Take notes about what you will say. Use these categories to help you.
   - opening question (polite request)
   - how much of an extension you want
   - why you deserve an extension
   - what you have done on your paper so far

2. **WRITE A FIRST DRAFT** Before you write your draft, read the checklist below. Write your draft using modals and phrases of request, permission, and desire.

3. **EDIT** Read your work and check it against the checklist below. Circle grammar, spelling, and punctuation errors.

| DO I... | YES |
|---|---|
| begin with a polite request using *could* or *may* to ask for an extension? | ☐ |
| provide one or more reasons to explain why I need an extension? | ☐ |
| use *would like* to express a desire? | ☐ |
| use *please* and language that is polite and appropriately formal for the situation? | ☐ |
| finish by thanking my professor for considering my request? | ☐ |

4. **PEER REVIEW** Work with a partner to help you decide how to fix your errors and improve the content.

5. **REWRITE YOUR DRAFT** Using the comments from your partner, write a final draft.

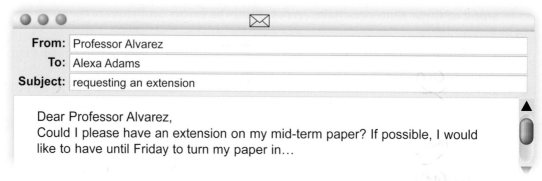

From: Professor Alvarez
To: Alexa Adams
Subject: requesting an extension

Dear Professor Alvarez,
Could I please have an extension on my mid-term paper? If possible, I would like to have until Friday to turn my paper in…

# 11

# Modals and Phrasal Modals of Advice, Necessity, and Prohibition

# Tips on Being a Good Dinner Guest

## A1 Before You Read

 Discuss these questions.

Do you go to dinner at friends' homes and invite friends to your home for dinner? What are these dinners like? What is polite behavior for hosts and guests?

## A2 Read

CD1 T56 Read these tips for some ideas about what to do and not do when you're a dinner guest in another country.

*Consejos Para ser un buen huésped*

 ## Tips on Being a Good Dinner Guest

When you travel or live in another country, it's an honor to be invited to dinner at the home of
5 someone from that country. This meal may be the first of many great experiences you'll have in that country. Before
10 accepting a dinner invitation, however, you'd better know the cultural "rules" for guests. Although you don't have to follow these rules, by following them you show
15 respect for your hosts and are more likely to have a really good time.

Every country has its own "rules." Here are some examples:

## Turkey

- You <u>must not</u> wear your shoes in the house. Your hosts will offer you
20 slippers.

- You <u>had better not</u> eat too much before you go to dinner. Your hosts will probably offer you a big dinner followed by nuts, fruit, cake, and tea
25 and coffee. <u>You should accept</u> all this food; <u>you shouldn't</u> say that you cannot eat more.

## Mexico

- You must not arrive early. In fact, you have to be at least a little late.
30 Your hosts will expect this.

- Don't leave too soon after the meal. Mexicans feel that a good guest <u>ought to</u> stay and talk for a while after all the eating is finished.

## China

35 - You <u>should be on</u> time. This shows respect for your hosts.

- You <u>must</u> take off your shoes before you enter the house.

- You <u>should</u> leave a little food on
40 your plate because you want to show that your hosts are generous.

## General

In many countries, you are expected to give your hosts a small gift. Of course, you <u>ought to</u> find out what
45 kind of gift is appropriate.

Finally, because these customs can be so different from country to country and culture to culture, look and listen carefully. Follow the lead
50 of your hosts.

---

**honor:** something special and a reason for feeling proud

**respect:** politeness, a feeling that you value and appreciate someone

**generous:** kind, willing to give a lot to others

## A3 After You Read

**Write *T* for true or *F* for false for each statement.**

___F___ **1.** The tips are for dining in restaurants.

___F___ **2.** According to the tips, being on time is especially important in Mexico.

___T___ **3.** According to the tips, taking your shoes off before entering the house is important in both Turkey and China.

___F___ **4.** In Turkey, when your hosts offer you more food, they expect you to say "no."

___T___ **5.** In many countries, guests sometimes bring a small gift.

## B | FORM

# Modals and Phrasal Modals of Advice, Necessity, and Prohibition

### Think Critically About Form

**A.** Look back at the online tips on page 201 and complete the tasks below.

1. **IDENTIFY** An example of the modal *must* is underlined. Find another example. What form of the verb follows *must*?

2. **IDENTIFY** Find an example of the modal *should*. What form of the verb follows it?

3. **IDENTIFY** Find an example of each of these phrasal modals: *have to*, *ought to*, and *had better*. What form of the verb follows each of them?

4. **COMPARE AND CONTRAST** Find the negative forms of *must*, *should*, and *have to*. How is the negative form of *have to* different from the negative forms of *should* and *must*?

**B.** Discuss your answers with the class and read the Form charts to check them.

▶ **Modals of Permission**

ONLINE PRACTICE

#### AFFIRMATIVE STATEMENTS

| SUBJECT | MODAL | BASE FORM OF VERB | |
|---------|-------|-------------------|---|
| You | could might should must | buy | a gift. |
| He | | | |
| They | | | |

#### NEGATIVE STATEMENTS

| SUBJECT | MODAL + NOT | BASE FORM OF VERB | |
|---------|-------------|-------------------|---|
| You | should not shouldn't must not | buy | a gift. |
| He | | | |
| They | | | |

#### YES/NO QUESTIONS

| MODAL | SUBJECT | BASE FORM OF VERB | |
|-------|---------|-------------------|---|
| Should | I | buy | a gift? |

#### SHORT ANSWERS

| YES | SUBJECT | MODAL | | NO | SUBJECT | MODAL + NOT |
|-----|---------|-------|---|----|---------|-------------|
| Yes, | you | should. | | No, | you | shouldn't. |

#### INFORMATION QUESTIONS

| WH- WORD | MODAL | SUBJECT | VERB | |
|----------|-------|---------|------|---|
| Where | should | we | go | for dinner? |

- *Could, might, should,* and *must* are used to give advice. *Should* and *must* are also used to express necessity. *Must not* is used to express prohibition.
- Like all modals, *could, might, should,* and *must* are followed by the base form of the verb and have the same form for all subjects.
- The contracted form *mustn't* is not usually used in American English.
- Do not use *couldn't* in negative statements of advice.
- *Could, might,* and *must* are not usually used in questions of advice.
- We usually use *have to* (see below) instead of *must* in questions of necessity.

## ▶ Phrasal Modals of Advice and Necessity

| AFFIRMATIVE STATEMENTS | | | |
|---|---|---|---|
| SUBJECT | PHRASAL MODAL | BASE FORM OF VERB | |
| I | have to have got to | | |
| She | has to has got to | call | him. |
| They | have to have got to | | |

| NEGATIVE STATEMENTS | | | | |
|---|---|---|---|---|
| SUBJECT | *DO/DOES* + *NOT* | PHRASAL MODAL | BASE FORM OF VERB | |
| I | do not don't | | | |
| She | does not doesn't | have to | call | him. |
| They | do not don't | | | |

| CONTRACTIONS | | | |
|---|---|---|---|
| I've | got to | call | him. |
| She's | | | |

| CONTRACTIONS | | | | |
|---|---|---|---|---|
| I | don't | have to | call | him. |
| She | doesn't | | | |

| AFFIRMATIVE STATEMENTS | | | |
|---|---|---|---|
| SUBJECT | PHRASAL MODAL | BASE FORM OF VERB | |
| I | | | |
| She | ought to had better | call | him. |
| They | | | |

| NEGATIVE STATEMENTS | | | |
|---|---|---|---|
| SUBJECT | PHRASAL MODAL + *NOT* | BASE FORM OF VERB | |
| I | | | |
| She | had better not | call | him. |
| They | | | |

| CONTRACTIONS | | |
|---|---|---|
| I'd better | call | him. |

| CONTRACTIONS | | |
|---|---|---|
| I'd better not | call | him. |

*(Continued on page 204)*

| | YES/NO QUESTIONS | | | |
|---|---|---|---|---|
| *DO/DOES* | SUBJECT | PHRASAL MODAL | BASE FORM OF VERB | |
| **Do** | I | | | |
| **Does** | she | **have to** | **call** | him? |
| **Do** | they | | | |

| | SHORT ANSWERS | | | | | | |
|---|---|---|---|---|---|---|---|
| *YES* | SUBJECT | *DO/ DOES* | | *NO* | SUBJECT | *DO/DOES* + NOT |
| | you | **do.** | | | you | **don't.** |
| **Yes,** | she | **does.** | | **No,** | she | **doesn't.** |
| | they | **do.** | | | they | **don't.** |

| | INFORMATION QUESTIONS | | | |
|---|---|---|---|---|
| *WH-* WORD | *DO/DOES* | SUBJECT | PHRASAL MODAL | BASE FORM OF VERB |
| **Who** | **do** | I | | |
| **What** | | | **have to** | **pay?** |
| **When** | **does** | she | | |
| **Why** | | | | |

- *Have to, have got to, ought to,* and *had better* are used to give advice. *Have to* and *have got to* are also used to express necessity.

- Unlike other phrasal modals, *have to* and *have got to* have different forms for the third-person singular.

- *Had better* looks like a past form, but isn't. It is used to talk about the present and the future.

  You**'d better** call him now.    We**'d better** leave tomorrow.

- In spoken English, we usually use contracted forms of *had better* and *have got to*. The contracted form of *had* for all persons is *'d. Have to* does not have a contracted form.

  You**'d better** call him.    You**'ve got to** call him    x You've to call him. (INCORRECT)

- We do not usually use *have got* to or *ought to* in negative statements or in questions.

- We do not usually use *had better* in questions.

## B1 Listening for Form

CD1 T57 Listen to these sentences. Circle the modal forms you hear.

1. a. should
   b. shouldn't *(circled)*

2. a. has to
   b. doesn't have to

3. a. We'd better
   b. We'd better not

4. a. must
   b. must not

5. a. have to
   b. don't have to

6. a. should
   b. shouldn't

7. a. You've got to
   b. You have to

## B2 Working on Questions

*Should = Debe*

A. Rewrite these statements as *Yes/No* questions.

1. He should buy a new car. Should he buy a new car?
2. We have to eat at 12:00. Do we have to eat at 12:00?
3. They should bring a gift. Should they bring a gift?
4. She has to go to class today. Does she has to go to class today?
5. You have to get a new passport. Do I have to get a new passport?
6. He should see a doctor. Should he see a doctor?

B. Write an information question about each underlined word or phrase.

1. Susan should give us the money. Who should give us the money?
2. He has to write a paper for his history class. What does he have to write?
3. You have to stay in the hospital for two days. How long do I have to stay in the hospital?
4. We should go to the gym on Monday. When should we go to the gym?
5. They have to take this form to the Registration Office. Where they have to take registration form?
6. You should talk to the professor after the class. When should I talk to the professor?

## B3 Writing Contracted Forms

Rewrite these sentences with contractions where possible. If you cannot use a contraction in a sentence, write *No contraction possible*.

1. You had better tell her the truth. _You'd better tell her the truth._

2. You have to look for a better job. _____

3. She ought to see a doctor. _____

4. He has got to study more. _He's got to study more._

5. You should not wear jeans to work. _____

6. She has to spend more time with the kids. _She's_ _____

7. You had better not argue with him. _You'd better_ _____

8. You have got to take a trip to the Caribbean! _You've got to ta_ _____

9. He should not waste any more time. _Shouldn't_ _____

10. You do not have to call. _____

## B4 Writing Negative Statements

Rewrite these affirmative statements as negative statements. Use contractions where possible.

1. You should ask him to help. _You shouldn't ask him to help._

2. Jake has to do his homework now. _____

3. Visitors must park here. _____

4. You had better tell your roommate the news. _____

5. Employees have to attend the sales meeting. _____

6. They should buy their son a car this year. _____

7. You must get on that train. _____

8. You should ask for a raise. _____

9. He had better wait until tomorrow. _____

10. You have to be home early. _____

## Informally Speaking

**Reduced Forms of *Ought To*, *Has To*, *Have To*, and *Have Got To***

Look at the cartoon and listen to the conversation. How are the underlined forms in the cartoon different from what you hear?

> I <u>ought to</u> get back to the library.

> Yeah, I <u>have to</u> go to class, anyway.

In informal speech, *ought to* is often pronounced as /ˈɔtə/, *has to* as /ˈhæstə/, *have to* as /ˈhæftə/, and *have got to* as /hæv ˈgɑtə/ or /ˈgɑtə/.

| Standard Form | What You Might Hear |
|---|---|
| I **ought to** go. | "I /ˈɔtə/ go." |
| She **has to** do the work. | "She /ˈhæstə/ do the work." |
| We **have to** see him now. | "We /ˈhæftə/ see him now." |
| You**'ve got to** finish today. | "You've /ˈgɑtə/ finish today." |
| | OR "You /ˈgɑtə/ finish today." |

## B5 Understanding Informal Speech

Matt and Linda are getting married today. Listen to their conversations. Write the standard form of the words you hear.

*Conversation 1: At Matt's house*

**Matt:** It's 9:00. We _____*ought to*_____ leave now.
                                    1

**Friend:** The wedding is at 10:00. We don't _____ leave until 9:30.
                                                        2

**Matt:** But we _____ be there before the guests arrive.
                        3

*Conversation 2: Later, at the ceremony*

**Linda:** Where's Matt? He _____ come soon! We're getting
                                        1
married in 15 minutes!

**Sister:** Maybe I _____ call him at home.
                          2

**Father:** Don't worry. He'll be here. We _____ stay calm and wait.
                                                    3

# Modals and Phrasal Modals of Advice

## Think Critically About Meaning and Use

**A.** Read the sentences and answer the questions below.

**a.** You ought to take that job.
**b.** You could take that job now, or you could wait awhile.
**c.** You had better take that job soon, or someone else will.
**d.** You have to take that job. You need a job!
**e.** You should take that job.

1. **EVALUATE** Which two sentences offer advice and have the same meaning? *a/e*
2. **EVALUATE** Which sentence expresses the strongest advice? *d*
3. **EVALUATE** Which sentence makes two suggestions? *b*
4. **EVALUATE** Which sentence expresses a warning? *c*

**B.** Discuss your answers with the class and read the Meaning and Use Notes to check them.

## Meaning and Use Notes

**ONLINE PRACTICE**

### Weak and Strong Advice

▶ **1**   Use *could, might, should (not), ought to, had better (not), have to, have got to,* and *must* to give advice, suggestions, and warnings.

|  |  |
|---|---|
|  | *It's Mary's graduation tomorrow.* |
| *Weak* • could, might | You **could buy** her flowers. |
| • should (not), ought to | You **should ask** her what she wants. |
| • had better (not) | You**'d better buy** something before it's too late. |
| • have to, have got to, | You **have to buy** her that new e-book. |
| *Strong*   must |  |

## Suggestions with *Could* and *Might*

▶ **2**  Both *could* and *might* are used to make casual suggestions, especially when there is more than one choice.

If you don't want to drive there, you **might** try taking the bus, or you **could** ride your bike.

You **could** meet for lunch or dinner.

## Advice with *Should* and *Ought To*

▶ **3A**  Use *should (not)* and *ought to* to give advice. *Should (not)* is more common than *ought to.*

You **should get** married in June, when the weather is warm.

You **ought to look** for a new job.

▶ **3B**  You can also use *should (not)* and *ought to* in general statements to express a personal opinion about something.

People **shouldn't** drive when they're tired.

The President **ought to** do more for the environment.

▶ **3C**  Use words such as *I think, maybe,* and *perhaps* to soften your advice or opinion.

I think the President **ought to do** more for the environment.

Maybe you **should get** married in June.

## Warnings with *Had Better*

▶ **4**  *Had better (not)* is stronger than *should (not)* or *ought to.* It is used to give advice with a warning about possible bad consequences. As with *should (not)* or *ought to,* you can use expressions such as *I think, maybe,* and *perhaps* to soften the meaning.

You**'d better study** for the test. If you don't, you'll fail.

You**'d better not make** so many personal phone calls at work, or you'll lose your job.

I think you**'d better see** the doctor, or your cold will get worse.

The roads are really icy. Maybe you**'d better stay** home.

*(Continued on page 210)*

| | Strong Advice with *Have To*, *Have Got To*, and *Must* |
|---|---|

▶ **5A**   *Have to*, *have got to*, and *must* are used to give strong advice. They often suggest that the situation is serious or urgent.

Your cough sounds terrible. You $\begin{cases} \text{have to} \\ \text{'ve got to} \\ \text{must} \end{cases}$ **see** a doctor immediately.

▶ **5B**   Another type of strong advice with *have to*, *have got to*, and *must* is more casual. It shows that the speaker has a strong opinion about something, even though the situation is not serious.

You $\begin{cases} \text{have to} \\ \text{'ve got to} \\ \text{must} \end{cases}$ **try** that new restaurant. I ate there yesterday and the food is great!

## C1 Listening for Meaning and Use

▶ Notes 1–5

CD1 T60

Listen to two people give advice. Who gives stronger advice: speaker A or speaker B? Check ( ✓ ) the correct column.

| | SPEAKER A | SPEAKER B |
|---|---|---|
| 1. | | ✓ |
| 2. | | |
| 3. | | |
| 4. | | |
| 5. | | |
| 6. | | |
| 7. | | |
| 8. | | |

## C2 Making Suggestions

▶ Note 2

Write two suggestions for each question or statement. Use *could* in one suggestion and *might* in the other.

1. **Friend:** My grades in French are really bad. What should I do?

   **You:** <u>You could study harder.</u>

   <u>You might get a tutor to help you.</u>

2. **Friend:** I need to e͏arn some extra money this summer. How can I find a job?
   (garoʳ)

   **You:** _____

   _____

3. **Sister:** Let's go somewhere special for Mom's birthday. Where could we go?

   **You:** _____

   _____

4. **Friend:** I'm so bored. There's nothing to do around here.

   **You:** We could go see a movie?

   You might rent a movie

## C3 Giving Your Opinion

▶ Notes 3A–3C

A. Work with a partner. Take turns asking and answering questions using these words and phrases. Use *should* in your questions. Use *should* or *ought to* in your answers. You can soften your opinions with *I think, maybe,* or *perhaps.*

1. college students/take courses in many different subject areas?

   *A: Should college students take courses in many different subject areas?*

   *B: No, they shouldn't. I think college students should take most of their courses in just one subject area.*

2. students/have a job while they're in school

3. students/take more online courses

4. teachers/give less work

5. students/spend a semester studying abroad

B. Work on your own. Make up two more opinion questions with *should.* Then ask your classmates for their opinions.

## C4 Giving Advice  ▶ Notes 3A, 3C, 5A

A. **Work with a partner. Give two pieces of advice to the person(s) in each situation. Use *you should* in one and *you ought to* in the other. You can soften your advice with *maybe*, *perhaps*, or *I think*.**

1. Sasha has an old car. The car is making a strange noise.

   *You ought to buy a new car. Maybe you should fix your car.*

2. Today is Monday. Emily has to work today, but she woke up with a sore throat.

   _____

3. Dan isn't doing very well in his math class.

   _____

4. Mr. and Mrs. Chen love their apartment, but it's a little expensive.

   _____

B. **The situations have become worse. Give two pieces of strong advice for each situation. Use *you have to*, *you've got to*, or *you must*.**

1. Now Sasha's car has broken down.

   *You must not fix this car. You've got to buy a new car.*

2. It's Monday night. Emily has a high fever. She feels very sick.

   _____

3. Now Dan is failing math. If he fails, he won't graduate.

   _____

4. The Chens' landlord has increased the rent and they can't afford it.

   _____

 C. **Work by yourself. Write down three situations of your own. Then ask your partner to give advice.**

## C5 Giving Warnings

Look at the pictures and write a warning for each one. Use *had better* or *had better not*.

1. _He had better stop the car._

4. _He had better jump_

2. _They had better not fish._

5. _He had better take the umbrella_

3. _He had better not run._

6. _She had better not play with the cat._

## Modals of Necessity and Prohibition

### Think Critically About Meaning and Use

**A.** Read the sentences and answer the questions below.

**1a.** Students must show ID to enter the building.
**1b.** You have to show ID to enter the building.

**2a.** Students must not bring food into the library.
**2b.** You shouldn't bring food into the library.

1. **EVALUATE** Which sentence in each pair is formal, and sounds like a rule or a law?

2. **EVALUATE** Which sentence in each pair sounds more conversational?

**B.** Discuss your answers with the class and read the Meaning and Use Notes to check them.

## Meaning and Use Notes

ONLINE
PRACTICE

| **Necessity** |
|---|
| ▶ **1A** *Should, ought to, have to, have got to,* and *must* express necessity. *Must* expresses the strongest necessity and is used in formal or more serious situations. We often use *should, ought to, have to,* and *have got to* in conversation to avoid sounding too formal.<br><br>Students **should study** their notes before the exam.<br><br>I **have to hurry**. I'm going to be late!<br><br>We**'ve got to send** out the invitations today. The award ceremony is next week.<br><br>You **must take** the final exam if you want to pass the course. |
| ▶ **1B** Use *must* to express rules, laws, and requirements, especially in written documents.<br><br>Bicyclists **must obey** all traffic lights in the city.<br><br>All couples **must apply** for a marriage license in person. |
| ▶ **1C** *Should, have to,* and *have got to* are often used instead of *must* to talk about rules and laws in less formal English.<br><br>The manual says that cyclists **should obey** all traffic lights in the city.<br><br>I found out that we **have to apply** for a marriage license in person. |

## Lack of Necessity vs. Prohibition

▶ **2**  *Don't/doesn't have to* and *must not* have very different meanings. *Don't/doesn't have to* means that something is not necessary—there is a choice of whether to do it or not. *Must not* means that something is prohibited (not allowed). There is no choice involved.

| ***Don't/Doesn't Have To* (Not Necessary)** | ***Must Not* (Prohibited)** |
|---|---|
| Your children **don't have to take** these vitamins. If they eat a healthy diet, they'll be fine. | Your children **must not take** these vitamins. They are for adults only. |

## D1 Listening for Meaning and Use

▶ Notes 1A, 1B, 2

CD1 T61   Listen to these conversations between an employee at the Department of Motor Vehicles and people who call with questions. What does the employee say about each of the topics in the chart? Check ( ✓ ) the correct column.

|  |  | NECESSARY | NOT NECESSARY | PROHIBITED |
|---|---|---|---|---|
| 1. | take an eye test | ✓ |  |  |
| 2. | take the eye test at the Department of Motor Vehicles |  |  |  |
| 3. | need a California license to drive in California |  |  |  |
| 4. | pay with a credit card |  |  |  |
| 5. | go to driving school |  |  |  |
| 6. | drive alone with a learner's permit |  |  |  |

## D2 Explaining Signs

A. Read these public signs. Then explain the signs by completing the statements with *must*, *don't have to*, or *must not*.

1. SWIMMING POOL FOR APARTMENT RESIDENTS ONLY

   This means that you _____ *have to* _____ be a resident of the apartment

   building to swim in the pool.

2. NO BICYCLES ALLOWED

   This means that you _____ ride your bike in the park.

3. CHILDREN UNDER 12 FREE

   This means that children under 12 years old _____ pay

   to go in.

4. NO APPOINTMENT NECESSARY

   This means that you _____ make an appointment.

5. NO EXIT

   This means that you _____ go out this door.

6. ID REQUIRED

   This means that you _____ show identification.

7. HOSPITAL ZONE—NO HORNS

   This means that you _____ blow your car horn in this area.

8. NO FOOD OR GLASS BOTTLES

   This means that you _____ take food into this place,

   but you _____ take a plastic bottle.

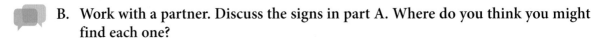

B. Work with a partner. Discuss the signs in part A. Where do you think you might find each one?

## D3 Writing About Rules and Laws ▶ Notes 1B, 1C, 2

A. Look at each sign and write a sentence to explain its meaning. Use *must* and *must not*.

1. <u>You must wear a seat</u>
   <u>belt.</u>

3. _____

5. _____

2. _____

4. _____

6. _____

 B. Work with a partner. What other signs have you seen? Write down the words. Draw the images and show them to your classmates. Explain each sign using *have to*, *have got to*, or *must not*.

*You have to turn right.*

## D4 Stating Necessity, Lack of Necessity, and Prohibition ▶ Notes 1A, 2

Work with a partner. Think about your English class. Write sentences about what is necessary, what is not necessary, and what is not allowed. Use *have got to*, *have to*, *don't have to*, *must*, and *must not*.

1. <u>We have to speak English in class.</u>

2. _____

3. _____

4. _____

5. _____

## Think Critically About Meaning and Use

**A.** Choose the best answer to complete each conversation.

1. **A:** Emergency Room. How can I help you?

   **B:** My daughter fell down the stairs and she's unconscious! Should I bring her in?

   **A:** _____ wait for an ambulance.

   **a.** You'd better

   **b.** You could

2. **A:** Do you like my new dress?

   **B:** _____.

   **a.** Not really. You shouldn't wear that color.

   **b.** Yes, you don't have to wear that color.

3. **A:** I'd like to pick up my car. Is it ready?

   **B:** Yes, but you _____ come right away. We're closing in a few minutes.

   **a.** might

   **b.** should

4. **A:** I don't have my glasses. What does that sign say?

   **B:** It says, "Visitors _____ check in at the front desk."

   **a.** must

   **b.** ought to

5. **A:** Can we put posters on the wall in our dorm room?

   **B:** Yes, but you _____ make holes in the walls. It's against the rules.

   **a.** don't have to

   **b.** shouldn't

6. **A:** My boss will fire me if I come late again.

   **B:** _____

   **a.** Then you'd better be on time from now on.

   **b.** Then maybe you must not be late.

7. **A:** What do you want for dinner?

   **B:** I don't care. _____

   **a.** You should make hot dogs.

   **b.** We could have spaghetti.

8. **A:** Look at all those people at the exit. We'll never get out.

   **B:** We _____ use that exit. There's another one in the back.

   **a.** don't have to

   **b.** must not

**B.** Discuss these questions in small groups.

1. **ANALYZE** Look at conversations 1, 3, 4, and 7. Which three use strong modals of advice? Which uses a weaker modal of advice?

2. **EVALUATE** Look at B's reponses in 5 and 8. Which gives a warning about something that might have bad consequences? Which expresses lack of necessity?

## Edit

**Find the errors in this paragraph and correct them.**

There are many wedding traditions in the United States. One of them is that the bride ought ^to^ wear "something old, something new, something borrowed, something blue, and a sixpence in her shoe." The old, new, borrowed, and blue parts are easy enough. However, a sixpence is an old English coin. It is impossible to find these days, so most people feel that the bride doesn't has to use a sixpence—any coin will do. Another tradition is that the groom must not to see the bride before the wedding. People think that it is bad luck. Many people think that brides ought ^to^ wear white. However, less traditional brides feel they must not do that. One final tradition is that when people get married, they've [they have] to save and freeze a piece of their wedding cake to eat on their first anniversary.

# Write

Imagine that you are the director of a small company. Follow the steps below to write a memo explaining the office rules to new employees. Use modals of advice, necessity, and prohibition.

1. **BRAINSTORM** Think about all the things a new employee needs to know. Make notes about what you want to say. Use these categories to help you.

   - office hours
   - lateness
   - appropriate clothing
   - lunch breaks

   - vacation policy
   - sick leave
   - personal phone calls
   - personal emails and Internet use

2. **WRITE A FIRST DRAFT** Before you write your draft, read the checklist below. Write your draft using modals and phrasal modals to express advice, necessity, and prohibition.

3. **EDIT** Read your work and check it against the checklist below. Circle grammar, spelling, and punctuation errors.

| DO I ... | YES |
|---|:---:|
| clearly explain the office rules to new employees in an appropriately organized memo? | ☐ |
| express rules, advice, and suggestions with modals and phrasal modals such as *must, had better, should, ought to, might,* and *could*? | ☐ |
| express prohibition with *must not* and lack of necessity with *don't have to*? | ☐ |
| use modals of the appropriate strength? | ☐ |
| use appropriate form for modals? | ☐ |

4. **PEER REVIEW** Work with a partner to help you decide how to fix your errors and improve the content.

5. **REWRITE YOUR DRAFT** Using the comments from your partner, write a final draft. Remember to include these features of a business memo.

> To: All New Employees          CC: Vilma Rodriguez
> From: Bob Chang               Date:
> Re: Office rules
>
> 1. Office hours are 9:00 to 5:00. If you are going to be late, you should always…

**Choose the correct word or words to complete each sentence.**

1. In the early 20th century, doctors _____ bacterial infections because antibiotics did not exist.

   **a.** cannot treat        **b.** could not treat        **c.** may treat        **d.** will be able to treat

2. There is no guarantee, but medical researchers _____ a cure for cancer someday.

   **a.** can be able to find        **b.** are able to find        **c.** will be able to find        **d.** may be able to find

3. I think Alex would _____ have Chinese food tonight.

   **a.** prefer to        **b.** prefers to        **c.** to prefer        **d.** prefer

4. Could you _____ me your car tomorrow?

   **a.** will lend        **b.** lending        **c.** lend        **d.** to lend

5. Joe _____ work the late shift.

   **a.** doesn't have        **b.** don't have to        **c.** doesn't have to        **d.** don't have

6. Takeshi _____ get to work on time every day or his boss will fire him.

   **a.** have to        **b.** had better        **c.** might        **d.** could

7. _____ Holly on Sunday?

   **a.** Should Carla visit        **b.** Ought Carla visit        **c.** Should Carla visiting        **d.** Ought to Carla visit

8. I'm not feeling well. I'd rather _____ go to the show.

   **a.** no        **b.** not        **c.** don't        **d.** not to

9. I think Naomi would _____ become the new manager.

   **a.** rather prefer        **b.** like to        **c.** prefer        **d.** likes to

10. _____ join us for dinner?

    **a.** Pedro would prefer    **b.** Pedro should        **c.** Could Pedro        **d.** Would Pedro like

11. Can Ana _____ our study group?

    **a.** to join        **b.** joins        **c.** join        **d.** joining

12. Library patrons _____ books from the reference section without permission.

    **a.** removing        **b.** may        **c.** may not remove        **d.** to remove

**Choose the correct response to complete each conversation.**

13. **A:** Is Keiko going on vacation next month?

    **B:** _____ but I'm not sure.

       **a.** She might be,    **c.** She will be going to,

       **b.** Maybe she can,    **d.** She is going to,

14. **A:** I'm sorry, but the attorney can't interview the witness today.

    **B:** _____

       **a.** When will she be able to interview him?    **c.** When was she able to interview him?

       **b.** When will she know how to interview him?    **d.** Why doesn't she know how to interview him?

15. **A:** _____ hear the music?

    **B:** Yes, it's beautiful.

       **a.** May you    **c.** Might you

       **b.** Can you    **d.** May be you

16. **A:** Could you help me with this?

    **B:** I _____ right now. I'll be there in a few minutes.

       **a.** can't    **c.** may not

       **b.** couldn't    **d.** might not

17. **A:** Would you rather drive or walk to school today?

    **B:** _____ It's beautiful out.

       **a.** Yes, I would.    **c.** No, I wouldn't rather.

       **b.** I'd rather walk.    **d.** Yes, thanks for asking me.

**Match the response to the statement below.**

_____ **18.** The vacuum is overheating.    **a.** I don't care. We could eat Greek food.

_____ **19.** You shouldn't eat a lot of salt.    **b.** I know. It's bad for your health.

_____ **20.** I'm taking the bus today.    **c.** Good. Then I don't have to order them online.

   **d.** You'd better study a lot.

   **e.** You should hurry. It's coming in a few minutes.

   **f.** You'd better not eat this dessert.

   **g.** Yes. According to the law, you have to be at least 16 years old.

   **h.** You'd better unplug it.

# Appendices

# 1 Spelling of Verbs and Nouns Ending in *-s* and *-es*

1.  For most third-person singular verbs and plural nouns, add *-s* to the base form.

    | Verbs | Nouns |
    |---|---|
    | swim — swims | lake — lakes |

2.  If the base form ends with the letter *s*, *z*, *sh*, *ch*, or *x*, add *-es*.

    | Verbs | Nouns |
    |---|---|
    | miss — misses | box — boxes |

3.  If the base form ends with a consonant + *y*, change *y* to *i* and add *-es*. (Compare vowel + *y*: obey — obeys; toy — toys.)

    | Verbs | Nouns |
    |---|---|
    | try — tries | baby — babies |

4.  If the base form ends with a consonant + *o*, add *-s* or *-es*. Some words take *-s*, some words take *-es*, some take both *-s* and *-es*. (Compare vowel + *o*: radio — radios; zoo — zoos.)

    | -s | Both -s and -es |
    |---|---|
    | auto — autos | tornado — tornados/tornadoes |
    | photo — photos | volcano — volcanos/volcanoes |
    | piano — pianos | zero — zeros/zeroes |
    | solo — solos | |

    **-es**

    do — does

    echo — echoes

    go — goes

    hero — heroes

    potato — potatoes

    tomato — tomatoes

5.  If the base form of certain nouns ends with a single *f* or *fe,* change the *f* or *fe* to *v* and add *-es*.

    calf — calves

    shelf — shelves

    knife — knives

    **Exceptions**

    belief — beliefs

    chief — chiefs

    roof — roofs

    scarf — scarfs/scarves

## 2 Pronunciation of Verbs and Nouns Ending in *-s* and *-es*

1. If the base form of the verb or noun ends with the sound /s/, /z/, /ʃ/, /ʒ/, /tʃ/, /dʒ/, or /ks/, then pronounce *-es* as an extra syllable /ɪz/.

**Verbs**

slice — slices      watch — watches

lose — loses        judge — judges

wash — washes       relax — relaxes

**Nouns**

price — prices      inch — inches

size — sizes        language — languages

dish — dishes       tax — taxes

garage — garages

2. If the base form ends with the voiceless sound /p/, /t/, /k/, /f/, or /θ/, then pronounce *-s* and *-es* as /s/.

**Verbs**

sleep — sleeps      work — works

hit — hits          laugh — laughs

**Nouns**

grape — grapes      cuff — cuffs

cat — cats          fifth — fifths

book — books

3. If the base form ends with any other consonant or with a vowel sound, then pronounce *-s* and *-es* as /z/.

**Verbs**

learn — learns

go — goes

**Nouns**

name — names

boy — boys

## 3 Spelling of Verbs Ending in *-ing*

1. For most verbs, add *-ing* to the base form of the verb.

sleep — sleeping      talk — talking

2. If the base form ends in a single *e*, drop the *e* and add *-ing* (exception: be — being).

live — living          write — writing

3. If the base form ends in *ie*, change *ie* to *y* and add *-ing*.

die — dying            lie — lying

4. If the base form of a one-syllable verb ends with a single vowel + consonant, double the final consonant and add *-ing*. (Compare two vowels + consonant: eat — eating.)

hit — hitting          stop — stopping

5. If the base form of a verb with two or more syllables ends in a single vowel + consonant, double the final consonant only if the stress is on the final syllable. Do not double the final consonant if the stress is not on the final syllable.

admı́t — admitting   begı́n — beginning   devélop — developing   lísten — listening

6. Do not double the final consonants *x*, *w*, and *y*.

fix — fixing           plow — plowing         obey — obeying

## 4   Spelling of Verbs Ending in -*ed*

1.  To form the simple past and past participle of most regular verbs, add -*ed* to the base form.

    brush — brushed          play — played

2.  If the base form ends with *e*, just add -*d*.

    close — closed           live — lived

3.  If the base form ends with a consonant + *y*, change the y to *i* and add -*ed*. (Compare vowel + *y*: play — played; enjoy — enjoyed.)

    study — studied          dry — dried

4.  If the base form of a one-syllable verb ends with a single vowel + consonant, double the final consonant and add -*ed*.

    plan — planned           shop — shopped

5.  If the base form of a verb with two or more syllables ends with a single vowel + consonant, double the final consonant and add -*ed* only when the stress is on the final syllable. Do not double the final consonant if the stress is not on the final syllable.

    prefér — preferred       énter — entered

6.  Do not double the final consonants *x*, *w*, and *y*.

    coax — coaxed            snow — snowed            stay — stayed

## 5   Pronunciation of Verbs Ending in -*ed*

1.  If the base form of the verb ends with the sounds /t/ or /d/, then pronounce -*ed* as an extra syllable /ɪd/.

    | /t/ | /d/ |
    | --- | --- |
    | start — started | need — needed |
    | wait — waited | decide — decided |

2.  If the base form ends with the voiceless sounds /f/, /k/, /p/, /s/, /ʃ/, /tʃ/, or /ks/, then pronounce -*ed* as /t/.

    | | | | |
    | --- | --- | --- | --- |
    | laugh — laughed | jump — jumped | wish — wished | fax — faxed |
    | look — looked | slice — sliced | watch — watched | |

3.  If the base form ends with the voiced sounds /b/, /g/, /dʒ/, /m/, /n/, /ŋ/, /l/, /r/, /ð/, /v/, /z/, or with a vowel, then pronounce -*ed* as /d/.

    | | | | |
    | --- | --- | --- | --- |
    | rob — robbed | hum — hummed | call — called | wave — waved |
    | brag — bragged | rain — rained | order — ordered | close — closed |
    | judge — judged | bang — banged | bathe — bathed | play — played |

# 6 Irregular Verbs

| Base Form | Simple Past | Past Participle | | Base Form | Simple Past | Past Participle |
|---|---|---|---|---|---|---|
| arise | arose | arisen | Crecer | grow | grew | grown |
| be | was/were | been | | hang | hung | hung |
| beat | beat | beaten | Tener | have | had | had |
| become | became | become | Escuchar | hear | heard | heard |
| begin | began | begun | Esconder | hide | hid | hidden |
| bend | bent | bent | | hit | hit | hit |
| bet | bet | bet | | hold | held | held |
| bind | bound | bound | | hurt | hurt | hurt |
| bite | bit | bitten | Mantener | keep | kept | kept |
| bleed | bled | bled | Saber | know | knew | known |
| blow | blew | blown | | lay (= put) | laid | laid |
| break | broke | broken | | lead | led | led |
| bring | brought | brought | Marchar | leave | left | left |
| build | built | built | | lend | lent | lent |
| buy | bought | bought | | let | let | let |
| catch | caught | caught | Mentir | lie (= recline) | lay | lain |
| choose | chose | chosen | | light | lit | lit |
| come | came | come | Perder | lose | lost | lost |
| cost | cost | cost | Hacer | make | made | made |
| creep | crept | crept | | mean | meant | meant |
| cut | cut | cut | | meet | met | met |
| deal | dealt | dealt | Pagar | pay | paid | paid |
| dig | dug | dug | Provar | prove | proved | proven/proved |
| dive | dove/dived | dived | Poner | put | put | put |
| do | did | done | Renunciar | quit | quit | quit |
| draw | drew | drawn | Leer | read | read | read |
| drink | drank | drunk | | ride | rode | ridden |
| drive | drove | driven | | ring | rang | rung |
| eat | ate | eaten | | rise | rose | risen |
| fall | fell | fallen | Correr | run | ran | run |
| feed | fed | fed | Decir | say | said | said |
| feel | felt | felt | Ver | see | saw | seen |
| fight | fought | fought | Vender | sell | sold | sold |
| find | found | found | Enviar | send | sent | sent |
| fit | fit | fit | | set | set | set |
| flee | fled | fled | | sew | sewed | sewn |
| fly | flew | flown | | shake | shook | shaken |
| forget | forgot | forgotten | | shine | shone | shone |
| forgive | forgave | forgiven | | shoot | shot | shot |
| freeze | froze | frozen | | show | showed | shown |
| get | got | gotten | | shrink | shrank | shrunk |
| give | gave | given | | shut | shut | shut |
| go | went | gone | | sing | sang | sung |

| Base Form | Simple Past | Past Participle | | Base Form | Simple Past | Past Participle |
|---|---|---|---|---|---|---|
| sink | sank | sunk | | sweep | swept | swept |
| sit | sit | sit | | swim | swam | swum |
| sleep | slept | slept | | swing | swung | swung |
| slide | slid | slid | | take | took | taken |
| speak | spoke | spoken | | teach | taught | taught |
| speed | sped | sped | | tear | tore | torn |
| spend | spent | spent | | tell | told | told |
| spin | spun | spun | | think | thought | thought |
| split | split | split | | throw | threw | thrown |
| spread | spread | spread | | understand | understood | understood |
| spring | sprang | sprung | | undertake | undertook | undertaken |
| stand | stood | stood | | upset | upset | upset |
| steal | stole | stolen | | wake | woke | woken |
| stick | stuck | stuck | | wear | wore | worn |
| stink | stank | stunk | | weep | wept | wept |
| strike | struck | struck | | wet | wet | wet |
| string | strung | strung | | win | won | won |
| swear | swore | sworn | | write | wrote | written |

*(Handwritten Spanish annotations in the margins: Sentar (sit), Dormir (sleep), Hablar (speak), Robar (steal), Jurar (swear), Tomar (take), Enseñar (teach), Decir / Pensar / Tirar (tell / think / throw), Entender (understand), Enojar / Despertar / Poner (wake), Mojar (wet), ganar (win), escribir (write))*

# 7  Common Stative Verbs

| Emotions and Attitudes | Senses and Sensations | Knowledge and Beliefs | Descriptions and Measurements |
|---|---|---|---|
| admire | ache | agree | appear |
| appreciate | burn | believe | be |
| care | feel | consider | cost |
| desire | hear | disagree | equal |
| despise | hurt | expect | look (like) |
| dislike | itch | feel (= think) | measure |
| doubt | notice | find | resemble |
| envy | see | forget | seem |
| fear | smell | guess | sound (like) |
| hate | sound | hope | taste |
| like | sting | imagine | weigh |
| love | taste | know | |
| mind | | mean | **Possession and Relationships** |
| need | | notice | belong |
| prefer | | realize | consist of |
| regret | | recognize | contain |
| respect | | remember | depend on |
| want | | suppose | have |
| | | think | include |
| | | understand | own |
| | | | possess |

# 8 Common Irregular Plural Nouns

| Singular | Plural |
|----------|--------|
| child | children |
| fish | fish |
| foot | feet |
| man | men |
| mouse | mice |
| person | people |
| tooth | teeth |
| woman | women |

# 9 Common Adjectives Ending in -ed and -ing

| -ed | -ing | -ed | -ing |
|-----|------|-----|------|
| amazed | amazing | relaxed | relaxing |
| amused | amusing | satisfied | satisfying |
| annoyed | annoying | shocked | shocking |
| bored | boring | surprised | surprising |
| confused | confusing | terrified | terrifying |
| depressed | depressing | tired | tiring |
| disappointed | disappointing | | |
| embarrassed | embarrassing | | |
| excited | exciting | | |
| fascinated | fascinating | | |
| frightened | frightening | | |
| interested | interesting | | |

# 10 Spelling Rules for Adverbs Ending in -ly

1. Many adverbs of manner are formed by adding -ly to an adjective.

   careful — carefully      quick — quickly

2. If the adjective ends with a consonant + y, change the y to i and add -ly.

   easy — easily      happy — happily

3. If the adjective ends in le, drop the e and add -y.

   gentle — gently      suitable — suitably

4. If the adjective ends in ic, add -ally.

   fantastic — fantastically      terrific — terrifically

## 11 Adjectives with Two Comparative and Superlative Forms

| Adjective | Comparative | Superlative |
|---|---|---|
| common | commoner<br>more common | the commonest<br>the most common |
| friendly | friendlier<br>more friendly | the friendliest<br>the most friendly |
| handsome | handsomer<br>more handsome | the handsomest<br>the most handsome |
| happy | happier<br>more happy | the happiest<br>the most happy |
| lively | livelier<br>more lively | the liveliest<br>the most lively |
| lovely | lovelier<br>more lovely | the loveliest<br>the most lovely |
| narrow | narrower<br>more narrow | the narrowest<br>the most narrow |
| polite | politer<br>more polite | the politest<br>the most polite |
| quiet | quieter<br>more quiet | the quietest<br>the most quiet |

## 12 Irregular Comparative and Superlative Forms

| Adjective | Adverb | Comparative | Superlative |
|---|---|---|---|
| bad | badly | worse | the worst |
| far | far | farther/further | the farthest/furthest |
| good | well | better | the best |
| (a) little | (a) little | less | the least |
| much/many | much/many | more | the most |

# 13 Gerunds

## Verb + Gerund

These verbs may be followed by gerunds, but not by infinitives:

| | | | |
|---|---|---|---|
| acknowledge | detest | keep (= continue) | recall |
| admit | discuss | loathe | recollect |
| anticipate | dislike | mean (= involve) | recommend |
| appreciate | endure | mention | regret |
| avoid | enjoy | mind (= object to) | report |
| can't help | escape | miss | resent |
| celebrate | excuse | omit | resist |
| consider | feel like | postpone | resume |
| defend | finish | practice | risk |
| defer | go | prevent | suggest |
| delay | imagine | prohibit | tolerate |
| deny | involve | quit | understand |

## Verb with Preposition + Gerund

These verbs or verb phrases with prepositions may be followed by gerunds, but not by infinitives:

| | | |
|---|---|---|
| adapt to | believe in | depend on |
| adjust to | blame for | disapprove of |
| agree (with someone) on | care about | discourage (someone) from |
| apologize (to someone) for | complain (to someone) about | engage in |
| approve of | concentrate on | forgive (someone) for |
| argue (with someone) about | consist of | help (someone) with |
| ask about | decide on | |

## *Be* + Adjective + Preposition + Gerund

Adjectives with prepositions typically occur in *be* + adjective phrases. These phrases may be followed by gerunds, but not by infinitives:

| | | |
|---|---|---|
| be accustomed to | be familiar with | be nervous about |
| be afraid of | be famous for | be perfect for |
| be angry (at someone) about | be fond of | be proud of |
| be ashamed of | be glad about | be responsible for |
| be capable of | be good at | be sad about |
| be certain of/about | be happy about | be successful in |
| be concerned with | be incapable of | be suitable for |
| be critical of | be interested in | be tired of |
| be discouraged from | be jealous of | be tolerant of |
| be enthusiastic about | be known for | be upset about |

## 14 Infinitives

These verbs may be followed by infinitives, but not gerunds:

### Verb + Infinitive

| | | | |
|---|---|---|---|
| agree | decide | offer | struggle |
| aim | decline | plan | swear |
| appear | demand | pledge | tend |
| arrange | fail | pretend | volunteer |
| care | hope | refuse | wait |
| claim | intend | resolve | |
| consent | manage | seem | |

### Verb + Object + Infinitive

| | | | |
|---|---|---|---|
| advise | get | persuade | tell |
| command | hire | remind | trust |
| convince | invite | require | urge |
| force | order | teach | warn |

### Verb + (Object) + Infinitive

| | | | |
|---|---|---|---|
| ask | desire | need | want |
| beg | expect | pay | wish |
| choose | help | prepare | would like |
| dare | know | promise | |

## 15 Verb + Infinitive or Gerund

These verbs may be followed by infinitives or gerunds:

| | | | |
|---|---|---|---|
| attempt | continue | neglect | start |
| begin | forget | prefer | stop |
| can't bear | hate | propose | try |
| can't stand | like | regret | |
| cease | love | remember | |

# 16 Contractions with Verb and Modal Forms

## Contractions with *Be*

| | | |
|---|---|---|
| I am | = | I'm |
| you are | = | you're |
| he is | = | he's |
| she is | = | she's |
| it is | = | it's |
| we are | = | we're |
| you are | = | you're |
| they are | = | they're |
| | | |
| I am not | = | I'm not |
| you are not | = | you're not / you aren't |
| he is not | = | he's not / he isn't |
| she is not | = | she's not / she isn't |
| it is not | = | it's not / it isn't |
| we are not | = | we're not / we aren't |
| you are not | = | you're not / you aren't |
| they are not | = | they're not / they aren't |

## Contractions with *Be Going To*

| | | |
|---|---|---|
| I am going to | = | I'm going to |
| you are going to | = | you're going to |
| he is going to | = | he's going to |
| she is going to | = | she's going to |
| it is going to | = | it's going to |
| we are going to | = | we're going to |
| you are going to | = | you're going to |
| they are going to | = | they're going to |
| | | |
| you are not going to | = | you're not going to / you aren't going to |

## Contractions with *Will*

| | | |
|---|---|---|
| I will | = | I'll |
| you will | = | you'll |
| he will | = | he'll |
| she will | = | she'll |
| it will | = | it'll |
| we will | = | we'll |
| you will | = | you'll |
| they will | = | they'll |
| | | |
| will not | = | won't |

## Contractions with *Would*

| | | |
|---|---|---|
| I would | = | I'd |
| you would | = | you'd |
| he would | = | he'd |
| she would | = | she'd |
| we would | = | we'd |
| you would | = | you'd |
| they would | = | they'd |
| | | |
| would not | = | wouldn't |

## Contractions with *Was* and *Were*

| | | |
|---|---|---|
| was not | = | wasn't |
| were not | = | weren't |

## Contractions with *Have*

| | | |
|---|---|---|
| I have | = | I've |
| you have | = | you've |
| he has | = | he's |
| she has | = | she's |
| it has | = | it's |
| we have | = | we've |
| you have | = | you've |
| they have | = | they've |
| | | |
| have not | = | haven't |
| has not | = | hasn't |

## Contractions with *Had*

| | | |
|---|---|---|
| I had | = | I'd |
| you had | = | you'd |
| he had | = | he'd |
| she had | = | she'd |
| we had | = | we'd |
| you had | = | you'd |
| they had | = | they'd |
| | | |
| had not | = | hadn't |

## Contractions with *Do* and *Did*

| | | |
|---|---|---|
| do not | = | don't |
| does not | = | doesn't |
| did not | = | didn't |

## Contractions with Modals and Phrasal Modals

| | | |
|---|---|---|
| cannot | = | can't |
| could not | = | couldn't |
| should not | = | shouldn't |
| | | |
| have got to | = | 've got to |
| has got to | = | 's got to |

## Separable Transitive Phrasal Verbs

Many two-word transitive phrasal verbs are separable. This means that a noun object can separate the two words of the phrasal verb or follow the phrasal verb. If the object is a pronoun (*me*, *you*, *him*, *her*, *us*, *it*, or *them*), the pronoun must separate the two words of the phrasal verb. Pronoun objects cannot follow the phrasal verb.

| Noun Object | Pronoun Object |
|---|---|
| She **turned** the offer **down**. | She **turned** it **down**. |
| She **turned down** the offer. | x She **turned down** it. (INCORRECT) |

These are some common separable transitive phrasal verbs and their meanings:

| Phrasal Verb | Meaning |
|---|---|
| bring (someone) up | raise someone (a child) |
| bring (something) up | introduce a topic |
| brush (something) off | remove something by brushing |
| call (something) off | cancel something |
| call (someone) up | telephone someone |
| clean (something) up | clean something completely |
| do (something) over | do something again |
| dry (something) off | dry something with a towel |
| fill (something) out | complete a form with information |
| get (someone) up | awaken someone |
| give (something) back | return something |
| hand (something) in | give something to a person in authority |
| hold (something) up | delay something |
| leave (something) out | omit something |
| let (something) out | alter clothes to make them larger |
| look (something) over | examine something carefully or review it |
| look (something) up | look for information in a book or on the Internet |
| make (something) up | invent something |
| mark (something) down/up | decrease/increase the price of something |
| pick (something) out | choose something |
| pick (something/someone) up | lift something or someone; stop to get something or someone |
| put (something) away | put something in its usual place |
| put (something) off | postpone something |
| put (something) together | assemble something |
| take (something) away | remove something |
| take (something) back | return something |
| take (something) off | remove an article of clothing |
| talk (something) over | discuss something |
| tear (something) up | destroy something by ripping |
| think (something) through | consider something thoroughly |

| Phrasal Verb | Meaning |
|---|---|
| throw (something) away | get rid of something |
| try (something) on | put on clothing to see how it looks |
| turn (something) down | refuse a request; lower the heat or volume |
| turn (something) in | give something to a person in authority |
| turn (something) off | stop a machine or a light |
| turn (something) on | start a machine or a light |
| turn (something) over | turn something so that its top is facing down |
| use (something) up | use something until no more is left |

## Nonseparable Transitive Phrasal Verbs

Some two-word and most three-word transitive phrasal verbs cannot be separated. This means that a noun object or pronoun object cannot separate the parts of the phrasal verb.

| Noun Object | Pronoun Object |
|---|---|
| The teacher **called on** Sally. | The teacher **called on** her. |
| x The teacher **called** Sally **on**. | x The teacher **called** her **on**. |
| (INCORRECT) | (INCORRECT) |

These are some common nonseparable transitive phrasal verbs and their meanings:

| Phrasal Verb | Meaning |
|---|---|
| break into (something) | enter something illegally, such as a car or house |
| call on (someone) | ask someone to speak, especially in a class or meeting |
| come across (something) | find something unexpectedly |
| come by for (someone) | pick someone up, especially in a car |
| count on (someone) | depend on someone |
| cut down on (something) | use less of something |
| do without (something) | manage without having something |
| drop out of (something) | quit something, especially school |
| end up with (something) | have or get something in the end |
| find out (something) | discover something |
| get around (something) | avoid something |
| get on with (something) | continue something |
| go along with (someone/something) | agree with someone/something |
| get over (something) | recover from something, such as an illness |
| go over (something) | review something, such as a report |
| look after (someone) | take care of someone |
| look into (something) | research a subject |
| look up to (someone) | admire someone |
| put up with (something/someone) | tolerate something or someone |
| run into (someone) | meet someone unexpectedly |
| take after (someone) | resemble someone; act like someone |

## Intransitive Phrasal Verbs

Intransitive phrasal verbs do not take objects.

My car **broke down** yesterday.          What time do you usually **get up**?

These are some common intransitive phrasal verbs and their meanings:

| Phrasal Verb | Meaning |
| --- | --- |
| blow up | explode |
| break down | stop working properly |
| burn down | burn completely |
| catch up | find out the latest news |
| come back | return |
| come over | visit |
| drop by | visit, especially unexpectedly |
| eat out | eat in a restaurant |
| fall down | suddenly stop standing |
| get up | get out of bed |
| give up | stop trying, lose hope |
| go down | (of computers) stop functioning; (of prices or temperature) become lower; (of ships) sink; (of the sun or moon) set |
| go off | (of lights or machines) stop functioning; (of alarms) start functioning; explode or make a loud noise |
| grow up | become an adult |
| hold on | wait on the telephone |
| look out | be careful |
| make out | manage or progress |
| move out | stop living somewhere, especially by removing all of your possessions |
| pass out | lose consciousness |
| show up | appear |
| start out | begin |
| take off | leave (usually by plane) |
| talk back | answer in a rude way |
| turn up | appear or arrive |
| wake up | stop sleeping |
| work out | exercise |

# 18 Phonetic Symbols

## Vowels

| | | | | | |
|---|---|---|---|---|---|
| i | see /si/ | u | too /tu/ | oʊ | go /goʊ/ |
| ɪ | sit /sɪt/ | ʌ | cup /kʌp/ | ər | bird /bərd/ |
| ɛ | ten /tɛn/ | ə | about /əˈbaʊt/ | ɪr | near /nɪr/ |
| æ | cat /kæt/ | eɪ | say /seɪ/ | ɛr | hair /hɛr/ |
| ɑ | hot /hɑt/ | aɪ | five /faɪv/ | ɑr | car /kɑr/ |
| ɔ | saw /sɔ/ | ɔɪ | boy /bɔɪ/ | ɔr | north /nɔrθ/ |
| ʊ | put /pʊt/ | aʊ | now /naʊ/ | ʊr | tour /tʊr/ |

## Consonants

| | | | | | |
|---|---|---|---|---|---|
| p | pen /pɛn/ | f | fall /fɔl/ | m | man /mæn/ |
| b | bad /bæd/ | v | voice /vɔɪs/ | n | no /noʊ/ |
| t | tea /ti/ | θ | thin /θɪn/ | ŋ | sing /sɪŋ/ |
| t̬ | butter /ˈbʌt̬ər/ | ð | then /ðɛn/ | l | leg /lɛg/ |
| d | did /dɪd/ | s | so /soʊ/ | r | red /rɛd/ |
| k | cat /kæt/ | z | zoo /zu/ | j | yes /jɛs/ |
| g | got /gɑt/ | ʃ | she /ʃi/ | w | wet /wɛt/ |
| tʃ | chin /tʃɪn/ | ʒ | vision /ˈvɪʒn/ | | |
| dʒ | June /dʒun/ | h | how /haʊ/ | | |

# Glossary of Grammar Terms

**ability modal** *See* **modal of ability**.

**action verb** A verb that describes a thing that someone or something does. An action verb does not describe a state or condition.

> Sam **rang** the bell.
> I **eat** soup for lunch.
> It **rains** a lot here.

**active sentence** In active sentences, the agent (the noun that is performing the action) is in subject position and the receiver (the noun that receives or is a result of the action) is in object position. In the following sentence, the subject **Alex** performed the action, and the object **letter** received the action.

> Alex mailed the letter.

**adjective** A word that describes or modifies the meaning of a noun.

> the **orange** car
> a **strange** noise

**adverb** A word that describes or modifies the meaning of a verb, another adverb, an adjective, or a sentence. Many adverbs answer such questions as *How? When? Where?* or *How often?* They often end in **-ly**.

> She ran **quickly**.
> a **really** hot day
> She ran **very** quickly.
> **Maybe** she'll leave.

**adverb of degree** An adverb that makes adjectives or other adverbs stronger or weaker.

> She is **extremely** busy this week.
> He performed **very** well during the exam.
> He was **somewhat** surprised by her response.

**adverb of frequency** An adverb that tells how often a situation occurs. Adverbs of frequency range in meaning from *all of the time* to *none of the time*.

> She **always** eats breakfast.
> He **never** eats meat.

**adverb of manner** An adverb that answers the question *How?* and describes the way someone does something or the way something happens. Adverbs of manner usually end in **-ly**.

> He walked **slowly**.
> It rained **heavily** all night.

**adverb of opinion** An adverb that expresses an opinion about an entire sentence or idea.

> **Luckily**, we missed the traffic.
> **We** couldn't find a seat on the train, **unfortunately**.

**adverb of possibility** An adverb that shows different degrees of how possible we think something is. Adverbs of possibility range in meaning from expressing a high degree of possibility to expressing a low degree of possibility.

> He'll **certainly** pass the test.
> **Maybe** he'll pass the test.
> He **definitely** won't pass the test.

**adverb of time** An adverb that answers the question *When?* and refers to either a specific time or a more indefinite time.

> Let's leave **tonight** instead of **tomorrow**.
> They **recently** opened a new store.

**adverbial phrase** A phrase that functions as an adverb.

> Amy spoke **very softly**.

**affirmative statement** A sentence that does not have a negative verb.

> Linda went to the movies.

**agreement** The subject and verb of a clause must agree in number. If the subject is singular, the verb form is also singular. If the subject is plural, the verb form is also plural.

> **He comes** home early.
> **They come** home early.

**article** The words **a**, **an**, and **the** in English. Articles are used to introduce and identify nouns.

   **a** potato    **an** onion    **the** supermarket

**auxiliary verb** A verb that is used before main verbs (or other auxiliary verbs) in a sentence. Auxiliary verbs are usually used in questions and negative sentences. **Do**, **have**, and **be** can act as auxiliary verbs. Modals (**may**, **can**, **will**, and so on) are also auxiliary verbs.

   **Do** you have the time?
   I **have** never been to Italy.
   The car **was** speeding.
   I **may** be late.

**base form** The form of a verb without any verb endings; the infinitive form without *to*. Also called *simple form*.

   sleep    be    stop

**clause** A group of words that has a subject and a verb. *See also* **dependent clause** and **main clause**.

   If I leave, . . .
   The rain stopped.
   . . . when he speaks.
   . . . that I saw.

**common noun** A noun that refers to any of a class of people, animals, places, things, or ideas. Common nouns are not capitalized.

   man   cat   city   pencil   grammar

**comparative** A form of an adjective, adverb, or noun that is used to express differences between two items or situations.

   This book is **heavier than** that one.
   He runs **more quickly than** his brother.
   A CD costs **more money than** a cassette.

**complex sentence** A sentence that has a main clause and one or more dependent clauses.

   When the bell rang, we were finishing dinner.

**conditional sentence** A sentence that expresses a real or unreal situation in the *if* clause, and the (real or unreal) expected result in the main clause.

   If I have time, I will travel to Africa.
   If I had time, I would travel to Africa.

**consonant** A speech sound that is made by partly or completely stopping the air as it comes out of the mouth. For example, with the sounds /p/, /d/, and /g/, the air is completely stopped. With the sounds /s/, /f/, and /l/, the air is partly stopped.

**contraction** The combination of two words into one by omitting certain letters and replacing them with an apostrophe.

   I will = **I'll**   we are = **we're**
   are not = **aren't**

**count noun** A common noun that you can count as an individual thing. It usually has both a singular and a plural form.

   orange — oranges   woman — women

**definite article** The word the in English. It is used to identify nouns based on information the speaker and listener share about the noun. The definite article is also used for making general statements about a whole class or group of nouns.

   Please give me **the** key.
   **The** scorpion is dangerous.

**dependent clause** A clause that cannot stand alone as a sentence because it depends on the main clause to complete the meaning of the sentence. Also called *subordinate clause*.

   I'm going home **after he calls**.

**determiner** A word such as **a**, **an**, **the**, **this**, **that**, **these**, **those**, **my**, **some**, **a few**, and **three** that is used before a noun to limit its meaning in some way.

   **those** videos

**direct object** A noun or pronoun that refers to a person or thing that is directly affected by the action of a verb.

   John wrote **a letter.**
   Please buy **some milk.**

**first person** One of the three classes of personal pronouns. First person refers to the person *(I)* or people *(we)* who are actually speaking or writing.

**future** A time that is to come. The future is expressed in English with **will**, **be going to**, the simple present, or the present continuous. These different forms of the future often have different meanings and uses.

> I **will** help you later.
> David **is going to** call later.
> The train **leaves** at 6:05 this evening.
> I**'m driving** to Toronto tomorrow.

**general quantity expression** A quantity expression that indicates whether a quantity or an amount is large or small. It does not give an exact amount.

> **a lot of** cookies    **a little** flour
> **a few** people    **some** milk

**general statement** A generalization about a whole class or group of nouns.

> Whales are mammals.
> A daffodil is a flower that grows from a bulb.

**generic noun** A noun that refers to a whole class or group of nouns.

> I like **rice**.
> **A bird** can fly.
> **The laser** is an important tool.

**gerund** An -ing form of a verb that is used in place of a noun or pronoun to name an activity or a state.

> **Skiing** is fun.    He doesn't like **being sick**.

**if clause** A dependent clause that begins with **if** and expresses a real or unreal situation.

> **If I have the time,** I'll paint the kitchen.
> **If I had the time,** I'd paint the kitchen.

**imperative** A type of sentence, usually without a subject, that tells someone to do something. The verb is in the base form.

> **Open** your books to page 36.
> **Be** ready at eight.

**impersonal *you*** The use of the pronoun **you** to refer to people in general rather than a particular person or group of people.

> Nowadays **you** can buy anything on the Internet.

**indefinite article** The words **a** and **an** in English. Indefinite articles introduce a noun as a member of a class of nouns or make generalizations about a whole class or group of nouns.

> Please hand me **a** pencil.
> **An** ocean is **a** large body of water.

**independent clause** *See* **main clause.**

**indirect object** A noun or pronoun used after some verbs that refers to the person who receives the direct object of a sentence.

> John wrote a letter **to Mary**.
> Please buy some milk **for us**.

**infinitive** A verb form that includes **to** + the base form of a verb. An infinitive is used in place of a noun or pronoun to name an activity or state expressed by a verb.

> Do you like **to swim**?

**information question** A question that begins with a **wh-** word.

> Where does she live?
> Who lives here?

**intonation** The change in pitch, loudness, syllable length, and rhythm in spoken language.

**intransitive verb** A verb that cannot be followed by an object.

> We finally **arrived**.

**irregular verb** A verb that does not form the simple past by adding -*d* or -*ed* endings.

> put — put — put
> buy — bought — bought

**main clause** A clause that can be used by itself as a sentence. Also called *independent clause*.

> I'm going home.

**main verb** A verb that can be used alone in a sentence. A main verb can also occur with an auxiliary verb.

> I **ate** lunch at 11:30.
> Kate can't **eat** lunch today.

**mental activity verb** A verb such as **decide**, **know**, and **understand** that expresses an opinion, thought, or feeling.

> I don't **know** why she left.

**modal** The auxiliary verbs **can**, **could**, **may**, **might**, **must**, **should**, **will**, and **would**. They modify the meaning of a main verb by expressing ability, authority, formality, politeness, or various degrees of certainty. Also called *modal auxiliary*.

> You **should** take something for your headache.
> Applicants **must** have a high school diploma.

**modal of ability** **Can** and **could** are called modals of ability when they express the ability to do something.

> He **can** speak Arabic and English.
> **Can** you play the piano?
> Yesterday we **couldn't** leave during the storm.
> Seat belts **can** save lives.

**modal of necessity** **Should** and **must** are called modals of necessity along with the phrasal modals **ought to**, **have to**, and **have got to**. They express various degrees of necessity in opinions, obligations, rules, laws, and other requirements.

> Students **must** take two upper-level courses in order to graduate.
> Employees **should** wear identification tags at all times.
> We**'ve got to** arrive before the ceremony starts.

**modal of possibility** **Could**, **might**, **may**, **should**, **must**, and **will** are called modals of possibility when they express various degrees of certainty ranging from slight possibility to strong certainty.

> It **could / might / may / will** rain later.

**modal of prohibition** **Must not** is called a modal of prohibition when it means that something is not allowed (prohibited).

> Drivers **must not** change lanes without signaling.

**modal of request** **Can**, **could**, **will**, and **would** are called modals of request when they are used for asking someone to do something. They express various degrees of politeness and formality.

> **Can** you **pass** the sugar, please?
> **Would** you **tell** me the time?

**modify** To add to or change the meaning of a word. Adjectives modify nouns (expensive cars). Adverbs modify verbs (very fast).

**negative statement** A sentence with a negative verb.

> I **didn't see** that movie.
> He **isn't** happy.

**noncount noun** A common noun that cannot be counted. A noncount noun has no plural form and cannot occur with **a**, **an**, or a number.

> information     mathematics     weather

**nonseparable** Refers to two- or three-word verbs that don't allow a noun or pronoun object to separate the two or three words in the verb phrase. Certain two-word verbs and almost all three-word verbs are nonseparable.

> Amy **got off** the bus.
> We **cut down on** fat in our diet.

**noun** A word that typically refers to a person, animal, place, thing, or idea.

> Tom     rabbit     store     computer
> mathematics

**noun clause** A dependent clause that can occur in the same place as a noun, pronoun, or noun phrase in a sentence. Noun clauses begin with **wh**-words, **if, whether**, or **that**.

> I don't know **where he is**.
> I wonder **if he's coming**.
> I don't know **whether it's true**.
> I think **that it's a lie**.

**noun phrase** A phrase formed by a noun and its modifiers. A noun phrase can substitute for a noun in a sentence.

> She drank **milk**.
> She drank **chocolate milk**.
> She drank **the milk**.

**object** A noun, pronoun, or noun phrase that follows a transitive verb or a preposition.

> He likes **pizza**.
> She likes **him**.
> Go with **her**.
> Steve threw **the ball**.

**particle** Words such as **up**, **out**, and **down** that are linked to certain verbs to form phrasal verbs. Particles look like prepositions but don't express the same meanings.

> He got **up** late.
> Tom works **out** three times a week.
> They turned **down** the offer.

**passive sentence** Passive sentences emphasize the receiver of an action by changing the usual order of the subject and object in a sentence. In the sentence below, the subject (**The letter**) does not perform the action; it receives the action or is the result of an action. The passive is formed with a form of **be** + the past participle of a transitive verb.

> The letter was mailed yesterday.

**past continuous** A verb form that expresses an activity in progress at a specific time in the past. The past continuous is formed with **was** or **were** + verb + **-ing**. Also called *past progressive*.

> A: What **were** you **doing** last night at eight o'clock?
> B: I **was studying**.

**past participle** A past verb form that may differ from the simple past form of some irregular verbs. It is used to form the present perfect, for example.

> I have never **seen** that movie.

**past progressive** *See* **past continuous**.

**phrasal modal** A verb that is not a true modal, but has the same meaning as a modal verb. Examples of phrasal modals are **ought to**, **have to**, and **have got to**.

**phrasal verb** A two- or three-word verb such as **turn down** or **run out of**. The meaning of a phrasal verb is usually different from the meanings of its individual words.

> She **turned down** the job offer.
> Don't **run out of** gas on the freeway.

**phrase** A group of words that can form a grammatical unit. A phrase can take the form of a noun phrase, verb phrase, adjective phrase, adverbial phrase, or prepositional phrase. This means it can act as a noun, verb, adjective, adverb, or preposition.

> The **tall man** left.
> Lee **hit the ball**.
> The child was **very quiet**.
> She spoke **too fast**.
> They ran **down the stairs**.

**plural** The form of a word that refers to more than one person or thing. For example, **cats** and **children** are the plural forms of **cat** and **child**.

**possibility modal** *See* **modal of possibility**.

**preposition** A word such as **at**, **in**, **on**, or **to**, that links nouns, pronouns, and gerunds to other words.

**prepositional phrase** A phrase that consists of a preposition followed by a noun or noun phrase.

> on Sunday
> under the table

**present continuous** A verb form that indicates that an activity is in progress, temporary, or changing. It is formed with **be** + verb + **-ing**.
Also called *present progressive*.

> I'm **watering** the garden.
> Ruth **is working** for her uncle.
> He's **getting** better.

**present perfect** A verb form that expresses a connection between the past and the present. It indicates indefinite past time, recent past time, or continuing past time. The present perfect is formed with **have** + the past participle of the main verb.

> I've **seen** that movie.
> The manager **has** just **resigned**.
> We've **been** here for three hours.

**present progressive** *See* **present continuous**.

**pronoun** A word that can replace a noun or noun phrase. **I**, **you**, **he**, **she**, **it**, **mine**, and **yours** are some examples of pronouns.

**proper noun** A noun that is the name of a particular person, animal, place, thing, or idea. Proper nouns begin with capital letters and are usually not preceded by **the**.

> Peter  Rover  India  Apollo 13  Buddhism

**purpose infinitive** An infinitive that expresses the reason or purpose for doing something.

> **In order to operate this machine,** press the green button.

**quantity expression** A word or words that occur before a noun to express a quantity or amount of that noun.

> **a lot of** rain
> **few** books
> **four** trucks

**real conditional sentence** A sentence that expresses a real or possible situation in the **if** clause and the expected result in the main clause. It has an **if** clause in the simple present, and the **will** future in the main clause.

> If I get a raise, I won't look for a new job.

**regular verb** A verb that forms the simple past by adding -**ed**, -**d**, or changing **y** to **i** and then adding -**ed** to the simple form.

> hunt — hunted
> love — loved
> cry — cried

**rejoinder** A short response used in conversation.

> A: I like sushi.
> B: **So do I.**
> C: **Me too.**

**response** An answer to a question, or a reply to other types of spoken or written language.

> A: Are you hungry?
> B: **Yes, in fact I am. Let's eat.**
> A: I'm tired of this long winter.
> B: **So am I.**

**second person** One of the three classes of personal pronouns. Second person refers to the person (**you**, singular) or people (**you**, plural) who are the listeners or readers.

**separable** Refers to certain two-word verbs that allow a noun or pronoun object to separate the two words in the verb phrase.

> She **gave** her job **up**.

**short answer** An answer to a **Yes/No** question that has **yes** or **no** plus the subject and an auxiliary verb.

> A: Do you speak Chinese?
> B: **Yes, I do. / No, I don't.**

**simple past** A verb tense that expresses actions and situations that were completed at a definite time in the past.

> Carol **ate** lunch.
> She **was** hungry.

**simple present** A verb tense that expresses general statements, especially about habitual or repeated activities and permanent situations.

> Every morning I **catch** the 8:00 bus.
> The earth **is** round.

**singular** The form of a word that refers to only one person or thing. For example, **cat** and **child** are the singular forms of **cats** and **children**.

**stative verb** A type of verb that is not usually used in the continuous form because it expresses a condition or state that is not changing. **Know**, **love**, **resemble**, **see**, and **smell** are some examples.

**subject** A noun, pronoun, or noun phrase that precedes the verb phrase in a sentence. The subject is closely related to the verb as the doer or experiencer of the action or state, or closely related to the noun that is being described in a sentence with *be*.

> **Erica** kicked the ball.
> **He** feels dizzy.
> **The park** is huge.

**subordinate clause** *See* **dependent clause**.

**superlative** A form of an adjective, adverb, or noun used to compare a group of three or more people, things, or actions. The superlative shows that one member of the group has more (or less) than all of the others.

> This perfume has **the strongest** scent.
> He speaks **the fastest** of all.
> That machine makes **the most noise** of the three.

**tag question** A type of question that is added to the end of a statement in order to express doubt, surprise, and certainty. Certain rising or falling intonation patterns accompany these different meanings.

> You're feeling sick, **aren't you?**
> He didn't leave, **did he?**

**tense** The form of a verb that shows past, present, and future time.

> He **lives** in New York now.
> He **lived** in Washington two years ago.
> He**'ll live** in Toronto next year.

**third person** One of the three classes of personal pronouns. Third person refers to some person (**he**, **she**), people (**they**), or thing (**it**) other than the speaker/writer or listener/reader.

**three-word verb** A phrasal verb such as **break up with**, **cut down on**, and **look out for**. The meaning of a three-word verb is usually different from the individual meanings of the three words.

**time clause** A dependent clause that begins with a word such as **while**, **when**, before, or after. It expresses the relationship in time between two different events in the same sentence.

> **Before Sandy left,** she fixed the copy machine.

**time expression** A phrase that functions as an adverb of time.

> She graduated **three years ago**.
> I'll see them **the day after tomorrow**.

**transitive verb** A verb that is followed by an object.

> I **read** the book.

**two-word verb** A phrasal verb such as **blow up**, **cross out**, and **hand in**. The meaning of a two-word verb is usually different from the individual meanings of the two words.

**used to** A special past tense verb. It expresses habitual past situations that no longer exist.

> **We used to** go skiing a lot. Now we go snowboarding.

**verb** A word that refers to an action or a state.

> Gina **closed** the window.
> Tim **loves** classical music.

**verb phrase** A phrase that has a main verb and any objects, adverbs, or dependent clauses that complete the meaning of the verb in the sentence.

> Who **called you?**
> He **walked slowly**.
> I **know what his name is**.

**voiced** Refers to speech sounds that are made by vibrating the vocal cords. Examples of voiced sounds are /b/, /d/, and /g/.

> **b**at **d**ot **g**et

**voiceless** Refers to speech sounds that are made without vibrating the vocal cords. Examples of voiceless sounds are /p/, /t/, and /f/.

> u**p** i**t** i**f**

**vowel** A speech sound that is made with the lips and teeth open. The air from the lungs is not blocked at all. For example, the sounds /a/, /o/, and /i/ are vowels.

**wh- word** Who, whom, what, where, when, why, how, and which are **wh-** words. They are used to ask questions and to connect clauses.

**Yes/No question** A question that can be answered with the words **yes** or **no**.

> Can you drive a car?
> Does he live here?

# Index

This Index is for the full and split editions. Entries for Volume A are in bold.

# Grammar Sense

## ONLINE PRACTICE

### How to Register for Grammar Sense Online Practice

Follow the steps to register for *Grammar Sense Online Practice*.

1. Go to www.grammarsensepractice.com and click on **Register**

2. Read and agree to the terms of use. **I Agree.**

3. Enter the Access Code that came with your Student Book. Your code is written on the inside back cover of your book.

   ☐  ☐  ☐  ☐   **Enter**

4. Enter your personal information (first and last name, email address, and password).

5. Click on the Student Book that you are using for your class.

> It is very important to select your book. You are using Grammar Sense 2. Please click the **BLUE** Grammar Sense 2 cover.

If you don't know which book to select, **STOP**. Continue when you know your book.

6. Enter your class ID to join your class, and click NEXT. Your class ID is on the line below, or your teacher will give it to you on a different piece of paper.

   _____   **Next**

   You don't need a class ID code. If you do not have a class ID code, click Skip. To enter this code later, choose Join a Class from your Home page.

7. Once you're done, click on Enter Online Practice to begin using *Grammar Sense Online Practice*.

**Enter Online Practice**

Next time you want to use *Grammar Sense Online Practice*, just go to www.grammarsensepractice.com and log in with your email address and password.